Finding HER Stuff

HEALING.
ENCOURAGEMENT.
RESTORATION.

 FriesenPress

Suite 300 - 990 Fort St
Victoria, BC, V8V 3K2
Canada

www.friesenpress.com

ISBN
978-1-5255-3782-0 (Hardcover)
978-1-5255-3783-7 (Paperback)
978-1-5255-3784-4 (eBook)

1. SELF-HELP, GENERAL

Distributed to the trade by The Ingram Book Company

I do not sit down at my desk to put into verse something that is already clear in my mind. If it were clear in my mind, I should have no incentive or need to write about it. We do not write in order to be understood; we write in order to understand.

~ C. S. Lewis

Many souls have fortified these words and meditations of my heart. Endless love and bottomless thanks for generously sharing your time, thoughts, energy, wisdom and dreams that have encouraged me to complete this writing. I am so grateful, humbled and fortunate to walk this life amidst your beauty, grace and wit. Thank you for investing your life into my story.

Mum... this book is dedicated to your quiet courage, your steadfast presence, and your general kickass-ed-ness.

AJ

TABLE OF CONTENTS

AUTHOR'S BIO

At 22 years old, AJ lost her beloved mum suddenly to a brain tumor, an event that ignited the unravelling of her seemingly solid family. Feeling abandoned and alone, she sought solace in the company of an older man, quickly married him, and began fourteen years of an oppressive marriage. Enduring physical, verbal, emotional, spiritual, psychological and sexual abuse, AJ changed from a bright, free spirit, to an empty shell.

All attempts to escape this chaos were hindered by her loyalty to vows, her love for their children and being dependent on a man who had taken away her career, her family connections and her identity. Finally, after his insistence she become a police officer, AJ successfully completed her law enforcement training and found the courage to escape for good.

For two years, she hid from healing. Wantonly chasing happiness, she ran from anything resembling her married life and tried to drown out the pain with alcohol, sex and living without rules. This set her on a downward spiral toward more heartbreak and loss. Her children were acting out, responding to their own trauma and the upheaval of the only perspective they knew: Conflict.

Criminal and family court appearances dragged on for three years, resulting in a highly divisive custody ruling. Ultimately, the kids chose with their feet, further dividing the ties AJ had with her children. It was time to stop hiding—to stop avoiding the hurts—and start building a better life, but how?

AJ chose new priorities and patterns to establish a balance between too many rules, and not enough. She sought healthier relationships, fell in love, and became a stepmom in a blended family. Even though she married a beautiful man, true healing remained elusive. She battled episodes of depression after one child ran away, and her physical health was compromised by three significant head injuries.

Being triggered by light, sound and motion, her world ground to a halt. She literally sat still in the darkness for months to recover.

With only her thoughts and a deep desire to be well, she began to write, and a blog was born. "*Finding 52*" became the conduit for expressing her suffering, for processing her worry and for emancipating her dreams of a fulfilled life.

AJ's blogging exploration has been lovingly compiled in this book format.

INTRODUCTION

This is exciting! Today is a perfect day for adjusting sails, setting a new course, and beginning a new, scary adventure toward LIFE.

Why today?

Because I am fifty-two weeks away from being the same age my mother was when she succumbed to brain cancer, and it weighs on me heavily. I have had many years to think about her passing—twenty-four, to be exact. A few years ago, I passed the milestone of living more years on this earth *without* her, than *with* her. She was 47 years old when she died, seemingly ancient in my then 22-year-old mind—yet so very, VERY young in my now 46-year-old understanding. She was not present for my college graduation, my wedding day, or for any of my children being brought into this world. Her life ended before mine really began.

She did not get adequate time to pass along important details to me, for in my youth, I was not listening. Attempts to recall meaningful moments of her quiet life are fading over time, with only a few nuggets remaining from years spent trying to be *nothing* like my mother.

Now, as my age creeps up, I feel a desire to release stiffened, weathering bits that have been growing ridges inside of me from traumatic storms of my past. I want to challenge these unwelcome ruts and resist the progression of their grooves from digging deeper into my heart—a heart that wants *greater* warmth, needs *infinite* hope, and demands *ultimate freedom*.

WHY? Because…

If fifty-two weeks *is* the remaining time I have on this earth to create a life I believe worthy of living…

If fifty-two weeks *is* the time I have left to *say* and *do* important things with the ones I love…

If fifty-two weeks *is* the last chunk of time I have to establish how the rest of the world sees *who* I am, *what* I stand for, and *why* I make the choices I do...

... then I had better get started!

I have many fears of failing and not being able to commit to this course. Some memories may be too daunting or frightening to face. If I somehow gather enough courage to conquer this pain, I then must carve out time from my busy life to evaluate and record any outcomes that decree success. The fear is real!

But if I close my eyes, breathe deep, and listen to the murmurs arising from a heart longing for more—a mind pleading for an answer—my anxiety begins to slip away.

It must be now.

No more waiting. No more wondering if this *is* my best life. No more wondering if I can be my best. I can. I must. I have fifty-two weeks to discover it. But how? So much baggage stands in my way:

- I am a singer who did not become a star.
- I am a survivor of domestic abuse.
- I am a mother to five beautiful children, two have chosen to live with me, one has been forced by a second marriage, and another two who have chosen estrangement.
- I have survived and still manage significant bouts of depression.
- I am recovering from a third major concussion.
- I am a police officer not currently able to fulfil my duty in the uniform.

Ouch!

All these scars and hurts—old and new—managed or mismanaged, are stiffening my heart muscle. I had hoped to miraculously be unscathed by these challenging obstacles but am realizing this is not possible. While I appreciate the lessons learned, the wisdom gained, the character built through all these experiences, I feel the tightening grip from leftover scars, hindering my freedom to love, to laugh, and to flex with a dynamic, changing life.

Perhaps I will never entirely lose these scars. So, it is my goal to open them up, give them a chance to bleed out their worst, and gently love them back into being only faded markers from a struggle-filled, but hopeful life.

WILL YOU JOIN ME ON THIS ADVENTURE?

*(This is a space for scribbling, writing, doodling, blotting, or skipping to the next page, while deciding **if and why** this is your time to mend.)*

THE PLAN

I will probably require many reminders to keep me on track throughout the weeks. I have two baskets, one empty, and one filled with fifty-two items that were Mum's or were given to me by her. I will set these in a central part of my home as a visual reminder to focus and reflect on my words and actions.

One item will be chosen for an icon each week, then placed into the now-empty basket. At the end of fifty-two weeks, the empty basket will be full, and I will have reached my destination. Sticky notes, mantras, and theme songs will make this a fun, intentional, and ultimately impactful year for myself and any others who might choose to take this trek with me.

There are thirteen qualities I am wishing to grow within my daily life:

PATIENCE
POSITIVITY
SENSITIVITY
KINDNESS
CURIOSITY
GRACIOUSNESS
GRATITUDE
HUMOR
STRENGTH
ENCOURAGEMENT
CLEVERNESS
GENEROSITY
CREATIVITY

Each quality will get a four-week focus, examined and put into practice from four different perspectives:

ME: I am going to do my best to begin the first week of each topic with an internal and vulnerable reflection on how the characteristics manifest towards, and within, myself.

YOU: For the second week of each topic, I will attempt to build on any initial discoveries and look at how the qualities show up with my safe and closest relationships.

US: Hoping for some confidence to grow by the third week of each chosen quality, I will focus my attention within my family setting, and the people with whom I invest greater amounts of time.

THEM: Finally, as the fourth week concludes, having worked almost a month on each quality, I am hoping to expand the reflection into my community, my country, and perhaps... the world.

CHAPTER ONE

PATIENCE

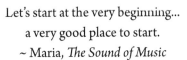

Let's start at the very beginning...
a very good place to start.
~ Maria, *The Sound of Music*

Week One

IT BEGINS WITH A LOCKET

This is going to be a fun and rewarding fifty-two weeks, although I must admit, I am experiencing strong uncertainty about going the distance. I can start projects like a champion, but finishing? No champion here.

So, if you have picked up this book and decided to join this exploration of living a maximized, beautifully flawed life—know that we are in this *together* and trust that the only experience or skills necessary are already inside of us.

This week starts my discovery of PATIENCE. More specifically, it is about me... being patient... with ME.

The icon I have chosen to help remind me of my focus on patience is a gold locket inherited from my mum. Inside this locket, are two pictures. Dear Mum rests on the right. On the left is my precious, oldest boy—the first child who chose to be estranged from me. I thought they were both lost to me forever. Mum was lost in her battle with cancer and my son was lost in a nasty custody battle. I put both their faces in this locket to remember loving moments we shared and silently plead for their return into my life.

Okay, I am not suggesting a Lazarus-style resurrection will occur for Mum *(a little weird after twenty-four years)*, although in the throes of initial mourning and a deep denial stage of grief, I could not help but hope it was possible. I understand the physical barriers death imposes upon relationships. However, I believe emotional connections are still very strong and vibrant after loved ones die. Perhaps this is why the other mourning phases of anger and sadness take so long to process. This kind of trauma could be attached to our emotional wiring, and therefore not easily recognized as needing to be healed.

If it were a physical scrape or bruise, torn muscles or protruding bones, or an ailment visible to the naked eye, we would know what to do. Our physical stuff usually gets a lot of attention and often can be fixed. For confusing and complex emotions, an appropriate course for healing is not as straightforward.

I think emotional pain requires love and space to heal, but it must be sought. We can seek help for all our wounds or choose not to heal. It seems like some people decide to remain raw and sore for years, sometimes decades, making a strong case for *time not* being the ultimate healer. Some ignore their emotional wounds, creating a buildup of scar tissue so immobilizing that it can surpass the initial impact of the original wound.

This is all part of my old story. A saga that went on—and on—until I'd had enough.

Moping

Agonizing

Stumbling

Lamenting

These moments were hope stealers—joy stealers—life stealers—because I am *still* living. Since I know life can be cut short, I want my best life *now*. My best self *now*. If I want a clear, honorable picture painted of the lady I am—I must BE that lady.

So, if I want to be described as a patient lady, I must *be* patient. Hah! Imagine that. *Being* what I strive to be. Acting how I *want* to act. If I don't, it may say on my epitaph:

"HERE LIES A SPAZZED LUNATIC
WHO FLIPPED OUT OVER LITTLE THINGS!"

Me—being patient—with me.

Sounds simple, right? Let us begin!

Choose your own ICON for Patience:
(If you prefer to use your own writing journal, please excuse this space, or skip choosing an icon entirely. No pressure from ME!)

PATIENCE WITH ME

I was not sure, at the beginning of the week, if I had much work to do in terms of being patient with myself. I self-describe as being open to identifying what attitudes are harsh to the esteem and believed my self-talk to be generally positive. I wondered if there would be enough chances to adequately test my actions, as I was already practicing what I thought was an enlightened discipline of self-care. I was half prepared to invent stuff to write about, but as luck *(life)* would have it, there were plenty of moments to practice being patient with me!

On Day One, I woke in a panic over an alarm clock not set, sunny weather had turned gloomy, and moody teenagers were annoyingly glum. I forgot to take a photo of the beautiful autumn leaves turning color on a vine growing outside our kitchen window, which are now ruined due to the cold and rain of a dismal morning. I also forgot to send my nephew his tenth-birthday card, after promising a time frame of when it would arrive. I began adding it all up in my head, and the verdict was—I fail at almost everything. A swift boot of judgement kicked me hard, and I thought: *Can't you do anything right?* And there it was. My work. It was all laid out for me in that single thought.

I am surprised to learn that my default for negative feelings within an experience is judgement. I am either trying to convince myself I am not supposed to be feeling a particular way or am just too inferior a human to feel any other way. It is also easy to jump to a conclusion that someone else is to blame. *They* made me feel upset, and therefore, *they* need work.

I noticed the kind of language I use to talk to myself when I am upset with something going wrong. I accuse myself in the "you" tense, like there is another person inside who is responsible for failing, instead of the actual me. I get mad at *her* and repeat lies I have heard from past accusers.

By Day Three, my pattern became too common to ignore.

Trigger

Upset

Blame Someone

Feel Bad

More Triggers

REPEAT

I realized—the work needed was indeed *my own*.

Some of my really good, hot buttons got pushed during this week. Raising teenagers is enough to warrant intensive therapy, but lots of other challenges emerged as opportunities to practice. Here are some honorable mentions:

- Moving furniture into different rooms within the house without a definite plan
- A night of no sleep *(see earlier comment about teens)*
- Being hungry at a *long* school parent meeting, heavily regretting skipping lunch, and not a single emergency granola bar or gummy snack left in my bag *(the teens again, they raided my snacks!)*
- PMS *(enough said?)*
- A significant disagreement in parenting between me and hubby, nothing new, but very emotionally draining

It does not stop there, but since I want to spare myself the rehash, I will skip ahead to the number one trigger of the week, which was facing the fact that I may have a hoarding problem. This was difficult to ignore while attempting to switch entire contents from various rooms. Even the message at church on Sunday addressed how joy is sacrificed in our lives by holding onto 'stuff'.

And—I am realizing I may have passed that trait down to my children, whose spaces are piled with treasures, just like their mama's. I was clearly getting nudged to deal with this very personal issue, because my guilt was thick. I did not want to look around, afraid I would be comparing my collections with hubby's minimalistic tendencies. Pride tried to choke out a faint voice calling for release of my guilt—for letting go of my judgements—for transforming how I intersect with conflict.

A new pattern had to emerge.

So, I reached for the gold chain hanging around my neck until anxious fingers held Mum's locket. Rubbing its smooth, slim surface, I kept asking myself to go further than what was bothering me outside.

I changed the language I used to label myself.

Not "you" anymore—I introduced myself to "me".

This trigger is somehow about me—and for me.

Then it felt right to say, "*Hello, Me. It is okay to feel this way, even if you don't know **why** you do.*"

Aaahhh! A shift in my heart. It *is* okay to feel anyway I feel. I *do* have reason to be bothered, but so what? Is my goal to become a martyr or victim? I adopted that kind of behavior in the past because it helped me survive, but does it serve me now?

Does having another person feel bad about what I perceive as their offensive behavior make *me* feel better? Can beating myself up with shame or bitterness manifest the patience I fervently desire?

No.

So—just breathe a bit. Allow love the space to seep into this feeling.

This is patience.

When I was most successful in remembering to be okay with my feelings, calmness ruled. It did not just rule—it rocked! Calmness carried over into the days and situations that followed, building faster connections to the goal of patiently accepting myself wherever I was.

But conflict also carried over. When I was *least* successful at being able to gently guide my response from a trigger, a cloud of conflict lingered over my head until

I could accept *that* cloud as okay—breathing it away with loving reminders of why I started down this road.

I am learning—ME is learning—to move through tense, sometimes unresolved feelings, without *assuming* the situation is unsolvable.

Breathe. Love. Create Space.

Patience begins and ends—with ME.

Week Two

BABY GOT BONNETS

This week I am searching for what it means to be patient with the people I have in my immediate circle. I bump into the same close family and friends more frequently than anyone else, but not necessarily in a consistent manner. My goal would be to increase our positive interactions and decrease the negative. One of my favorite quotes from Maya Angelou suggests that people forget what was said but remember how interactions made them feel.

Too many times, I suspect I have left my closest loved ones *feeling* like they were not accepted, not loved—that they did not belong or live up to my standards. I have justified my actions by considering all the times I kept a tight tongue and *not* said what I was thinking. I told myself that this was okay, because the person had no idea how I *truly* felt. I convinced myself they were oblivious to a counterfeit smile and a short response. It is doubtful to be in fact fooling anyone, so I must strive for better.

The icon I will be using this week is a baby bonnet of Mum's. Approximately 71 years old, it is stored inside a woody, aromatic cedar chest, alongside other well-preserved family items, including many things saved from when I was a child:

- My dancing shoes (*not the Friday-night-dancing kind, but rather ballet slippers and their accompanying accoutrements for the only lessons my conservative mum deemed "appropriate for a young girl"*)
- Diaries from junior high school
- Favorite elementary school projects
- Posters from my childhood room
- A ripped pair of deeply faded Levi's
- My favorite pre-teen books…

Clearly, this is another space in need of some hoarding control!

Mum's bonnet, being old and fragile, will have to be held inside a clear baggie this week, if I am to carry it as a reminder. It has a matching sweater and booties with delicate pink ribbons, and if that isn't cute enough, there is a whole other set, made for Mum's twin, Aunty R, who is also a great collector of important old stuff. So—Aunty R, if you are reading this—*I don't know anything about any crocheted booties!*

PATIENCE WITH YOU

At the beginning of this chapter, I should have pointed out one very important fact: I am not educated through any academic process, about the topics I am tackling during this fifty-two-week sojourn. I have lived in and through some very dynamic personal experiences that have twisted, torn, compressed, molded, and churned me out, leading me to want to become a better person, inside and out … but I am NOT an expert.

Sharing my encounters with others, from the perspective of one who is living amidst the mess, is the only schooling I know. I am in the cold, wet trenches, tossing out personal garbage and grasping to a few sparkling gems, just like many of us are. We are in the muck daily—for ourselves and for the ones we love. I humbly admit that I am not up to the task of writing to assist, guide, direct, or transform anyone's life—except my own.

With that in mind—and assuming you are still reading—I press on.

A draft chapter was almost ready to go yesterday; Just needing little edit tweaks before being deemed complete. It was an easy week, perhaps because of the work from the previous week, with only small triggers showing up to manage without too much effort.

Being patient with people I love the most seems very similar to being patient with myself.

To be patient with YOU, I must understand that YOU have an inner ME—just as I do. As such, I should treat you as I would treat myself—with gentle curiosity. Sounds like the golden rule—which is taught to young kids—so it *must* be easy. Right?

When I understand how other people's MEs have pain/worry/fear/judgement/sorrow running as a default program through the backdrop of their own lives, my reaction is softened, less judgmental, and I am less likely to feel offended.

As the week went on, I quietly listened for any ME-type voices and managed to stay in the chill zone. This is great! I have a tangible strategy which stops me from entering dangerous territory of enflamed emotional responses that end with me feeling bad about myself. Only twelve hours left before ending Week Two.

There is only one thing left on the agenda before giving myself a hardy pat on the back: DATE NIGHT!

Celebrating our fourth wedding anniversary is not just a regular evening out. Anniversary dates remind us of the sacredness of vows, the joy of union, and the magic of true love! So, there are some expectations attached to the planning and execution of this night. For those of you with busy households and kids, you know how infrequent date nights can be, but also how pivotal they are in remembering who you are as a couple.

Just for a few hours, you are not a parent, an employee, a colleague, or a slave to household chores. These nights require some planning, perhaps some specially budgeted money set aside, and the complete anticipation of it being amazing!

Which it was—except I was bothered. Little triggers were creeping into the evening, subtle looks, teasing remarks that felt not-so funny, each of us bringing up things the other person did not want to talk about. This was not meeting my expectation of how our special night should feel.

Hubby is the closest person to me. My best friend—a great travel companion, a super supporter of my wildest schemes—and he was bothering ME. I could feel my blood pressure growing into the evening, past the point of listening to and accepting our mutual ME's.

I tried another strategy to suppress my annoyance—joking *(because that sometimes works—laughing nervously to release tension building within my core)*. Hubby is so good at letting it roll. He stays cool, as I start to look for a bucket of ice water to douse the little flames licking through my guts. No bucket is available, so I smolder away.

Twelve hours is not enough time to turn this around! How do I write about patience in a few hours, feeling this way?

Humbly. That's how. And maybe it is also the key to this week's discovery. As we drove home from our anniversary evening, all my senses were ready to pounce should one more trigger appear. My anxiety loomed about what writing would come in the morning, so I stared out the window to avoid a torrid outcome should I engage any further with hubby.

As I gazed unfocussed at passing billboards and traffic lights, it dawned on me: I am just reading signs. I have not designed city infrastructure or considered how to make safe streets for traffic. I can only explain how I got to where I am, and share where it is, I am trying to go. The signs are placed for all to see and use. Heed them or ignore them—it is a choice. My choice. Signs are neither good nor bad.

They are just indicators of experiences past and predictors of outcomes ahead. So, what are these signs telling me?

Pause. Read the signs. Breathe. Choose where you want to go.

How did the evening end? Hubby thinks we had a great night—true. **I** think we had a great night—also true. But it took a big yield sign for me to realize that my feelings were not pointing out a good direction. This sign slowed my words from rushing out like toxic waste, letting ME pause long enough to avoid disaster with YOU.

This is not the whole answer, I suppose. But it seems a worthy place to start.

Authentic. Imperfect. Non-academic. There is much work to be done.

Week Three

HARDCORE PATIENCE

We are picking up right where we left off, with the late lesson learned last week, continuing down this road of increased awareness for reading signs.

This week's icon is a delicate piece of cloth Mum worked on for months. It is an old Nordic craft called 'hardanger' *(insert pun here for 'hard anger' being appropriately paired with patience)*. This crafting skill is a mixed art of all needle crafts, but more intense! One wrong snip of the scissors, and the whole work is ruined.

Mum always had something in her hands: A recipe book, a crocheting hook, or a gardening hoe. She made good use of every waking moment, rarely relaxing or watching television and movies—but when she did sit down, there was a craft or task in her hand. I remember watching her execute this intricate pattern, and as she anchored it into the canvas, I thought: *This work takes a lot of patience!*

I did not have this item in my hoard of her possessions until very recently. Mum had made it for a family friend, so I had forgotten it existed. During the fourteen years of an isolating marriage, I was disconnected from our family history. Regrettably, important stories and memories were lost during those traumatic years.

Mum was often a topic of ridicule for my former spouse, who mocked me for showing any symptoms of mourning. He tore apart the character of a lady he never met and assured me that Mum had never *really* loved me at all. It became easier to stop thinking about Mum than to defend my grief.

To preserve any belongings of hers inside this hostile home, I had to convince him that I was not sentimentally attached to them, and that they only served a practical function. He voiced contempt for the relationship I described with Mum, labeling me erroneously loyal. He was so convincing that I eventually believed she did not love me, that she was not a good mother, and was not the virtuous person I remembered her to be.

He was partially right. She was not a saint!

But that is how loved ones tend to be pictured after they are no longer with us. Through my policing career, even the worst criminals involved with unconscionable gangs and leading merciless lives, have family members who remember their good qualities and praise their strengths when they meet an early demise.

Yes, Mum had faults, but it did not diminish the works of love she performed every day for the people around her. That is who I am concentrating on this week.

"Patience with US" is going to broaden the circle from my closest relationships, to those who intersect throughout my normal week. All my family and friends will be players in this week's discovery. I am going to ask 'US' two questions this week:

1. When in your life, have you experienced another person *purposefully* being patient with you?
2. How did *seeing* their patience, make you feel?

I don't know about your brain, but when I read this first question, I automatically flip to remembering times when people were impatient with me.

But that is not the question! I took another moment to reflect on more subtle indicators—almost intangible at times—to recall an exact moment of another person being patient with me.

I have my hardanger piece on display and it is ready to remind me.

PATIENCE WITH US

Sundays are a bit odd for me. As a child, it was the day we ate three family meals together instead of one and was the only day we were almost always doing the same things together. It also meant yummy breakfasts with fresh-baked biscuits or blueberry muffins and a big lunch meal that might have been put into the oven or slow cooker before heading out the door in a hurry to arrive almost on time for Sunday school and church.

Sundays often included company coming over to share our dinner spread or joining another family for coffee and dessert. I was expected to wear a dress or skirt, my brother wore his suit pants or slacks, my dad wore a suit and tie, and Mum—who normally wore a skirted suit to work—would switch up her colors for Sunday, choosing softer hues instead of the power colors she wore to run an office. And sometimes she wore a hat—a proper British-style hat, like the queen might wear to go out for a morning stroll.

That was our retro Sunday mixdown from about 1976-1986. Flash forward to Sunday mornings now.

We are a blended family with different religious views, the males choose to be home doing chores and watching TSN while the gals head off to church wearing anything but 'holey' jeans, to sing and visit with other folks that burn for Jesus. For breakfast—well, if hubby and I get back in time from our early Sunday morning grocery-store date, we settle on some jointly created concoction of whatever needs to be used up in the fridge—and pancakes—because EVERYTHING goes with pancakes.

Everyone does their own thing Sunday afternoon, but we all come together for a big Sunday supper, sometimes inviting the in-laws or other family members who happen to be nearby. It is a day that displays how different each family member is from the others, doing things we have the *least* in common. I do not sit comfortably with this comparison of my youthful family dynamics to our present day.

What does this have to do with my task this week of looking for opportunities to find patience within our family? I have uncovered a very startling truth: I am a family snob!

It is so easy to look around at other people, hear their stories about their family lives; See the struggles they endure with rebellious teens, look at their over-bearing parenting styles, observe a diversity of rejection or abandonment issues, and witness quagmires of complexities to the moon and back—and then say to myself, *So glad that's not our world. Those folks are messed up!*

Trust me, I know how that sounds, which is why graciousness is on the agenda in the weeks to come. But this is still the topic of patience, and I must process these thoughts, for this week.

In my old, rigid story, a twisted authority led me into loveless obedience, where it was drilled into me—we were the BEST family. We were more righteous, more health conscious, more clean living, more enlightened, more hard-working, more resourceful, more responsible—more, more, MORE—and it was a lie. And not just a teeny, white, half-lie. It was gigantically untrue.

I lived it, believed it, proclaimed it, and spun it, so that anyone who might challenge our warped reality would get hit with a barrage of data to support our claim. Doing this made life more peaceful between me and my ex, and sometimes avoided a fight all together, if I had defended us well. When I left that relationship, I purposefully did things to an opposite extreme, avoiding anything remotely connecting me to those lies, which means I was a rotten parent for a while. Really rotten. No rules, no worries, no deadlines, no expectations, no stability—Wow!

The kids are *still* revealing precarious stories from those wild couple of years. I remember thinking, as we were riding that chaotic wave of raw living—*At least we don't* **act** *like we are better than anyone else*. I was so sick of proving to people how healthy, wise, spiritual, good, and structured our family was—and so, no matter what madness we found ourselves swallowed up in after the divorce, at least now our family was *real*.

Raw and real—until it needed to be different.

Yes, the pendulum did swing back and forth for a while, trying to gain a grip on becoming a family with balance. It was not easy taking back the reigns offered to children who'd felt the power of liberation after living under extreme control. But slowly, a firmer grip on ourselves and each other started to take shape. What remained was the decision to never hold judgment over anyone's life again. I would walk humbly in my own shoes, knowing we are *all* doing our best and no one is perfect—until things started to feel pretty perfect.

I fell in love with a wonderful man and our kids were getting along. We took a leap of faith, bought a house together, and jumped into blended-family bliss by deciding to also get married. I felt so blessed! Sure, we had some bumps, but this was a new and exhilarating shot at a life I had feared was impossible. Hubby and I had stable jobs, we travelled with the kids to Disneyland, went camping in the summer—all was good.

We are **pretty** *awesome—maybe... even a superfamily!*

I surmised that, because things were going so well, it was somehow due to the genius parents at the helm—and that felt good! Because our family was crushing the details that *looked* messy in other blended situations, and because I was comparing it to the disaster I had left, my sense of superiority started to grow—and then it all came crashing down.

One child ran away. Despite endless pursuits, creative resolutions, and desperate pleas, that child stayed away. Darkness began to consume me. I was not able to function at work. The other kids and hubby were on edge. We had a wedding to plan, and I felt miserable. Where was that superfamily? Where was that parent who was doing everything right? I churned out another few years, battling depression and guilt, until a new normal could be established, and I was able to start climbing out of that pit.

After battling through those emotional struggles, I assumed this week would be an easy sail, having practiced much patience with our fractured family. It took eight years for my first estranged child to reconnect with our family, and now I wait for yet another one to adjust their current course of separation from us. Even after *years* of evidence to the contrary, I still want to see 'US' as perfect.

PERFECT—IS A LOT A PRESSURE!

This week—only Week Three of my fifty-two-week challenge—one of our kids completed their confinement at a secure facility *(which is a nice way of saying they got out of jail)*, one was caught in some dangerous lies, one came home high, one travelled close to home but did not plan to visit us, and one gave me so much attitude that I thought I was being 'punked' for Snapchat! *I am learning the give-away phrase as "Mom, can you say that again", which is my clue there is a digital device capturing the insanity of this moment.*

"Patience with US" is knowing that 'WE' are not perfect. It is accepting our strengths and flaws and not caring who else has something better going on. It is seeing our darkest bits and loving them anyway. It is not pressuring ourselves to be perfect, so I can brag about it on Facebook or on coffee breaks at work. My gut tells me to relax and just trust—WE are not done. Not yet.

Patience is believing our family is good—*and* lousy—but that our love does not quit. I need to stop competing with other people for who can sound like the best parent and or look like the family with no problems. I must stop competing with friends, colleagues, extended family—and even with hubby.

*But wait, I can't let **him** be a better parent than **me**! NO WAY!*

Well—actually—yes. He does need to be a better parent than me, when I am triggered and only want to scream and fight. My friends need to be better parents than me, when I need to see love modelled through fresh eyes. My colleagues need to be better parents than me, as examples of how to voice healthy pride. My extended family need to be better parents than me, so that our children are well cared for when they spend time together.

Accepting US is big work. Letting US be okay, right where we are, is a *bigger* work. And loving US in the messy midst of now is the *best* work.

Love—Your—US.

Week Four

PINS AND NEEDLES

This is it! My final week of patience. My family is probably hoping it will *not* be the end of my patience. Crossing my fingers...

During this week, not only will I attempt to keep practicing all the learning from earlier weeks but will also seek a grander vision for what patience might mean in the context of 'THEM'.

During some leadership training at work, I took note of the buzz language swirling around, using the concept of 'US vs. THEM'. It was meant to showcase how people often cannot see another's perspective because we miss the commonalities we share. The message was to break down any barriers that stop true collaboration and increase valuable diversity of thought. If this is accomplished, effective solutions to issues that impact our communities are potentially found. Sounds like I am busting out a BIG can of worms—and yes—I am!

Our country just had a leadership election. There were some unhappy people exaggerating the platforms of each political party, posting their views on multiple social-media sites. Opinions got stronger after the election results, evidence that an age-old adversity between the West and the East still exists. There is a clear geographical divide within our country when it comes to culture and values. This is a perfect example of what 'US vs. THEM' is all about.

Voting was tough! When I read all the promises and platforms of the candidates, I wanted to be convinced that one party was clearly in line with my beliefs. But frankly, they all left me a little disappointed. I kept wishing for one candidate's platform to be: "Vote for me, and I will work tirelessly WITH the opposition to come up with solutions for things we ALL think are important." Since I did not find this rhetoric on the ballot, perhaps I should toss my name in the ring for the next go around.

But this is not *Politics* and Patience, so let's get a move-on to the pins.

Why have I decided to use Mum's old pin keeper as my icon this week? It is a bit of a stretch but stick with me. *Pins... Stick...*

I don't know where the tin came from, but I know the story of some things inside.

The black round object is a magnet. My brother and I used these for our music lessons when we were small. We memorized how to read notes by placing the magnets onto a painted tin board with appropriately represented musical lines. Mum sat with us at the piano, not able to play herself, but reading out the notes and encouraging us to continue learning this valuable skill.

The shiny, oval, silver-headed pin is a hatpin used by ladies a few generations ago, to hold their hats in place on their hairdo's. I think it belonged to one of my great grandmas.

Several safety pins are here, as they were in constant supply on top of Mum's dresser, in her purse, or pockets. It was her version of duct tape. If anything went wrong, she had a safety pin. I'm that way too, but not with duct tape or safety pins. I use twist-ties. Nobody is allowed to throw these out in our house. Twist-ties are magic.

There is also a sewing-machine needle inside the tin, blending in with all the other shiny sharps. It was from Mum's old sewing machine, and the only remaining part of that faithful gadget, responsible for so many costumes and crafts created by Mum for me and my brother. She sewed patches on our jeans *before* it was cool, much to my displeasure. I still have some of the patches she didn't use in my ever-so-interesting hoard collection.

I watched Mum sew right through her thumb with that sewing machine, and she did not cry out in pain. If that had happened to me, I might have uttered a few choice words, and screamed a lot before vomiting or fainting *(or both)*. But *she* just shook her head, reversed the sewing needle wheel, and walked to the bathroom for a bandage. What a warrior!

All the other pins are from various home-economics classes. I used them in high school and so did my daughters—adding and losing pins along the way until we were left with this assorted gaggle of pointy reminders of past endeavors.

Pins link two separate pieces of fabric jutted up against the other. These fabrics are not yet bound by thread, so the pins remember where the fabrics are supposed to connect. Sometimes the fabrics are identical but facing in opposing directions. Sometimes the weight and texture are so different that the pins will accommodate more slack from one fabric while stretching the other. Pins secure what shape these two fabrics might form, keeping everything aligned until the seams are secure.

If you know the basics of sewing, you understand how hard it is to keep some fabrics matched up *without* pins. Too many times, I have tried to skip this pivotal step, going pin-less to speed the progress of my project, wasting more time tearing out and re-sewing a wonky seam than if I had pinned it in the first place. Pins are pillars for good outcomes, but how do they show up in establishing my "Patience with THEM"?

Week number four—here I come!

PATIENCE WITH THEM

WOW! Four weeks of practicing patience is under my belt!

Remember the fear-driven voices from Week One, worrying if I could find the discipline to do this—agonizing over the technological details of building a blog-site—doubting whether I even had anything meaningful to discover?

All gone.

Which finds me here at the end of Week Four, considering the scope of patience with THEM. Pins are what keep the diverse fabrics of our world together, until a permanent seam can be put in place. I have spent a lot of time with Mum's pin tin this week.

Hubby bought three new pairs of dress pants and asked if I would hem them. I spent six years in home-economics classes, so the question was not whether I *could* hem the pants. It was a question of whether I *would* hem them. He asked several weeks ago, so I had some time to deliberate, procrastinate, and 'hypothesignate'. *Okay, I made up that word, but it describes the time it took for me to just hem the pants, already!*

I thought about the financial gains of saving money by doing it myself. Since I do not know the going rate for hemming pants at a tailor's shop, I guessed the savings would be around $50. That is more money than I give myself for a bi-weekly allowance, so it seemed a fair motivator.

I thought about the things I would do for a loved one 'just because' they asked. Not necessarily things I would enjoy doing, but things in my wheelhouse that I could do without breaking a sweat. There is no price tag attached to these acts, so that alone seemed like a good reason for some inspiring needle action.

Another motivator is my brand-new sewing machine! I was so happy to get rid of the clunky, stiff, loud, held together by twist ties *(See! I **do** use them for magic)* sewing machine, which I bought at a grocery store when desperate for some curtains I could not afford to buy. Only 5 years old, that machine was a wreck, not like Mum's old Pfaff, which functioned for years after its prime.

This newest machine is digital and has all the bells and whistles. It has embroidery and quilting features, even a version of surging is possible… and I haven't used it in the ten months since I bought it. A few months ago, it made it out of the box, but I had yet to read the manual. And I could not be a dedicated home-economics student without practicing on some scraps first, so there it sat. Such simple steps, needing only my time and focus. So why the big stall?

I was ready to concede the pants to a professional when this week began. Saving money was not enough incentive. Having an altruistic motive was not enough reason. Having beautiful equipment with a full pictorial manual—also not doing it for me. So, what does it take?

Discipline. That was my first thought. I just need to get tough with myself. *Pretty sure that strategy failed in Week One. Next.*

How about a pay-it-forward kind of approach? Like handing out cookies to the city workers in our neighborhood park as they cleaned up autumn leaves or being overly generous to my fellow drivers while navigating traffic. Sure.

Did it. Done. The pants—still not hemmed.

I whined to myself about it taking *sooo looong* and being *soooo boring*. Who has energy for sewing when you are constantly picking your bottom lip off the floor, too bummed-out for hemming?

Finally, I shocked myself with a deadline. I declared—the pants would be finished in three-days' time *(sounds like the start of a good fairy-tale)*—then waited until the end of the first day to begin. But, since I do not like to start projects that require calculations or brain work later in the evening, I decided to start fresh the following day.

Sounds like a good plan, avoiding potential mistakes from tired eyes and fingers. However, just like the day before, I waited until everything else had been tackled and again, not much hemming was accomplished.

As I went to sleep that second night, I realized—if I did not begin my day with this sewing affair, it might not get finished. *Prioritizing* was going to be necessary to honor my deadline. So, on the third day, for two hours in the morning and three hours in the afternoon, I dedicated myself to this task, with only a few interruptions of other essential tasks.

I would like to say that I felt like a superhero or had a rush of dopamine when I was finished, but it simply was not the case. 'Whiney' AJ had been right! It was boring *(waaah!)*. It did take a long time *(boo-hoo!)*. And there was nothing 'in it' for me, except maybe getting asked to hem pants again someday. *Oh, goody!*

How does knowing this help me to be patient in a global sense, where I have seemingly little in common with others, or separated by barriers of language or what looks like insurmountable and opposing cultural and political differences? If I use a relatively current global issue, like the Syrian crisis, how does *my* patience have any kind of impact?

Perspective. Priorities. Deadlines.

> *"My priority to DISCOVER the best version of me*
> *collides with a consuming desire to BE discovered."*

No spotlight, no boardroom accolades, no witnesses to my tired hands at work, no glory. Just me in a basement corner, working toward one little goal. My longing to be the hero instead of filling a supporting role, seems to be the reason I balk at contributing when the efforts are *hidden*. For me, patience with THEM means this: Changing my *perspective*.

Any role that accomplishes good, that moves a greater action into fruition, is cause for celebration. There is a time to use my strength, to shine a light bright enough for others to see—and there is a time to put my strengths toward a power source that can reach farther than my own, to become *part* of something.

I can only do this if my *priorities* change with my perspective. As mindful as I try to be, I always seem to find tasks that suit my needs. I have already discovered my inclination to be a family 'snob', but could that tendency carry over into other things?

Sign me up for the diva roles; I wouldn't want to break a nail.

This is a strange evolution. It seems I have strayed from the work-hard-in-the-dirt ethics that raised me. It is time to carefully line up my values against my selfish wants, put those diva desires in their rightful place, and then pin it all down long enough to get some permanent stitching.

As for a deadline… well, this word can cause considerable stress, so I shall re-label it as a goal, a target, a destination, or an intention—anything that leads me to a place of accountability to myself. Even though the point of this pilgrimage is to live in a way that allows others to clearly see what I am about, I am *most* accountable to myself and my Creator. Since I do not know when my ultimate deadline will be reached—each task counts.

If each task, no matter how small, is treated like it could be my last, I will happily concede time in the limelight to be an ember supporting the flames of greater works.

AJ

What are some of your current perspectives that need to be challenged?

CHAPTER TWO

POSITIVITY

Life may not be the PARTY we signed up for,
but while we are here, we may as well dance.
~ Attributed to Jeanne C. Stein

Week Five

CLIP-ON EARRINGS AND OTHER HAPPY STUFF

I am excited to dive into a new topic. This week, I am checking in to see how positive I am with myself. I have a suspicion that some of this next discovery has already been unearthed by practicing patience in Week One. I also know there is a whole other layer of stuff lurking under my smiling exterior, disguising itself as positivity. I am going to find out what that stuff is, but before I begin, here are some ideas of how other people and cultures perceive living positive, happy lives.

When a comparison of dictionaries from thirty nations looked at how happiness is defined, it was found that Western and East Asian cultures view happiness quite differently. Western culture sees happiness as an individual's feeling of pleasure, while East Asian cultures define happiness by social harmony, or an association with good luck and fortune.

In Milan, Italy, citizens are required by an antiquated law to wear smiles on their faces. *Exceptions are made for people working at hospitals and attending funerals.*

Denmark has the happiest people in the world! Why? Apparently, it is due to their stable population, social-class cohesion, great educational system, energy independence, fine health care, available jobs, a retirement system for everyone, comfortable housing, lovely countryside pastimes, and plenty of leisure time to enjoy it.

I thought it would be because of those fresh chocolate-filled pastries!

This is a glimpse of happiness in our world, but is being positive the same as being happy? I think 'happy' is a tricky word.

It assumes things like: If a person is happy, they smile.

Or: If a person is smiling, they are happy.

The way western society sometimes models happiness has convinced me to think I am inferior or am lacking something. I have felt saddened and inadequate for not being or having everything equal to friends and neighbors.

Seems my definition of happiness needs an overhaul. Since I am driven to chase what *feels* happy, I am easily influenced by what people around me are doing and saying. Feeding these temporary and unfulfilling impulses consumes me. My teens are drowning in impulses of what feels good, right now!

In my late thirties, I was immersed in my own impulse-driven mayhem. It was not the most attractive time of life to be wantonly seeking pleasure, but understandable considering my recent departure from a traumatic marriage. Fortunately, it took less than two years of throwing myself into the phantom arms of happiness before I grew too tired, too hung-over, too chaotic, too sexed-up, and too used-up to continue.

This was clearly not a route to wellness. There was no healing in sight—no glow of distant light promising the dawn of a restored inner-self, just darkening moments that created more hiding, more chasing, and more frantic searching for a disappointingly allusive happy place. That is where an appetite for something else began.

Healthiness.

My icon this week is one of Mum's clip-on earrings, which she wore during her chemotherapy. Instead of waiting for clumps of her thick, straight, naturally auburn hair to fall out while the chemicals surged in her body, she bravely chose to shave it all off. She wore a scarf or wig over her bald head, and sometimes, when her scalp got too itchy, she wore nothing at all. Wearing big, chunky earrings helped her feel like she was maintaining her dignity as a put-together woman.

These dangly, black and gold, daisy-shaped earrings were hideous to me then and twenty-four years later, my opinion of them has not changed. But I am a good hoarder, so have held on like a champion. Wearing them as actual earrings is simply out of the question, but they handily clip onto lapels, anchor on zippers, and make decent bookmarks. *I do not recommend using one as a pillow embellishment, as they leave a terrific imprint on your face in the morning.*

I am hoping to chase a new definition of happiness in this chapter. Positivity starts now!

Choose your own ICON for Positivity:

POSITIVELY ME

"All negative, unhelpful, and obsessive thoughts,
are hereby cancelled."

This quote summarizes Week Five. It's not quite enough for me to end it there though. Over the past five years, I have had the good fortune to interact with the youth in our city. Mostly, I work in a supportive role, alongside teachers and parents, helping them create the best environment possible to raise and guide those entrusted to their care. This has been the focus:

- Be a trustworthy adult who demonstrates authentic interest in each child
- Have something meaningful to explore, about what is going on inside of them
- Let their voice be the most important resource on how they interpret their world
- See each child through a lens that focusses on what they do *well*
- And *(maybe most importantly)* be their biggest fan

Thankfully, the careers and compassions of some very insightful Canadian doctors have influenced this focus, and I recommend every parent, youth worker, or teacher to check out their social forums:

Dr. Michael Ungar – The Resilience Research Centre

Dr. Gabor Mate and Dr. Gordon Neufeld – *Hold On to Your Kids*

The reasons I think these experts are important to mention here—in relation to "Positivity with ME"—are two-fold:

The first reason may not seem obvious, but if I have not *really* grown up, research on developing brains is very applicable to me. While training to become better at my work, I am also gaining insight into being an adult.

The second reason the latest research is important is because I have needed to reframe professional and personal negativity a lot recently. So, Week Five is right on time. Another perfectly landed topic, somewhat simple—yet so, so hard.

The *easy* part is having an optimistic outlook and a stubborn belief that my glass *(even if bone-dry)* is always half full. If being positive comes somewhat naturally to me, it might mean I do not know how to work for it.

I remember moments in my life that have not been glossy and bright, could not have been reframed positively, and have taken me into darkness so deep I feared I would never return. Remembering this felt like I had not found the right avenue to go down or was 'doing the week wrong'. As I waited for the gloominess of my not-so-distant despair to burn off, I realized that I am not living in my old reality.

Physically removing myself from an unhealthy environment was the easier part. The tough stuff was removing the emotional mountains that were attached to my backside, weighing me down with every step, and blocking every breakthrough. My physical reality had changed, but my emotional reality stayed the same.

Waves of change challenge every aspect of what I think is true. Sometimes it knocks me flat on my face and sometimes I am floating along smoothly toward the freedom I am desperate to attain.

The waves that rock me are reminders—I am more than a physical body. I am also spirit, soul, and mysterious breath, all of which has brought me through foggy, lost moments that physical eyes could not navigate.

These two aspects of ME are equal. One is full of things I can see, taste, touch, plan, and act. It tests my physical abilities and strength to achieve a fulfilling life, filled with curious and *happy* adventures. The other place is where I spend time thinking, feeling, being, knowing, wondering, and sensing how to best understand why I am compelled toward certain directions. Here, I determine whether my compulsions are healthy.

These two places could be called "Happy ME" and "Healthy ME". At their worst, they compete against each other, sabotaging and stopping growth of the other while trying to ultimately be the only one in control.

At their best, they live in *balance* with one another. They can completely disappear, letting the other dominate without a struggle, then reappear the instant it looks like their help is needed.

Happy Me is extroverted, makes nineteen coffee dates in a week, finds plenty of humor during dull days, spontaneously breaks into loud song (*Queen or ABBA, depending on the situation),* and exhibits affection and general frivolity. Hubby likes Happy ME—but only to a point. He does not buy-in completely, because this is not all there is to me.

I like this part of me! I am alive, and fun, and carefree, and it feels like I am sailing through time, untouchable—but it does not last. I crash from this heightened happiness into an arena of accusations:

Insincere

    Flighty

        Lazy

            Stupid

                Irresponsible

                    Incompetent

When I am in the prime of Healthy ME, I exercise, read, actively listen to every conversation, eat wholesome foods, say yes to everything, sponsor more children in South America, and de-clutter the house (*which is a hoarder's way of saying they organize stuff to make the house look emptier*). I volunteer, make multiple meals to freeze for later, and work a side job to increase our income. These are all worthy and good things. BUT...

This kind of output can only last so long before I turn into a freaking-out, angry, closed-off, shut-down, zombie version of ME. This is what broods in my head during this phase:

Pessimism

> *Blame*

> > *Rage*

> > > *Pity*

> > > > *Self-Righteousness*

> > > > > *Helping Santa complete his Naughty List*

Now, I have inquired, and it turns out—Santa does not need any help with his naughty list, nor does karma have a shortage of subjects to visit. This has not stopped me from tirelessly and repeatedly nominating the same name for the worst, most naughty person I know:

Me.

But not *this* week.

Somehow, this focus on positivity has created an absence of negativity about who I am, what I am doing, and what motivates me to breathe. Maybe, the secret for silencing my brain's negative committee is finding some balance between happy and healthy.

I do not know what next week will hold, but I will gently remind myself that having positivity with ME may not always feel stable. It may be wobbly and shaky. I may be stretched from one end of my happy to the other side of my healthy, and it will be okay. Even if I faceplant while attempting the next step, at least I will still be moving forward. Adjusting my crown and getting right back onto that sketchy tightrope, is positively, ME.

Week Six

HOW DOES THE COOKIE BOOK CRUMBLE?

Baking is in my blood! It ranks topnotch on my love-to-do list, judging from the amount of time I devote to stirring, mixing, measuring, and tasting whatever plunks onto a shiny sheet or pan. Not only does it remind me of times spent with Mum, licking batter-covered spatulas while watching her bake, it also helps me remember a lesson I learned a few years after Mum passed. This is the story of 'The Cookbook'.

A year and a half into first marriage and a baby in my arms, I was on benefits for a maternity leave, which meant money was not plentiful. I had already been warned by ex-husband that, if I did not find more work while pregnant, I would be responsible for figuring out how to pay my share of the bills. I am not sure if this is commonly known, but getting a job is difficult when it looks like you swallowed a bass drum.

I was just starting a theatre career, so did what most actors do: I supplemented my income by working at a restaurant. Because people smoked in public buildings in the early nineties, I opted out of continuing as waitstaff and instead found two part-time retail jobs while finishing a three-month run of a musical-theatre show. I hoped this would be enough to cover my share of expenses.

There was NO extra money. I forbade myself to eat any of the more expensive items I was expected to purchase for him, like raw cashews, cheese, freshly squeezed juice, and soya milk. I bought only enough for what the ex would consume in a week. I stopped buying toiletries for myself, making remedies from scratch or not at all. I shopped at thrift stores for anything *really* necessary for me or baby.

As a result, I was a scrawny, frizzy-headed bag-lady, running frantically from store to store—newspaper flyers and coupon clippings waving in my hands, desperate for the lowest prices possible.

Besides looking odd, I was developing an unsettling behavior; Squirrelling away Mum's possessions. When my dad remarried, he and his new wife decided to relocate and auction off the contents of the house in which I had been raised. As the auction date loomed, I began filling up crannies and closets with stuff I was saving each time I made a trip to the farm. *Maybe this was the start of my hoarding?*

Mum had many, many cookbooks. I saved these books, knowing that cooking was one of the ways she displayed her love for her family. So, when ex looked in his usually bare cupboard for the singular cookbook he owned and saw a mountain of choices instead, he ordered them removed from the house. *Like store them in the garage?* Nope! He wanted them *gone* gone.

I boxed them up, sadly, after attempts to negotiate their merit failed. I tried to hide them for a while, pretending to have forgotten about them, being so busy with baby and coupon clipping, so he offered to put them out for the next garbage collection. *That* I could not stomach.

I took a breath, taped up the box, and gave over what felt like Mum's soul to the crowded, cold, cement dumping ground of a thrift store.

You might be screaming at me right now, wondering why I would give up those precious items, and not fight to keep those special connections to Mum.

It was a trade-off. Cookbooks were not the only items on the chopping block for removal or destruction. Knowing I would not be able to convince him to keep everything, I did my best to choose what had the most meaning.

We moved twice in our first three years of marriage, which always involved intense arguments over my stuff. Important things were dumped or left behind, without my knowledge or consent. I really could not bear those books being treated as worthless garbage, so I freed them to a second-hand store, taking solace in knowing it was a place where Mum enjoyed hunting for treasures. It was not a happy goodbye, but at least it was not cruel.

I am thrilled to say there is a happy ending, but I am not going to give it away just yet. How this story ends *and* ties into this week's focus, "Positivity with YOU", goes something like this:

Life surprises me. People surprise me. Cookbooks surprise me.

POSITIVITY WITH YOU

What a busy week! Much has been accomplished—and not just baking:

- Host a support shower for a young, unwed, mother-to-be—Check.
- Bake fresh goods for a global-justice cause—Check.
- Attend my mother-in-law's favorite charity event—Check.

- Run kids to sporting games and activities—Check.
- Volunteer for my regular Sunday-morning nursery shift *(where eight babies show up)*, ready to rock and roll—Check.
- Cook a big family dinner, roast beef and all the trimmings— *Double* Check!
- Pick up a family member from the airport at midnight—*Triple* Check!

Did I mention my full-time job in there somewhere? So, before I fall down dead tired, I should finish telling the story I left dangling.

After abandoning Mum's cookbooks at a donation center for used household items, I left feeling a deeper sense of loss than when I walked away from her interment ceremony. Sure, more time had passed, and the initial numbing shock of grief was over, but I was still grieving in what seemed like interchanging phases of guilt, anger, and sadness.

Chasing after a performance career did not alleviate these feelings. Getting married offered no reprieve. Having my first child, and experiencing the joyful flood of new life, lifted my darkened state temporarily, but it returned during sleepless, new-mommy nights. This was a desperate place and was probably the reason I resisted letting go of things that kept memories of Mum alive.

Almost six months after donating the cookbooks, I was scrambling to make the budget on $87 a week, which paid for gas, groceries for the three of us, and the utility bills. I did cash returns for any unused wedding gifts and baby-shower presents to scrape up a little more dough. All my previous savings were spent making up for any shortfalls when I could not pay the bills.

Each week, there were fewer ways to scrimp, everything already scrutinized to maximum savings. I was hardly using the car, hardly eating, and hardly noticing the extreme shifts in my ex's oppressive opinions. My focus was on that sweet babe and figuring out our next meal. *What does it cost to make and how can I do it cheaper next time?* I was going to prove him wrong and make sure the budget worked.

With no reserves left and having reached the end of the frugal spectrum, I needed to accomplish buying a week of groceries with just over $20. Back then, it would take at least $50 to purchase the proper quantity and quality necessary to maintain the budgeted standard. Discouraged, I set out anyway, baby in tow, into the first grocery outlet where I would find a few items on sale. This store was connected to a small indoor mall, and as the days were getting colder, babe and I would often sit on a mall bench for a while, cooing and laughing back and forth to each other.

On this day, a flea market was set up in the middle of the mall with different artisans and dealers. I decided to head toward the market, instead of the grocery store, delaying the misery of meticulously prioritizing what items I could afford.

Crocheted toilet-paper holders, handmade quilts, wooden crafts, and jewelry tables were lined up to showcase all the unique wares. One table drew my eye from the rest. It had antique trinkets, so I went to take a closer look. There was a section of older-seeming books on one side of the table, and as I approached, one popped out at me, reminding me of a book I remember Mum owning.

The sight of it flooded my senses a bit, remembering my ex asking me to make cookies that were in one of those recipe books he had forced me to give away. Like lemon juice on a paper cut, his request stung, and I felt no joy, or spite, or satisfaction in telling him that he could not have what he wanted—the recipe was gone, because the book was GONE. And now, here was one like it on this flea-market table.

I mused on how rare it would be to find another book like Mum's existing anywhere; My assumption of it being a one-of-a-kind or limited edition was clearly false.

But I had to touch it.

I set baby down, nestled tight in his carrier. I reached out for the book and opened the front cover. My mouth dropped open! There, on the right top corner, was my mother's signature. She had labelled it in careful cursive script.

This is HER cookbook! One of my lost books!

I blinked in disbelief, then stared at the man behind the table looking apathetically into my stunned face.

I stammered, *This… this was my mother's… It was hers… She died… and I… uhhh… I… You see, I could not keep everything…*

"It's five bucks."

Pardon me?

"All the hardcover books are five bucks."

*But… This is actually MY book… and I don't have five bucks (well, I do) but…
REALLY, I don't!*

I put the book back down indignantly, stooped to pick up my beautiful son, who
was peering sweetly from his cozy blanket coverings, and was about to turn my
back on that cookbook once again—but my feet would not move.

NO! This is NOT how it ends. I had followed the rules of that cheesy seventies
poem and set something I loved, free. It came back to me, so it IS mine!

I reached into my pocket and handed the guy 25 percent of the money I needed
for food that week. With the other $15, I went on to buy a small bag of groceries
and headed home with the cookbook. While I slowly unpacked the measly items,
wondering how to use and stretch out ingredients without raising any flags from
ex about not having enough food, I heard the mailman come up the front stairs.
Baby and I went to the mailbox, and to my surprise, a benefit cheque had arrived.
It had come earlier than expected—maybe because of a holiday, maybe because
of an error, or maybe because *it just had to be this way.*

It felt like a reminder that I was not alone in my dilemma. My life, my hurts, my
joys, my struggles, my thoughts—I was not alone. Recovering this cookbook
showed me a different side of hope. It taught me to use just as much caution with
the word hope as I do with the word happy.

This kind of hope is tough, gritty, raw, and powerful. It will stand steady in the
wake of a rebelling teen. This hope screams silently when words that are trying
to escape would damage relationships already in jeopardy. It reframes personal
deficits as benefits.

The hope I am talking about does not contain an unlimited supply of smiles or a
guarantee of skipping over heart-wrenching tragedies. My picture of hope is not
a cartoon caricature of daisies and yellow button faces. My kind of hope is mighty
and deep, carrying weight upon weight of burden and care; It bleeds and cries out
for mercy, yet stays determined to not be beaten.

Hope takes the last five dollars out of my wallet and dares me to trust I will have
enough to eat. Hope returns things I cannot keep, relieving my shame and guilt.
Hope stares through the lies to see the good that will come. Hope sustains brave
and gutsy people when no bravery or guts remain. Hope reminds me that I am

not alone, not abandoned, and not forsaken. Hope delivered my icon this week before knowing it would be an important part of the story…

Positivity with YOU is grounded in *that* kind of hope.

Week Seven

TROPHIES FOR EVERYONE

Last week felt like I had launched from the earth into a stratosphere where wisdom and insight abound, only to tumble softly back into that stable reality of 'everything is temporary'. What I knew yesterday does not always apply today or transfer to tomorrow. Consistently, a twist in the details encourages me to keep working toward a good result. With this in mind, here is Week Seven's icon:

Mum and I won this trophy together for a log-sawing competition. For those non-lumberjack type people, log sawing consists of a raised horizontal tree trunk that is sliced by a two-person saw—and it is a *race* to be the first team who cuts through the bottom of the log.

This was considered entertainment and a celebration of our community's industrial roots, during an annual heritage festival of the friendly town where I grew up. There were several themed events in keeping with the logging and forestry industry that helped build our town.

Looking back, it seems implausible that Mum and I would compete on a team together. I was a self-appointed athletic diva, loving track and field, volleyball, badminton, softball, and—once a year—arm wrestling.

Mum's highest level of athleticism was attained on the curling rink ice, clenching a wobbly broom that seemed to be holding her upright. I remember thinking I would never win if Mum was my partner.

Perhaps sporting endeavors were not her calling, but she tended a very large garden, where she handled a rake and hoe like a machine. I watched her and Dad from a large tree branch which called me to climb and sit upon its wide, strong branches. I hid from their hard-working view amongst rustling leaves, until I was spotted and given a task.

But log sawing was different. This was not our farm work. It was happening in town, in front of an audience, and others would be participating. *The perfect criteria to awaken my competitive nature.* I was ready to pounce into action. I had already become the first female to scurry up the 20-foot high pole and ring the bell that waited for all who successfully navigated this tricky ascent. *Sorry, no photo available.* After scaling the pole in glorious victory, I did not want to lose my momentum by a defeat in the log-sawing event.

I observed our fellow competitors eagerly, carefully watching for signs of weakness. Crosscut saws are very bendy—and sharp! It takes a delicate balance of effort, then no effort, to optimize the energy in the saw. For best results *(winning)*, you can only pull towards yourself. If you push at the other person, the saw bends and stops the cutting action. This means losing time—and losing the race.

It takes focus and balance to be good at this skill, as well as plenty of restraint to avoid 'helping' your teammate slide their half of the blade through. Forcing the saw to do its work, or anxiously pulling before your partner has time to complete their pull, also creates snags and stoppage in the action.

You have a job, your teammate has their job, and neither can do what the other must. Mum and I put our observations to the test and made it easily to the next round. As the competitors got better, we had to focus intently on each other and even unconsciously co-ordinated our breathing to remain synchronized and relaxed. Were a trophy not sitting in my hand, I would be tempted to think I have false memories about this day. I mean, how could we have won? We did not practice or know anything about sawing, nor had we ever worked as a team like that before.

This is what I think it is like to be part of a family. We do not get a practice family to test out before getting thrown amid strangers. We look for clues from past experiences to teach us what works well and what does not. Just when we start to get our feet under us and some things are making sense, we get competitive and compare ourselves to other families we perceive as vying for an undisclosed prize. Being a family is tricky stuff!

Whatever helped Mum and I work together toward a common goal is what I want to replicate here, in terms of being "Positive with US". I will focus on figuring out *my* job, letting others do *their* jobs, and try my very, very best, not to push at the other person.

I am hopeful for a great discovery this week, possibly worthy of a trophy. And maybe… we will all get trophies.

POSITIVE WITH US

I am consistently amazed by the situations popping up, allowing for plenty of practice each week. I started this week recalling one of the finer memories I have of Mum. It occurred to me, our harmonious teamwork toward winning that trophy back then, could be an indicator of what kind of friendship we may have had if given more time. And as an extension, it is a gauge for the kind of relationship I hope to have with my adult children someday. For that, I am truly grateful.

This week's practice took me down a humble road. I already explored happiness, healthiness, and hopefulness—excellent pillars that help keep me in a positive mindset. Now humility has wiggled its way onto the scene, while focusing on my inner circles of influence.

Humility has been a trigger word for me since I was a kid.

First, in grade four, a boy told me I was conceited. I knew he was not flattering me, so I dove into a dictionary to find out what it meant. Since he was a 10-year-old boy and obviously not trying to enlighten me, and I happened to be a hot-headed, dramatic 10-year-old girl—I grunted at him and vowed we would never speak again. I think he obliged.

Then, as I got older, singing and performing became more regular and the size of my audiences grew. If I received accolades or awards for music, Mum would tell me not to get too proud, and stay grounded. Humble. She never complimented me on any achievements other than academic, which were few.

Lastly, and absolutely the most impactful impression upon my self-esteem, was the nagging of my ex about how to be a "humble, righteous woman". This was defined as:

- Neglecting my outward appearance
- Submitting to my husband
- Doing all the household and parenting chores
- Somehow making an income, but never leaving the house

Whenever I did not live up to this standard, *(almost daily)* I was rebuked for my lack of humility and implored to seek immediate forgiveness. He appointed himself as judge over my ultimate salvation, and I did little to stop him. I also let him convince me that the loving family and friends of my childhood were not amicable relationships. He made a case proving I was undeserving of love from others and therefore must rely on him solely for acceptance and love.

Unlovable.

That was my constant condition. Useless to anyone—and to God. How fortunate for me that this humble and righteous man took pity on my worthless, damned soul and 'loved' me anyway. He categorized and labelled my wretchedness from despicable to evil, citing his honor and benevolence as my only saving grace.

In real time, to say this felt like torture, would be incredibly understated. The pain eased when I stopped fighting his lies and accepted that he was right. Once I set my thoughts to align with his, the war inside my head diminished.

One thing felt certain—I was not lovable.

My heart breaks for this girl, this ME, and all other humans who have stopped listening to their feisty selves. That voice is placed there by the Creator of Love, so we might know how carefully and wonderfully we are made—and how mysteriously and completely we are loved. Really, truly loved.

Anything after that kind of life should be easy, right? The torture over—living free—loving free—makes it feel like paradise now, yes?

I should easily trust love in this moment, right?

This week, we are facing another teen prematurely heading out the proverbial door. The door is not slamming in our faces, but we have been clearly rejected and our love labelled void. This child wants to be somewhere free of people that would stop the ones we love from harming themselves. Well-meaning parenting has been blamed again, and our family dynamic is changing.

Hubby and I are devastated. We work, play, and love full-on! Our kids have all they could want and need—the answer almost always being "yes". We spend time with them, engage in meaningful conversations, and lay out reasonable rules with normal consequences. Family is a priority and both of us have held off on career moves that would decrease our time doing things the kids want to do. They know we love them and would do anything for them, yet they refuse to be parented. They run away, get high, break laws, and hurt themselves and others… all to be free of 'US'.

This stirs up a big question: How do I remain positive amidst this? The horizon looks stormy and scary. I want to take over, get everything under control, push my way into each corner, come out swinging, and beat this ugliness down.

Then I remember log sawing.

Effort—then no effort.

Pull—there can be no push.

With that, my breathing eases, my spirit settles, and fresh eyes see the rest of the picture.

We put our best parenting practice into play, pulling our weight with integrity and compassion, balancing restriction and release, responsibility and freedom. If we push and feel the blade bend, we wait and give space for our kids to pull back in their own strength and time.

In anticipation of snags that would hinder a smooth transition of blending our two little families, hubby and I opted for pre-emptive therapy. Originally, this was a strategy we employed to be able to help the kids adjust to their new living arrangements. But it soon became clear, the kids were quite adaptable and able to deal with tricky situations by simply living out their own individual days. They were accepting change, accepting new siblings, having fun despite of the hurdles on any given day, and smiling resiliently. It turned out that hubby and I were the ones who needed the most help figuring out our blended relationship and parental boundaries.

When our middle boy left, he *meant* to burn the bridge connecting back to us. His siblings felt confused, asking questions about what was going on. We did not know how to answer them, so they moved ahead and shaped their lives without him. Hubby and I still long for his return but have taken cues from the younger family members and work toward regaining our form, reshaping our structure, minimizing the gaping hole left by his abrupt departure—and being okay.

We let go of the pain, because hanging onto it, does not fix it. We could relive the hurt over and over and still not have what we really want; Our child back in his bed, safe and sound.

When I thought it was my duty, as the mourning mother of a runaway child, to suffer and grieve for the rest of my days, it did not bring him back. Being unwilling to release my suffering changed me, but not in a healthy way. I went from living a life of new love and gratitude to creating a life of neglect. I neglected myself, the other children, my work, my passions, and it did not stop the heartbreak.

I humbly admit, it took my other kids modelling their healthy adaption to change, to battle back from depression and other ugly places. As we stare long and hard down another loaded barrel of turmoil, here is what I know:

Our family is not perfect, but it is my favorite.

We do not have complete victories, but I like our spirit.

We send well wishes and wait with open arms for those who choose separation.

We plod along with our standard traditions, like Friday night pizza and movies, Sunday suppers, extreme-contact driveway basketball, and daily story telling.

> **"My desire is to LOVE**
> **beyond the broken, shambled bits of our lives."**

This is OUR positive place!

Joy is waiting. Love is infinite. Peace is here.

Week Eight

THE SHOE-BAG

This is week what!?

Incredible! This week completes two of thirteen topics toward my fifty-two-week sojourn, and it continues to be the richest, most meaningful undertaking I have experienced so far in my life. Not only do I get to observe and evaluate living to the fullest, but I also get to live it!

It. Is. Changing. Me.

This week is all about "Positivity with THEM". This morning, it is proving hard to find my focus with a moderately large spider hanging over the computer desk, looking like he is on a quest of his own, for a nice warm place to hide during winter months.

I see three different scenarios determining the fate for this corner dweller. Since one daughter is deathly afraid of spiders, I could leave the little fellow alone to surprise her while she is doing her homework…

OR I could keep him as a family pet—replacing the tortoise that has recently relocated to a family who actually thought he was an endearing companion—maybe wrapping the eight-legged black dude up under the tree for a happy Christmas-morning gift…

OR I could set him on a difficult expedition of his own, by either facing an outdoor Canadian winter or swimming happily down the toilet. Whatever I decide, it must be now. Although I am not afraid of this hideous species, I cannot tolerate its proximity, allowing for a potential descent upon me while I am absorbed in writing. Uhhh… nooo…

Critter lovers, rejoice! Spider and I had a chat, not so much in words but in the exchange of knowing glances. It readily agreed that, if I did not squish her, she would skirt away into the snow looking terrified—even though she had every intention of crawling right back up into our cozy house again.

Mother, Cop, Spider-whisperer—I do it all.

Now I can concentrate. This week's icon is a shoe-bag, which I thought was an out-of-date concept, likened to the rubber slip-ons men wore over their shoes in the 50s and 60s. However, a quick google search revealed that there is still a high demand for the protection of footwear against the elements. Surprisingly, men have more options than ladies, for shoe-carrying products.

My biggest surprise? Even after twenty-five years, google has a picture of a shoe-bag just like Mum's. If you are interested, use the words 'ladies black leather shoe bag' in a search engine and you just might find it.

Since the snow and cold have suddenly become our winter reality, I can use this shoe-bag appropriately. It has been placed in the front closet of every house I have lived in for the past twenty-four years, but has only been used twice: Once, when going to a Christmas party six years ago and the snow was coming down in buckets, and again yesterday to start my week of "Positivity with THEM". Since this shoe bag is completely under-utilized, why do I keep it—aside from the obvious answer of being a hoarder?

It looks nice.

It is well made.

I like its rich texture.

It smells like a keeper.

I remember Mum carrying it.

And, the day *may* come, when I carry a fancy pair of shoes to a party again.

On days when the wind howls, the snow blows, the commute to work is long, and the van's service light has been on for the last two weeks—it is a super good idea to wear full-out winter gear.

A few people looked oddly at my shoe bag, one brave enough to ask what it might be. I explained that a lot of the ladies I knew growing up had bags to put their shoes in, like we have hooks to hang our purses on now. It was a thing. A good thing. Toes stayed warm, and you had a better grip while walking.

Mum had premium taste in shoes and paid a hefty sum for pairs she decided would join her collection. Protecting them was top priority, making the shoe-bag a valuable resource year-round.

I share Mum's love of shoes, but how does this have anything to do with being positive with the rest of the world, reaching beyond the borders of family and close friends and into potentially the whole world? What will I be attempting to practice this week, other than spider protection and how to carry shoes from point A to B?

Leaving great footprints.

Have you ever noticed footprints in the snow left behind by someone unknown? I like to imagine who they are, what they look like, and what kinds of shoes they might have been wearing. Male or female—adult or child—I create a guessing game of what color they are wearing and to where they are heading.

If someone were to guess my direction from the footprints I leave behind, I would want there to be no mistaking that my life was heading towards a positive place. If they guessed a direction I was going, it would be UP. If they guessed the color I wore, it would be brilliant YELLOW. If they guessed the sound of my feet passing, it would be a sweet BELL ringing. If they summarized my life into a single word, it would be "YES".

Sounds like some big shoes to fill.

POSITIVITY WITH THEM

Over the last three weeks, I have probed the definitions and descriptions of being happy, healthy, hopeful, and humble. Using the word 'healthy' to determine whether something is positive for me, was vital. Chasing happy no longer draws me. I plunked into the mucky trenches of what true hope looks like in a torn apart life, only to realize that my idea of hope is intensely raw and tough, and never completely extinguished. Humility kicked up its heels by asking me to accept the differences within our family and be okay despite it all.

This is a lot! My life should look like a miserable string of suffering, and yet I see so much blessing in the messing.

I may not have appreciated the best relationship of my life, without the mis-marriage to someone cruel.

I may never have encountered this flood of goodness, joy, ambition, and dreams, had I not lost Mum at an early age.

Because the ex would not allow me to wear makeup, my skin had fourteen years free of aggravation, which I am sure contributes to my youthful glow now. *Ha ha.*

Because I have held the burden of loving troubled teens, my empathy has increased toward other struggling parents who are asking, "Where did I go wrong?"

My suffering has given me Knowledge.

It has given me Compassion.

Has given me Strength.

Given me Awareness.

Given me Endurance.

Given me Power.

The power to *be* better, *know* better, *do* better, *see* better, and *live* better.

Being positive with THEM is a sharing thing.

Just as I have found comfort in the company of fellow sojourners, I too must comfort others—and listen—and look for opportunities to connect or make appropriate eye contact. When someone else contributes to a healthier outlook in my challenges, it may not change the outcome, but it feels different. If a stranger starts a humorous conversation after accidentally stepping on someone's toes, or a person riding an elevator leaves the other occupants smiling as they disembark—mission accomplished.

Having positive interactions with people outside my usual circle reinforces that trouble is only temporary, akin to hitting a reset button.

Brains and hearts are powerful instruments. They want to function well for us in the role they were designed to perform. Sometimes it takes little adjustments to keep making progress. Sometimes, after a trauma, it takes a total reset to establish something normal again.

My brain is on pace for total healing from my third concussion. Writing is helping. I am not where I need to be yet, but I am closer than I was yesterday, so I know brains can heal.

My heart has been torn a million different ways yet continues to pump through each season of pain and grows stronger with each intentional step toward joy and peace.

If life's greatest hurts are temporary, why do I get so rattled by obstacles? I do not need to worry, because whatever odds are stacking up against me, against those I love, against anyone experiencing pain—it will pass.

This is wonderful news, but I think there is more! "Positivity with THEM" is also about removing judgements.

Being a woman of faith—raised on it, socialized around it, schooled through it, interested in it—I feel that a big part of living positively is intertwined with how I see God, or Spirit, or Soulfulness, Religion, Inner Beliefs—how you name it is not important. Whatever the *thing* is that connects us to power beyond ourselves, that is the stuff I am talking about.

My faith ventures have taught me there is a greater Love beyond me, with infinite strength and more knowledge than I could ever attain. Because of that, I have help when befriending a vulnerable girl who fears what people think, questions her worth, and longs for acceptance. Her frailty is mine. Together, we bear witness to our insurmountable value as people on this earth.

And finally, being positive with THEM is knowing that it is never 'the end'.

Pain and pressure are uncomfortable. I would rather back away than keep pressing past the hard stuff, but it means I am missing the most healing part of my life. And what story would be worth reading if the characters had nothing to fight against? Nothing to learn? Nothing to look forward to? A good story is worth the work.

I think humans are abundantly more fascinating than characters in a book. We have epic adventures and glorious endings waiting in all of our chapters. I am learning to look onward with anticipation, to wherever an obstacle will lead me next, because if the way seems blocked up ahead, I get to choose a different direction.

I am sure there would be a lot less fighting and more positive action in our world if this kind of thinking became contagious. When all else fails, and the plot in my life is getting intense with drama, I hope to look around, smile at my supporting characters, and remind myself—pain is temporary—and a great story is about to be told!

AJ

"The waves of change,
Fight 'em or float.
Your choice."

What are some of your stories that need changing?

CHAPTER THREE

SENSITIVITY

Life does not get better by CHANCE
It gets better by CHANGE!
~ Jim Rohn

Week Nine

TO BE... OR NOT?

Time for a new topic!

Week Nine finds me in the moments leading up to Christmas with my focus on SENSITIVITY.

I am so excited to get going on this topic. Not because I was getting bored with being positive but because it is a thrill to complete each week and month, realizing there is so much more to discover!

It is with great hope and gentleness that I begin testing the idea of being sensitive. I am eager to wrap my head around how to increase my sensitivity to the people around me, who seem to NEED a lot of consideration right now. Those people shall remain nameless for now...

I found myself running to catch up to the thoughts and ideas that were racing inside my head, excited to capture it all in words and basking in anticipated accomplishment, when I suddenly realized, I was not following the pattern. The first week of any topic is supposed to be internally focused, looking at my own sticky areas and then using that reflection toward an effective approach with others.

C'mon AJ, you are doing it wrong...

POP!

Hissssss… That is the sound of the wind leaving my sails, thoughts escaping from my head, and a heavy sigh being exhaled from my lungs—*well, this is no fun.* Maybe I am not finished yet with positivity.

Where to begin now? Maybe with a confession. This week took longer than a week to write, meaning I am now behind schedule for the fifty-two-week timeline. I have been attempting to incorporate a regular writing routine into an already jammed life. Setting time aside for this detailed and reflective task has not been easy. Writing is a fantastic addition to my busy life, and I truly crave the time spent scribing out thoughts. It is one of the healthiest things I can do for myself currently, but it does not always take priority.

Then December rolls into town…

Ho! HO! WOAH!

HELP! I know I am not alone in experiencing a marked amplification of 'busy-ness' occurring each year at holiday time, especially among people who have kids. I am a huge lover of this season, probably because Mum made it very special for us growing up, so I tend to dive into all activities and traditions with abandon. The memories of anticipating a thoughtful and beautifully wrapped gift from Mum was my favorite part of Christmas.

'Gift giving' was her language of love.

I did not hear affirming words. Quite the opposite, in fact. She demonstrated her feelings about my greatest passion, singing, by cringing. It was only *after* she was diagnosed with cancer that she became my biggest fan. *More on that story in the weeks to come.*

I did not get much quality time with her. Only rarely did she attend or participate in things that were important to me. It was hard for her to watch my performances (*see comment above*). She did not stick around to witness the sporting events she drove me to, always having a purchase or errand pulling her away. I thought it was because we lived in a small town, and when you have a chance to get into the city, to get what is not available where you live, you do it! As much I as tried to understand her priorities, all I wanted was for my mum to see me win at something—to show her I was good at stuff.

I did not receive affectionate hugs or touches. I did not hear her say "I love you." For me, being the kind of mother who grabs, cuddles, holds, hugs, and articulates my unwavering love for my kids constantly, *not* using these techniques to increase your bond with your children, is an alien concept. The closest thing to affection Mum could muster was the occasional pinch on my rear-end. Somehow, I knew that this sharp nabbing with her thumb against my buttocks was the best way she could express her feelings. I accepted this and did not hold it against her.

Her secondary language of love was performing acts of service; Sewing Halloween costumes, driving us to activities, preparing special Sunday-morning breakfasts and suppers, working unpaid overtime hours on community-enhancement projects, and hosting all our friends and neighbors with food, games, and more food. We put a plaque on her gravestone listing all the projects she spearheaded for the betterment of our town. Dad took it down recently. He thinks Mum wouldn't want that kind of bragging attention to her work. Now the plaque sits at my front door and is a real conversation starter for people as they come up our sidewalk.

The plaque lists the things she DID… not the things she *didn't* do, so it will be my icon this week.

I hope there is more to be learned about the things I am *doing,* even if that means seeing the stuff I am *not* doing, first. The plaque weighs over fifty pounds, so I have selected a smaller, secondary icon; A little bronze flowered broach.

Being sensitive. It begins now.

Choose your own ICON for Sensitivity:

SENSITIVITY WITH ME

BIG Surprise!

Exploring being sensitive with ME took a completely different turn than what I anticipated. I was pretty sure a large dump of sensitivity would come barreling down from opening skies of enlightenment and awesomeness—but the universe had alternate ideas.

Here is what happened:

Nothing.

Life was not bumpy this week. A couple little obstacles… a few baby potholes, but nothing like the twisty-turny terrain that usually shows up. Maybe obstacles have become the norm, so my navigation is on automatic until something tougher appears. So far, I have delved into things from my past that have already garnered some work or current stuff that has not been too challenging. Perhaps it is time to shake things up.

For the past six months, I have been diligently working toward healing from a concussion I received in a random fall that should not have knocked me senseless, but did. Not only did I stop working for a time, but I also entered intense rehabilitation to gain back the mental ability and physical strength I once took for granted. I am almost recovered and feel ready to do most tasks, but there is a lingering emotional barrier that is proving difficult to breach.

My therapy, or recovery, seems to have various levels. The surface level is just understanding what I need to know or do. The second layer is acting in a way that honors the knowledge gained. Thirdly, I must practice the action required to establish a new norm. And lastly, I must be okay with any reduced abilities and not judge myself for it.

I think all these levels have their snags, coaxing me to simmer at one stage or another before realizing, I am not moving on—have not shifted gears—am not finding the results I seek. At this stage though, I am just as likely to boil over suddenly as I am to scorch the bottom of my sanity pot with a slow, steady burnout, evaporating all my energy.

Emotionally, this concussion and the symptoms that accompany it are a real drag! It looks like a severe depression, and feels like it, too. It is not easy to talk about, and it is harder to explain. I am not comfortable disclosing my limitations to anyone. I assume people think I should have control over whether my brain will play nice or if it will blank out.

As much as I love having those rare days of putting my feet up, staying in jammies all day, and shutting off the world *(including technology)*, it is just not my thing. I like people, and working, and going places, and doing things, and have not been able to do any of this for months.

This is actual brain illness, a valid medical condition, and I cannot talk about it, or completely get over it. So, what is stopping me? Fear?

I could fall again.

I might look like a failure.

I will be weaker than before.

I cannot trust my brain.

People will label me.

I will label me.

The list could go on and on. Fear trumps my motivation, my creative vision, my raunchy motivational songs, and the triumphant life statements I vow to follow—for a while. But I get tired of fear.

"FEAR IS BORING!"

Fear wastes a whole summer spent at the beach by not dipping my toes into the ocean, not even for a second. Even though I am not entirely fond of the water, at a certain point, I simply must decide to get my hair wet, plunge down into the fleeting cold, and kick up some fun in the waves. When I let myself be tossed upon the turvy ocean, I always end up with a smile on my face.

Big waves make me a little nervous, though. I have been face-planted into the sand enough times to vividly feel their indiscriminate power. I compensate my feeble ability in the water with a strategy of facing the waves to see what is coming and always being able to reach the bottom with my toes. Even so, huge waves still catch me off-guard, and I desperately flail my body toward oxygen and the safety of my towel, where I rinse my sandy mouth and let the sun burn away my shivery goosebumps. So, why should fear be part of this storyline?

Because it *sounds* good. I cannot tell you how many conversations I have had where the foundation of what is being exchanged is the imagination of a million unfounded fears. I think I talk a lot about the worst things that can happen—and I think it is time to stop.

I search the catalogs of my memory to see how many of the worries, doubts, freak outs, rants, or breakdowns have affected the outcome of a difficult situation—and have come up with none.

My emotionally charged responses or actions are not an effective indicator of future events. This forces me to challenge my previous beliefs that this kind of verbal output is therapeutic.

I said at the start of the chapter that I had a BIG surprise.

This week, I anticipated getting more internalized and more in tune with my emotions, being discerning with whatever stimulus was driving my awareness, and becoming more sensitive, period. It did not work.

Like I said, nothing was happening this week other than regular life, regular triggers, and common annoyances. Intensifying my efforts to be more sensitive tipped the scales in the opposite direction of where I anticipated.

Instead of finding resolution to sensitive triggers, my hyper-awareness of feelings increased conflict. Instead of finding humor in little upsets or mistakes, I got offended. Staying tuned to only my feelings, I expected others to openly confess their wrongdoing. It did not stop there.

When I only considered myself—my own happiness, my own comfort, my own sense of wellness—not only did I want people to know they hurt me, but I also wanted them to suffer for it!

OUCH!

Lesson for Week Nine: Be LESS sensitive with yourself.

Puuuuu-llllease!

AJ, do the world a favor, and quit moping about stuff that goes wrong. Stop taking every action and word like an intentional attack and stop talking about every bump and curve like it is a tragedy. **Not everything is about ME.**

Maybe that is what I needed to find.

> **"Think a little LESS**
> **Live a Little MORE"**

Fear, anger, worry, doubt, regret—these feelings fade when I am LESS sensitive with ME.

Week Ten!

I am celebrating and glad *(very, very glad)* that this is the direction I get to walk today, on the way to a better tomorrow.

Before I begin with this week's topic, I am going to deviate from the normal pattern and instead attempt to give some insight into what is happening behind the scenes while I write.

Why? Because I cannot go any further down this road without being sure that everyone knows a couple of things about me and my life.

My problems do not disappear by typing upon a magical keyboard. I do not have it all together and do no approach these topics lightly. I have been writing through some struggle-filled moments and want to lay down some transparency about this reality.

While I believe in the privacy of the ones I love, I also believe in contesting a fake media presence that would serve to mislead others about who I am and what this book is all about.

So, without any further explanation, this is my actual life:

10 WEEK CHECK-IN:

September - December 2015

We are not starting anywhere fresh. We are bogged down in past labels, current trends, and future predictions—all certain of a negative outcome.

Too many relationship hurts are left open and raw, not knowing when they will be bandaged up.

Having not gone through this transition with my own mother, I do not know what to expect from a relationship that changes from daughter to friend. What I see as loving is not being received as such, which makes me wonder if love becomes void when the intended receiver rejects it.

Rejection has been too often a reality of my besieged bonds with my kids. Recently, one rare communication occurred with a child who has been estranged, and I could not have handled it worse. I stuck my big nose in the middle of a sibling conversation, causing their relationship to become strained, and potentially isolating that child from the last thread of connection to our family.

Why couldn't I stay the course of my rehearsed automated responses, instead of going down the fatal tunnel of guilt, shame, and past hurts? This only ends in anger and bitterness, and more rejection—and the pain of losing your child comes rushing back as though it had just happened.

One adult child is leaving the country, inspired to seek out adventurous territory and make their mark on the world scene. Having just found him again, it is hard to watch him go, yet this goodbye is heart-lightening in comparison to the alternatives of the past.

One child is straining to find their next steps after school and not sure of their direction. How can I sit by and not push just a little? They resist. I am starting to feel like a very unpopular mom, feeling far from being able to connect to my kids and them far from wanting to connect with me.

How am I supposed to love in this?

SENSITIVE WITH YOU

There is more to share regarding the emotional burdens of now, but at least this is a start in understanding why my writing goals are not always attainable within a span of seven actual days. Time is a bit symbolic for me now, not measured in units, but rather in emotional chunks. Maybe you have similar barriers to finding time to read, reflect, or journal. Let's not forget saving time to veg in front of a TV with a bowl of popcorn without feeling there is something else we should be doing!

Therefore, I declare that from now on, any and all deadlines shall be removed from this book's mandate of finishing within fifty-two weeks. It will take the time it takes.

No more. No less.

There. I am free—and so are you. Finish this book and YOUR weeks in whatever timeframe makes sense for your life.

ENJOY THE SHOW

Now, last week I wrote of the Christmas tidal wave that came crashing into town. So, I have decided to incorporate Christmas into my icon for this week:

A tablecloth made by Mum for a friend *(who recently returned it to me when she found out about my writing)*.

Because gift giving was Mum's language of love—for every holiday, not just Christmas—she gave many special presents to my brother and me. However, Christmas was the pinnacle holiday, where gifts were lavished upon us, and never once was the holiday season remotely disappointing or lame. *Except that one year when I desperately wanted roller skates and instead got a skate box cleverly weighted with books to make it feel like roller skates were inside—but no. It was an earring tree. Pretty sure my brother crafted that shyster gift.*

I love getting ready for Christmas. It brings to mind bright memories of growing up on a small farm, where skating, skiing, caroling, and visiting were all part of what felt like a regular and relaxed busy-ness throughout the winter. Maybe, as a kid, it did not seem so busy because I was not the one working, baking, cooking, planning, driving, or buying.

As a grownup, I realize Christmas doubles my normal amount of busy. Combine that with an acute awareness of other people's needs this week, and it confirms why quiet spaces to breathe are at a premium.

Something from last week struck an unfinished chord, so I continued to mull it over to see where it might go. It is this idea of wanting to emotionally punish others whom I feel have offended me. This was revealed when I intensified my sensitivity on how my feelings were being affected in any given situation. How many times in a day did those feelings occur? More than I care to admit!

I am offended when a colleague does not return a greeting that is as cheery and generous as my own.

I am offended when my kids do not appreciate the acts of service performed for them by two loving parents every day.

I am offended when a server at a coffee shop or grocery counter avoids eye contact, staring directly into their register while asking me questions they are trained to recite, but not caring about my answers.

I am offended when my hubby teases me about things that I believe actually bother him, while he claims he is just having fun.

Punish them! These offenses cannot be ignored. I *must* act emotionally cold, indifferent, and sometimes even rude, so there can be no mistaking that an offence has occurred. Only after the guilty party has profusely apologized and been adequately deprived of my approval, shall I be vindicated.

There is just one little problem with this justification... it is far from flattering.

My kind of vindication tends to look like:

- Muttering through a slow-motion workday that drags on in growing bitterness
- Stirring a big pot of tension at the family supper table, which everyone must slice through in order to have a conversation or else choose to eat in awkward silence
- Ignoring the "Always Kiss Me Goodnight" motto hanging above our bed, grunting out a flat *"love you"* before rolling to the far side of the mattress

So, I must ask—who is getting punished in this?

I am!

This default is a punishment for me. My day is not productive. I waste the few moments I get to spend with my family, and I do not sleep well. Most of the time, after the smoke settles and I look back at a scene that unfolded while trying to enlighten someone regarding *their* offense, I am clearly the one who ends up looking like the offender, half-crazed, petty, immature—and that is putting it nicely! I am sure there have been other terms used to describe me when I display this kind of behavior.

I used this idea of emotional punishment when approaching the people in my inner circle, as I analyzed how to be sensitive to YOU.

Many opportunities to practice came up this week:

1. Hubby and I are still reeling from having one less teen in the house. As parents of growing teens, we are getting used to the anxiety that comes when they become ready to take on independent ventures. We pray there have been enough good moments in their upbringing to keep them as safe as possible, but ultimately, we send them off in goodwill, and hope for their amazing future. These are good goodbyes.

The not-so-good goodbyes are tricky. Slamming a door that was opened freely, burning bridges built with good intentions and love, and spitting on the ground that offered nurturing for years—tricky does not adequately describe *that* kind of goodbye.

But our current parenting story is different because all the effort put into raising this fleeing child gets relentlessly interrogated... by us. Fear can grip every corner of your heart. Common worries, things which every parent tries to protect their precious babes from while under their wings, turn to terrors when a child leaves prematurely.

Facing another empty chair, staring into this aching absence, one question drowns out all others: HOW are we going to live without each other?

2. A close family member seems to be avoiding an emotional request I made of them, either not willing or not able to fulfill it. Yes, I know the tactic (*because I use it too*); Avoid the problem, and maybe it goes away.

My bid was carefully weighted, to be sure it was first necessary and then kind. Somethings are difficult to hear from people we love, since they are the last people we want to disappoint. Yet these are the very same people who will not stop loving and extending themselves toward us, right through our awkward and hurting bits and pieces. Extending myself to YOU feels unappreciated currently, so I look back to patience for some help on that.

3. One teen is critically sarcastic to me. I put myself back into Mum's shoes when she was dealing with me as a teenager (*or, more accurately, NOT dealing with me as a young, snarky gal*). She often stayed silent when

my gnarly looks or testy retorts flared up from an innocent question or interaction. But where did that come from?

I do not remember Mum and Dad modelling disrespectful language or manners to me and my brother. Occasionally, there were upsets when navigating who was spending more money than they should, or what was an appropriate time to arrive at any given destination, but nothing beyond what I know now as normal family conflicts.

My parents' failures in communication pale in comparison to the modelling my kids had from their biological father towards me. It is a wonder they knew to call me "Mom", as they regularly heard the derogatory names my ex had for me. Once those sweet babes understood the meaning of the words, they would come to my defense and explain to their grown father why I literally could not be the things he was calling me.

This is a classic example of verbal abuse. *Can't I just blame the ex for this parenting struggle, please?*

Understandable—but no.

UGGH!

The zingers are in full force lately. They sting because I am getting the result of a wish I heard Mum make once; For me to someday have a sweet girl "just like" me.

4. Last week, I said I was not going to mope about little things that seemed offensive. I was going to be less sensitive when people were just being people. And I have stuck to it. No verbal venting from me this week. I physically bit my tongue, cheeks, and lips to get through some family interactions, sometimes re-biting in response to a carried-over issue that had not healed, but I stayed the course.

RESULTS?

- A chance to repay the support hubby gave to me when I did not have hope, could not see light, and could not bear my own weight in our relationship. This describes the BIGGEST way in which I have been able to be sensitive this week. Trusting the ones I love enough to let them take all the withdrawals they need from our joint emotional bank account, knowing they will deposit again someday when they have more wellness and strength.

- Letting people come through on *their* timeline, not mine. Emotions and relationships are not on deadlines. Just because I am focused on the potential time left to create the best life I can envision, does not mean that everyone else should have the same focus.
- I get it. Teens go through their phases. Even though my adult-aged children have proved their phases will not last forever, it takes *mucho* effort to believe that the phase upon us now shall ever pass. If I look back upon young AJ—with all her impatience and sarcasm directed toward Mum—I would say she took a right turn, resulting in an entire year of blogging dedicated to dear 'ol Mum!
- When my tongue stops wagging, my legs start moving. Eliminating the verbal venting causes me to find other ways to deal with my inner tensions *(without completely chewing myself to bits)* like with exercise. Seems to be a fairly standard approach in recent generations, since we do less physically demanding tasks than our predecessors, to remind ourselves to move and work our bodies—okay, sometimes it is more than a reminder—I often must drag myself kicking and screaming toward fitness.

So, I made a deal with myself. If I complained out loud this week, I would do an additional workout. I guess I was super motivated to avoid an extra work out, because I did not break this deal. It feels a bit sad to know I can trick myself like this, but since it worked, that win is for ME, YOU, and anyone else who chances across my path!

Week Eleven

HOW TO CLEAN EVERYTHING

Do you wonder if your family is odd?

Ever get a feeling you have unusual issues?

Wondering why people keep asking if you have your own TV reality show?

This IS my life—this IS my family—this IS Week Eleven, and the examination of being "Sensitive with US".

I am going further back this week, looking at a time when US was very different. This felt like a looooong phase in my life, and one that I thought might never end, except with me or my ex inside a box and buried deep in the cold, dark ground. How often and desperate were my prayers, to escape from that madness, requesting either freedom or strength to manage the conflict. Since I remained in that spot for fourteen years, I guess the answer to my prayers was strength.

But I did not feel strong. I felt unworthy and lonely, having no close adult relationships other than with a person who believed it was his duty to save my unrighteous soul and point out the evil lurking in all my actions.

I felt abandoned and unloved, with Mum dead, Dad neutral, my brother distant, and friends prohibited. Guilt and shame were my constant companions, having ignored the sage advice given to not marry so soon after Mum's death—to not marry this complicated man.

Stubbornness (*or stupidity*) certainly ruled on the day we sat to write our premarital compatibility test. My signal should have been the sarcastic laughter prompted by the questions that were to reveal if we had similar beliefs. When the results were explained as having significant markers for a troubled relationship (*maybe even impossible*), I looked at it like a challenge. Within six weeks of exchanging vows, I was pregnant—and it began.

Upon hearing that he would soon be a father, whatever had been tinkering inside his mind as idyllic concepts became outward laws. What we discussed initially as good philosophies now needed to be acted on, and adhered to without question, because the health and wellness of the growing babe inside depended on it. Ex's contribution was already complete, having accomplished the miraculous task of fertilizing a healthy 23-year-old woman in her conceiving prime. He did not need to adhere to these new rules. He had already done his sacrificial service of donating highly optimal genes.

Do you sense a mocking tone? How about scornful? That would be correct. As much as I have tried to dial in my bitterness and anger over being treated cruelly, there is still a piece of me that has not completely forgiven.

It has been nine years since my emancipation. Maybe I need about five more years of peace, which will then be the equalizing number of years away from the pain, before forgiveness can completely take hold. Fortunately, through many blessings and generous relationships, I am starting to forget. I realize forgiving and forgetting are two very different actions. So, my work continues, as triggers from the past suddenly plunge hidden memories into acute awareness, clearly and obviously not forgotten—not forgiven.

For fourteen years, I believed his thoughts, followed his guidance, aligned my decisions, and submitted my will … mostly. Yes, there were knock-down, drag-'em-out, fights. Yes, I stood up for myself and my fading beliefs, even after the violence started. Yes, for years I refused to let anything or anyone—not even the abusive, unstable father of my children—to rip apart my family. Yes, it almost killed me. Yes, *he* almost killed me.

US was not happy. US was not healthy. US was not to be trusted. US made me sick!

When I finally left that marriage, life was not instantly transformed into a paradise of peace and freedom. Years of gnarly, twisted chains were cast around my heart and spirit, entrapping me emotionally, spiritually, physically, and sexually, even after the locks were already opened. Crawling out from under their weight has taken years—is *still* taking years. Yet, I keep clawing ahead, refusing to let them hold me forever, refusing to live as someone who was once held captive.

How will this affect the way I am currently sensitive to US?

Good question!

It would be easy to say that any sensitivity would be better than the ZERO sensitivity I once knew to be US—which is a very low standard, and not a good fit for making this life great. I think this is going to take a whole lot of gentleness, a strategy that is showing up consistently whenever it is time to roll up my sleeves for some good, old-fashioned, messy work.

Is messy frightening to you? I get anxious, nervous about disrupting my comfort zone. I worry about how long messes take to clean up, or who might see the mess. I do not want US to feel messy as it is a sad reminder of an awful part of my life. So, how will I navigate this messy, imperfect life?

Maybe my icon will help. It is a specialty book of Mum's, written for people who are interested in cleaning up messes. It is simply entitled: How To Clean Everything by Alma Chestnut Moore, last printed in 1968. Of course, the messes in this book are related to stained materials, like, carpet, clothing and furniture, but perhaps there will be more connections to this topic than would be obvious on the surface.

So, I take a deep breath, looking my past and present straight in the eye, and head in a direction I hope will reveal secrets about how to best be sensitive to US.

SENSITIVITY WITH US

"Please don't fix,
Please don't do,
Just sit so I know I am not alone."

I am tempted to end it right there. Seems clear enough. Let's just hold hands and everything will be fine—could be the equivalent of pressing the easy button. I am guessing there is another layer to explore, if my time processing and filtering the first ten weeks of rich experiences is any indicator.

Writing is helping healing thoughts to take root in my emotional memory. There is hope that the scarred and rigid hollows in my heart will become smooth again, pliable, softened, yet stronger, which is an addicting feeling!

It feels good to figure stuff out, to get to the bottom of a trench and realize that *you* are still *you*—a little wiser and a little muddier, but nothing a hot shower, a sudsy luffa and lots of loving care cannot fix.

Speaking of mud, let's pick up on the idea of how to clean everything. Specifically, how to be sensitive to the big, messy—US.

My family lives in a constant state of change. Our dynamics swell and shrink, whirl and crash, lay quiet and run wild, contingent upon which family members live within our walls and which live elsewhere.

WE are in a different world than the one I remember as a child. Living on a farm, my attempt to leave home when parents made me mad or tried to structure my adolescent floundering, looked like a typical runaway scene from images I saw in cartoons. A checkered hankie tied to a stick and slung over a droopy shoulder comes to mind.

At the tender age of 11 *(perhaps a magic number for this week)*, I stormed down our windy driveway that led to a gravel road. Depending on which direction I decided to walk, I could make it to town in about an hour or keep walking for days.

So, where was I actually going with my yellow skateboard tucked under my arm and an oatmeal cookie stuffed into my pocket? You guessed it—nowhere. I sat down after coming around the first bend of the lane, out of sight of the house, and waited to see who cared that I was gone.

Dad eventually came driving down the lane and saw me pouting, crossed-legged with my skateboard propping up my elbows. I had already eaten my cookie so had nothing to do but perfect the sour look on my face. He told me to 'git' home, and I did—probably to eat a few more cookies, but also because I was that kind of kid. I kicked up dust to raise a fuss, but ultimately, I did what I was told.

In blended families, many options exist to run away from your home and never look back. I have already alluded to one child doing just that. It feels like a lifetime has gone by in four and a half years. It was so painful, so frightening, so frustratingly helpless, and the hardest aspect was remaining sane while all hopes of his return were being ripped away.

As he got further and further from our reach and influence, I got more and more desperate to grab onto him and never let go. Calls in the night from concerned police colleagues, calls from him when he was cold and starving, and calls from complete strangers trying to help this vulnerable young teen who looked out of place. All this slowly drove me into the clutches of my first diagnosed depression. I hope to write more on that subject, but not this week.

This week is not about ME. It is about US.

Hubby and I had done the research, were proactively engaged in therapy for blended family help in navigating the potential trials of our new US. We followed a gradual method recommended for establishing levels of relationship between us and all the kids. In total, we took two years to fully blend our lives, the first six months of that figuring out whether hubby and I really *liked* each other, before deciding to introduce the children.

That could be what saved us from the gloomy statistics of second marriages not lasting more than two years. The stats also predict that if second marriages make it past the two-year test, there is a greater chance of staying together. Happily, we are into our eighth year together, our sixth year blended, and our fifth year of marriage.

WHOOPPEE!

Compared to the US in my first marriage, this US rocks!

And yet, here we are, not really rocking. We are rolling, though. Rolling through each day, holding on for another sunrise, another chance to create a day worth living, no matter how we feel and who is under the roof.

Now that two sons have fled, I am left to think, *Is it US? What are WE doing wrong?*

Too many rules?

Too many talks?

Too many activities?

Too heavily involved?

Too worried?

Too *not* worried?

WE have had more than four years to contemplate why first boy left, and slowly evolved our parenting into a version that looks almost completely opposite to the old one. You would think that this transformation of philosophy and approach would severely diminish any similar incidents from occurring. It did not.

WE changed—and second boy still left. Another sting for US. US is broken. US cannot be good. US does not rock.

More days than I care to remember have felt like we are hanging by a thread, clinging to a faint glimmer of hope, or almost losing grip with reality. But as I looked at US this week, I also saw laughter, love, patience, romance, encouragements, support, teamwork, problem-solving, general shenanigans, and one daughter returning home. Then something dawned on me:

I have been the one labelling messes as failures, but that was old language from my brainwashed mind. All had to appear pristine on the outside or I had failed and would suffer the consequences. Nothing could look messy, or feel messy, in that old life. Since these memories are attached to strong emotional pain, they are still able to blur my reality.

I have other memories to draw on, though. There was one very significant moment, early on in our blended family days, that started changing my twisted definition of 'mess'.

Hubby was sitting with the kids while I was singing with the police chorus for an elderly community audience. Drinks and dessert were being served to them while I sang, which seemed like a perfect set up for my young children to sit with a man they were just getting to know. My youngest girl, who was 7 at the time, ended up spilling her full glass of juice all over the table, chair, and herself. All my kids' faces turned pale, looking in horror for what this man left in charge of them, would do.

I saw them hold their breath, bracing for the coming wrath they were accustomed to receiving in these instances. My breath also left for an instant, as I watched this event unfold, helpless to respond from the stage. Hubby very lovingly took her by the hand, sat her in his chair, immediately gave her another drink, then cleaned up the mess without so much as a blink.

The mess really did not matter. WE spill. WE slip. WE wreck. It is time to finish this forgotten lesson now.

"Messes are NOT failures."

Hmmm... If WE are not failing in this mess, why does it hurt so much? I thought pain was a sign of something in need of fixing. When pain of this magnitude happens inside our family, it feels like a mistake, like something is very, very wrong. Yet, when I remained open to what else was present in the mess, I found joy and support. Both were just as present—just as sure. Maybe I need to be okay with all of it.

Pain. Pleasure.

Hurt. Humor.

Sadness. Smiles.

Being sensitive to this balance is what keeps US going and it ALL belongs on the spectrum. My conclusion?

"*Pain is not a MISTAKE.*"

WE have US in the pain and mess, so we are never alone. We may never know why we lived through certain difficulties or challenges, but we know without a doubt—it did not break US.

And I love US for that.

Week Twelve

MY MOTHER WAS RIGHT

This week was fun. Christmas dinners, Boxing Day visits, late night gab sessions—all with the people I lovingly include in the circle of US. I had so much US in the last seven days that my Week-Twelve introduction is going to be a little shorter than usual.

Before I cut to the good stuff, there are a few thoughts I am needing to fit into a bigger context. Sometimes nasty things that get drudged out of the past often look random or feel surprising. By now, maybe you are like me and nothing on this fifty-two-week odyssey, is surprising. So, I say...

Bring IT!

The icon I used this week is a poem Mum had written down when she was younger. It was preserved inside a scrapbook that had college-era photos and wedding-shower cards, so she may have been in her early 20s when she penned this:

> If you know the Lord, you'll need nobody else.
> He'll see you through, the darkest night.
> And keep you on the road marked right.
> Follow the light, His wonderful light.

Not much else I could do with this icon, except display it on our Christmas tree. This poem does not indicate who authored it, and I know very little about that time in her life. She did not speak often about college or school memories. I remember her bringing it up once, prompted by attending her twenty-fifth high-school reunion. She did not reminisce about friends or events that helped shape her view of the world. No stories or wild tales about living in a small town with a twin sister—no hints of a favorite teacher or subject—but instead Mum came home with a warning for me!

She advised me to be nice to all the nerdy people in my school. Those were the ones who became successful in business careers, were still married to their first partners, and seemed to be doting parents. I am guessing this was her criteria for a successful life.

Well, Mumma … I think I was already pretty nice to everybody *(except during that angry phase in grade three when I wanted to pulverize all the boys)*. As I was 16 years old at the time of her warning, and not really looking to settle down ever, I took her words to mean that I should be nicer to my brother, whom I regularly accused of being a nerd, and who *did* carve out his own business from scratch, and is a lovely husband and father. So, she was certainly right about that.

Continuing that note of mothers being right, let me share what showed up under the Christmas tree from one of the kids. A black and white sign with a red heart that reads:

"OH God, My Mother Was Right About EVERYTHING!"

This will hang perfectly ANYWHERE in our house, but I am thinking the bathroom the kids use is a good place. First thing they see in the morning—last thing before bed. *Mother is always right AND has a sense of humor!*

The caveat offered with the sign was that its message is not currently binding on the relationship I have with my kids, but rather a reminder for ME about the grandmother none of my kids met. Clearly the kids have their own sense of humor.

This is the stuff muddling through my mind as I prepared to be sensitive to THEM. It could not have come at a better time. I am reminded that this portion of the month is set aside to go beyond the scope of my closer connections and broaden my focus into career and community circles. A recap of the last three weeks would go like this:

- Don't be SO sensitive; People are just people
- If I am offended, I can choose my reactions
- Messes are not failures, and pain is not a mistake

I SURE needed all these lessons this week. I was fighting to keep my job!

SENSITIVITY WITH THEM

The down-turned economy has not threatened my employment, like so many other people in my city presently. It was not an illness or poor-performance standards that came calling for my resignation. It was not a booming voice from heaven, telling me to devote myself to the blog *(and nothing but the blog)*, remaining at the keyboard for the rest of my days, nevermore to wear a uniform or pack a lunch. No, these factors did not bid for my quitting papers this week.

It was a person. One customer, if you will, who was dissatisfied with how I had 'assisted' him seven years ago and has gone to every supervisor, level of rank, and now an executive board level to complain about my service.

I just want to make sure the timing is quite clear… SEVEN YEARS. That is how long this thing has been poking me. I have been prodded by reviews and appeals, written several explanations and statements, attended his ranting mediatory sessions whose format disallowed me to talk, which resulted in furthering his dissatisfaction, and finally ending up here. This week. 'On trial' to defend myself in a situation that happened a lifetime ago.

Now, this is not like a criminal trial, although the verdict will become public knowledge and could seriously jeopardize my reputation within the organization and community. To put it bluntly—the stakes are high!

The first day of trial was 'fun'. He told many lies, in an ironic attempt to prove I had been untruthful, which for policing careers is serious and could be grounds for immediate dismissal. I kept telling myself: *It's not personal; People are just people.* Since I knew his complaints were erred, this sensitive approach seemed to work well. I did not get upset or feel offended.

Day One—done.

The second day was really *not* fun. This would be the first time in seven years that he would hear me speak my testimony face to face and listen to my side of the story. I had prepared extensively with the legal representation offered from my employer. I was equipped to handle any possible attacks from this individual who was determined to have me fired. I was doing well, carefully listening for questions designed to trick me into admitting the guilt he wanted to prove. Halfway through the day, I felt confident I would come out in the right and true light, consistently saying what I have said for seven years—the truth.

Somewhere between the first three hours of answering questions and lunch, his lawyer turned up the heat. I was on his menu, and he tried to eat me alive! His tactics were dynamically different, making rude grunting noises after I responded, as if my words were disgusting. He scoffed out loud between my sentences, like they were idiotic, remarking that school children would be less obtuse. *I did not use literary license on that word. He actually said, OBTUSE.* He started to raise his voice with impatience when I asked him to rephrase his complex questions, designed to draw confessional evidence out of me.

It was getting messy. It hurt—so I kept repeating to myself: *This is not a mistake. I am not a failure.* But I totally wanted to crush this man!

After all, I had already taken my lumps. Against my better judgement and under pressure to make this complaint go away, I officially 'accepted' disciplinary measures for what 'they' said would be a great strategy to make this complainer stop for good. He did not go away. He was encouraged by this gesture and appealed for more to be done.

This ticked me off! Not only was I pushed into signing this paper by a couple of senior company men who thought they knew better—in a closed-door, surprise meeting, without a union rep or peer advocate present—it also did not have the promised effect! I lost significant trust in the organization and continue to process the residue of bad feelings about this unjust treatment. But back to the trial...

With smoke about to billow from my ears, and tears filling the corners of my eyes, I asked for a short recess from my testimony and set off for a brisk walk down a quiet hallway.

I know I am at my breaking point. My brain is still recovering from concussive symptoms, and not yet operating at 100 percent of my normal ability to focus. Still, I cannot let him get inside my head, cannot let him under my skin, and should not fall for the bait leading to an emotional reaction due to his unprofessional behaviors.

I can feel myself losing grip. Old voices in my head agree with this new attacker. They band together to become a continuous loop of guilt and inferiority.

How am I supposed to be sensitive to him—to this? I am innocent, and this has been hanging over my head for more than half of my career.

I have eaten crow—lost sleep—and have compounded heartache and heartbreak from other stressful life events happening in concert with this.

Steady girl… hold your ground, but I could not hear myself anymore.

After a few more hours of hard-hitting questions and delivering earnest answers, it came time for closing remarks. Not only did his lawyer concede to some of my version of the events, the judicator commended me for my reasonable and responsible earlier admission, a factor that would go favorably for me in the ultimate outcome.

I was stunned. My head spun backwards to the time when I had been coerced to accepting this inaccurate admission. It was a tremendous assault on my character, a dig at my work ethic, an offense to the core of my being, and one of the hardest things I had to do in my career, because I knew I was NOT guilty.

It was a BIG hurt, a BIG mess, and was unresolvable for a long time. How did it transform into the thing that would now likely save me?

I will not know for a while whether this situation is finally over. I leave that decision to a person in charge of weighing this issue, and ultimately—in the hands of the Divine.

After copious tears and a few expletives, I decided to have a good evening with my family despite a less than ideal day. We laughed, ate good food, enjoyed fond memories of the boys not with us, and I went to bed feeling loved and well.

My final lesson in sensitivity is this:

The hurtful people and situations I encounter in my community and career—that cause me to distrust my calling—would have me stop believing in the good of what I do. They try to convince me to harbor bitterness for the people I serve, to sabotage trust and safety at every interaction—and then this emerges:

"Pain has one job. It grabs our attention."

If the fear of getting hurt is holding me back from working and living with abundant and compassionate energy for others, let me remember this… pain is not permanent.

AJ

"If there be regrets,
Let it be for repeating a lesson already learned."

Who are your healthy influencers?

Would you let go of something sensitive to be transformed? How?

CHAPTER FOUR

KINDNESS

Be KIND whenever Possible.
It is ALWAYS Possible.
~ Dalai Lama

Week Thirteen

KINDNESS KICKS OFF

If you are anything like me, there is a point in the Christmas season where I would rather buy my own presents to save myself the effort of looking impressed during gift opening.

I know, I know. This is terrible, and not at all the point of what makes the exchange of gifts magical. So, instead of worrying about materialistic gifts, I am focusing on a more meaningful present I want to give to myself; Starting this new year with a focus of KINDNESS.

I am surrounded by people who believe in a 'religion' of kindness, who choose kindness when it is difficult, when it is politically incorrect, and when it would be easier to be bitter, cold, cruel, spiteful, or simply neutral. Their philosophy is straightforward, as far as I understand:

"Kindness matters too much to live any other way."

Early on in our dating relationship, hubby and I were careful to always speak kindly when we had something crucial to say. The more we got to know and trust each other, the less careful we became in voicing our thoughts and opinions. It got to a point where the deposits into our emotional bank accounts *(Remember those from Week 10?)* were not equal to the withdrawals we were making with our impatient responses or refusal to actively listen to the other. I am told relationships can only stay in a healthy balance if using the ratio of *ten* deposits of the good stuff for each *one* withdrawal of ill-placed behaviour.

10:1

That is a heavily *imbalanced* ratio for achieving balance!

Noticing an emotional wedge starting to form between us, we checked our approach to one another and found it lacking. We corrected our kindness level *(or lack of it)*, and the wedge dissolved. Whenever it returns, as it consistently has, we pay attention to our deposits of kindness.

My oldest son, now 22, had just turned 14 when I left his father. He felt loyal to his dad and ultimately decided to live with him full-time. His three younger siblings lived with me in an adjacent neighborhood, where he would visit often. It was not long before my son had completely turned his heart against me, quoting all kinds of untruths I can only assume came from his father. My son would ask, "Why did you leave my father?"

At first, my response was solely based on the abuse and how unsafe we were in that controlling environment. After a few years of soaking up the love of a supportive family and friend circle, I enhanced my answer to include *phrases like 'not being compatible'* and *'not good with each other'*. I explained how much his father had changed in the first year of our marriage, specifically after news of my conception with him.

As more years passed and my heart got braver, it was possible to go deeper into my answer, delving into layers not possible when wounds are too raw—too recent. The deeper I went, the simpler the answer became.

He was not kind.

I could have managed it all—the home-schooling of four kids, the strict dietary rules, the OCD cleaning rituals, the religious extremity, the squeaky tight budget, the isolation from family and friends—if only he had been kinder. My son used to raise many arguments about how his father was loving and righteous, but he could never disagree about how harsh and critical his dad behaved toward me.

It would not have been a happy life, but I would have stayed with his father unwaveringly had he not been so cruel. This cruelty paved a direct path to violence.

Because he saw me as an undeserving, worthless object, it was easy to strike me down or toss me about. As this lesser human being, I could be commanded to perform a multitude of absurd and demeaning tasks. Since no one could measure up to his unachievable standards, I was automatically used as a scapegoat for all that went wrong.

It wasn't the physical harm that did the most damage in our relationship, it was his emotional brutality. I could no longer live with it. The unkindness was killing me, robbing me of an urge to take another breath; Knowing that breathing meant continuing to live in a callous, merciless world.

Kindness matters this much!

It saves relationships. It validates people. It changes situations instantly. It sustains weary and hopeless travelers on distressing, uncertain pathways.

It heals.

As Week Thirteen starts, I have already found myself trying to create a loophole. During the first week of the last topic, I had trouble keeping the learning about ME, had to restrain myself from skipping forward to how it might look with others. With kindness as a topic, it seems different.

Instead of wanting to jump ahead, I am catching myself using the ME focus to excuse some borderline unkind behaviors. *Forget about THEM. This is MY week.*

Oh, the tricks I play to get away with stuff I do not want to take responsibility for, like:

Not using manners

Acting entitled

Serving myself

Thinking I am better than others

I was guilty of all of these in a space of a twenty-four-hour period, even considering my best Christmas cheer!

How do I find the right balance for being kind to myself—*when* to be kind to ME and *why* to be kind to ME—yet not forget about the standard kindness that should be shown to others? I will use my childhood pillowcase for my icon this week. It should help me center my first and last thoughts of the day, as I rest on it during nights of what could be an intriguing week.

Choose your own ICON for Kindness:

KINDNESS WITH ME

One week is NOT enough time to explore the depth of what being kind to myself might look like. This week has been tough! It was a good thing I had a soft place to start and end each day, with my faithful fluffy pillow absorbing an unusual amount of stress in the last seven days. If I am ever stuck for a topic to write about after these fifty-two weeks are finished, coming back to this challenging week would be a good start.

With a kindly note to myself: *You have a long way to go in terms of being kind to yourself*—I begin.

I have joined the ranks of millions of others deciding to create a healthier version of themselves this year. I started a diet. *Oh boy!* I am wondering now, after the first three miserable, detoxing days, if kindness to ME actually exists.

It began as a very kind thing, looking at my lifestyle, my eating habits, and my fitness goals and realizing that I am not on a good trajectory toward sustainable health. Some changes needed to happen, and although I have previously resisted the diet traps by increasing my exercise or making small changes to how I ate *(like no food after 6:00 p.m.)*, I find myself almost the same weight as when I had a full-term baby inside my belly—a whole other being inside of me waiting to be born. Wow!

It has been fifteen years since I carried the weight of an actual pregnancy, meaning in another fifteen years, I could potentially be carrying the weight of twins, if I do nothing about it now.

Please, do not get me wrong. I know weight is completely an individual perspective and my ideas about ideal weight or shape should not be compared to anyone else's ideas. I have people in my circle who have battled, accepted, or dismissed their excess or lack of weight, and I deeply respect our individual and unique approaches in sorting our complex perceptions surrounding body image.

I told hubby a few years back that we are getting older and can expect to have more blubbery bits here and there. But now that I am starting to bulge everywhere, I am not so sure I can accept this for my future. I think I need to fight a bit harder to avoid buying another pair of jeans in the double-digit size, since I no longer fit into pants that have been my standard for several years.

It has taken many months to get back into good health after a concussion took me out of regular work and activity. As my brain healed, I was not able to do much exercise. Getting back my energy levels is a priority for doing more vigorous exercise, which would be easier if I lost some weight. So around I go, back to the diet!

I enlisted hubby to join me in this mission, although he really does not need to lose weight and seems to have energy galore. Being the supportive and smart man that he is, he said his body could use a little freshening up on the inside. *Thank you, hubby.* Now, three days in, he is wondering if this was a good idea. Both of us are hungry and grumpy at the same time now, making polite conversations tricky. If this is our biggest worry this week, Mum would call it 'small potatoes'. If the kids heard us complain about being grumpy over a diet, they would call it an 'FWP' *(First-World Problem)*.

I am very aware of having the luxury to even contemplate reducing my daily food intake, when so many people in the world are desperate to increase it.

"It is a privilege to choose hunger."

Food has always been available to me in my lifetime, for which I am grateful. Growing up on a farm, we stored our garden harvest in freezers, on canning shelves, and inside cold rooms; The product of hard-working parents and two reluctant mini helpers.

From the time I was small, I understood how food ultimately ended up on the table—planning, tilling, tending, toiling—and longed for that kind of understanding for my own, city-raised children. I tried to integrate visiting farms into our homeschooling outcomes, and had the children help tend our tiny strawberry and carrot plots. These were easy enough to manage.

Tomatoes are difficult to grow. I tried several unsuccessful attempts when the kids were young, for science experiments but also for the price tag that would be eliminated from the weekly grocery budget. I would start them indoors early, transplant them twice, and maintain a consistent climate of humidity and warmth.

I must have drowned about a thousand plants before proudly watching a handful of successful vines sprout from the ground. Once the vines were established, I took great care to encourage the arrival of the blossom and budding stages.

Summer weather does not always play nice in my city. The skies open suddenly with thunder and hail, chasing people and vehicles toward adequate cover. I was too preoccupied with cooking to notice the dark clouds rolling quickly into our neighborhood. When the sound of heavy rain met my ears, it was already too late to set up the mounted roof for the hothouse storing these darling tomato plants. I rushed outside—*all instinct and no plan*—with only one goal in mind: Protect.

Cover and protect those precious vines—with my body first, then grabbing a piece of cardboard that was on the back deck. I did not have time to grab a coat or shoes. The children were startled when I bolted outside, so now stood watching curiously from the kitchen window. Their little eyes following my movement as I bent over the tomato plants, desperately willing myself to be wider, and hoping the cardboard roof I was holding would last through the storm.

The spot I chose to stand firm against the elements was facing into the house. I could see all my children's faces, pressing against the window, wondering what Mommy was doing. Their curiosity slowly turned to sympathy, as they watched huge hail stones pummel my bare arms and shoulders, with only a thin layer of cotton between these sharp, biting stones and the level surface of the stretched-out flesh on my back.

The stinging on my skin brought tears to my eyes—then it hailed harder.

I bawled, crying out when bigger stones contacted my exposed body; It lasted for what seemed like an eternity. All the while, those worried little eyes peered through the glass, so I kept shouting affirmations to them between gasps of anguish: *Mommy's okay... it's okay... I'm okay.*

What do tomatoes and kindness have in common? Nothing, I should think. But when I think about what it took to taste the reward of those juicy tomatoes—to get them to their full, amazing potential, the commitment needed to reap their harvest, I see a connection.

Kindness does not happen overnight. I have started the seeds this week and am trying to figure out a best way to keep them growing. I am guessing it could take about a thousand tries before seeing any success. There may be hailstorms to endure. I may have to comfort others when it feels like I am being tortured, but it will end. This kindness work has rewards that can be shared, that renew hope, that inspire planting seeds again next year… and that give me purpose.

Kindness is tough as nails!

Having kind thoughts, kind words, and kind acts takes an intensely determined mindset to accomplish. I have far to go, not only on this diet but also figuring out how to truly see kindness flowing freely within myself. My commitment to ME is this:

No negative judgments or internal backbiting for messing up, or for it taking longer than expected to arrive at the destination. You will arrive precisely when and how you are meant to; No sooner or different than is needed.

Kindness is a butt-kicker, but I am worth it. And so are you.

Week Fourteen

THE MEGA-LIFESTYLE

NO messing around, no fancy introduction, just straight down to business in Week Fourteen.

My icon this week is a pic of our family when I wanted to look JUST like Mum. I think I was 10 years old. I love this photo, not only for our fabulous hair but also because Mum had made my dress, and it was my one and only shot at being a flower girl. It may have also been the first day of my life when I looked like a girl—that's right. AJ was *(is)* a tomboy.

How are your reflections or resolutions going? For me, the diet is okay.

I am alive.

I have not eaten anyone.

And today... today, I feel good. Good enough to hit the treadmill AND push the snow off the driveway *(again)* before going to work. The whirly white flakes mesmerize for an instant, slowly falling to the ground while I watch from the front window. It is like they are inviting me to stretch and breathe in my focus for the day:

Kindness... kindness...

Even though last week's focus on ME was void of a significant victory, it was good to discover that the work must continue. I think that could be said of all these topics. More work is necessary and will never really be over. The whole point of discovery is to keep living in whatever knowledge I find, letting it change me, mold me, grow me—like those tomato plants. The care it took to find a way to grow them successfully, getting advice, and years of trial and error—that took determination.

It takes the same commitment to be on a diet or complete a project. If my mission is to change my life, I cannot look for temporary solutions. I must go deeper. The results I am pursuing inside and out—writing and dieting—all of it will be pointless, if I simply return to who I was and what I was doing before daring myself to be different.

I do not want to be changed for just a moment, or for this to be a fifty-two-week blip on my life-screen. I started this to permanently impact who I am and what I am about.

Forever.

Diets usually have temporary implications. I am writing as though my life depends on it, just like my body depends on what I give it to eat. Since I am the only one deciding what to feed my brain, my heart, and my body, I guess it makes sense to sync it all up and think long term. Whatever changes I make should continue to serve me until the end, or why am I investing in them? I am going to call this my 'mega-lifestyle' with an intentional architecture that is built to last.

Choosing habits to make life better reminds me of certain parenting strategies employed for kids who challenge the norms. Since I have a few of those personalities in my nest, I have drafted a couple different blueprints for building sanity during parent vs. child conflicts. For one son, I drafted many plans, trying to reign in his unpredictable behaviors.

He was almost 10 when I split from his dad. He welcomed the change as a reprieve from the wrath he felt from his father in greater frequency than any of his siblings. His almost equaled the wrath I received, though not quite. There were less ways for my ex to mistreat the children than to mistreat me. I made sure of it. Except for one time, which I hope to get back to, if the weeks will allow.

My son started standing up to his father and me from the time he could physically stand. I was opposed to spanking in general but was overruled when it came to what discipline methods should be imposed on kids who did not obey—or got dirty—or made mistakes. This kid was good at messes and mistakes, so he got walloped—a lot.

For reasons I am not aware of, my ex-husband thought that it wise to send the boys to a semi-private school, maybe to feel privileged or maybe because he distrusted my home-teaching, but off they went. My younger son was in grade one then, and I kept homeschooling the girls.

He rightly disclosed to his teacher that his daddy had whipped him with a belt, which raised the alarm and a home visit from a social worker followed.

I was caught in the middle. I did not agree that discipline should be administered in this manner to any of our sweet children, but I was pressured to defend my spouse and his twisted interpretation of a book I deemed Holy. If I did not agree with him in public, I would be punished later. So, this lovely government lady argued with my ex, explained the law, and noted we would be monitored in the future. I felt like she left knowing there would be no change in his discipline methods, even though he eventually appeased her by saying a belt would no longer used.

Brace yourself for this:

HE LIED.

I felt abandoned and helpless. This was not the first time an intervention had been attempted, and not the first time I watched a person who was trying to help, walk away. Was no one able to stop this from happening in my family? If I felt this way as an adult, it had to be worse inside a young, tender brain.

When I split from ex, I had no idea how I wanted to parent, except that spanking would not be an option. I know lots of parents are divided on this subject, but when coming from a violent beginning, I think my choice is understandable.

No spanking. Okay. Then what instead? My kids only knew to modify their behavior to avoid being spanked, so what did I do? I yelled. I yelled my head off at them! They screamed back. We yelled and screamed for months before I saw that habit needed to be different. Back to the drawing board.

Plan B: Ignore the undesirable behavior until it goes away. This is a time I called myself "Zombie Mommie"—thanks to shift work, and single parenting, and partying. The kind of patience it takes to ignore a kid who enjoys stirring the pot with all his siblings and with a zombie lady in charge, well—let's just say ignoring was not always a viable option. Combine that with all the kids going through emotional upsets like revolving doors and voila! The undesirable behaviors never went away. Plan failure. Next.

Plan C: Have another caring adult talk to them individually. Police officers, school counsellors, therapists, pastors—all had a turn with my toughest kid, with little result. How about a trusted friend who was volunteering to be a mentor? Good thing I regularly debriefed these little interactions or would not have learned how she was planting seeds I did not want taking root inside my children.

This is starting to sound like growing tomatoes.

So, I try—and try again.

Plan D: Design a privilege program. This was meant to capture all actions and attitudes, desirable and undesirable, giving them a numeric value to be added up at the end of the week, establishing what level of privileges would be allowed that child for the following week. Time on screens, time with friends, and number of chores, all were at stake for each level of privilege.

This system was flawed from the start, as it solely relied on my ability to record any actions necessary to create an accurate scoring. Then my whipper-snipper son calculated how many awful days he could have in a week to stay on the plus side of his privileges. He gave me two and a half angelic days, while the rest of the week I ripped out my hair *(or laughed hysterically when he was not looking)*. This kid had a crazy sense of humor, even when he was acting out.

All it takes is a little cleverness, or a shift of intentions, to thwart goals from being realized. I do not want to calculate my fifty-two weeks to get what I want for now. I do not want a temporary diet that ends right back where I started. It needs to be more.

When I think of more, I think of a feast. Not a food feast but a life feast; Full of health, balance, and faith that never ends.

Second week of kindness and a high veggie content starts NOW!

KINDNESS WITH YOU

Kindness… is challenging.

Yes, I said it.

Okay, in a larger picture, I might be judging myself too harshly, so I will suggest that I was certainly *nice* to everyone this week—but kind? I am not so sure.

NICE is easy! I can do nice all day long, every day; In my sleep, hanging from the moon, blindfolded, with a 150-pound anchor dragging behind and the worst spin-class instructor hurling insults in my face—and I will still be nice. Kindness, as I am learning, is on another level, and not an easy one. Let me explain...

When I first introduced kindness as a topic, I described it as being a crucial factor in a few close relationships. Some relationships were already relatively healthy, and one was not healthy at all, but kindness had an impact on whether those relationships lasted. I want to explain one of those relationships now.

My older son stayed estranged from me for over eight years after the divorce. His reasons included, remaining loyal to the twisted logic he had grown up with and not wanting to interrupt his participation in a sport he loved. Since he was coached by his father, there was some persuasion that he could not achieve his goals if he lived with me. He also feared ejection from the training club, as his coach-dad threatened to do, should our son have regular ties or communication with me.

As a result, my boy would initiate visits with his siblings, have a magnificent time playing with them, and when it was time to go, would rattle off a script meant to rebuke the unrighteousness in my house. It was clearly a strategy necessary for him to continue his visits. I recognized the tone in his speech as being coined by my ex. The fact that this script included returning to the cruelty from which we fled was enough of a giveaway. Good logic—going back so he can keep humiliating and rejecting us. *Sounds like ex kind of logic.*

At first, I said nothing. I hoped the advice I was given in the first stages of separation was true and attempted not to talk badly about the other parent. It did not work. I refused to talk about their father, while my ex said whatever he thought made him look good. This is a common storyline for nasty marriage breakups, which is probably why the original advice was given. But I think this approach only works if there are two relatively healthy adults in the mix. When one is abusive, how do you say nothing, while watching your impressionable kids believe in something sick?

So, I started battling back in my defense, appealing to my son's sensitive nature with the wrongs committed against me for fourteen years. This was also not a successful approach. It drove him further into the trench being dug between us.

Knowing I needed to find another strategy, I tried establishing boundaries for acceptable topics while he was with us. We were not to talk about his father, the divorce, my personal life, or how I should parent his siblings. It broke my heart when I had to ask him to leave a few times, when he could not stay within that boundary.

He too created a loophole around my behavior modifier; Coming over to play games, running around the house, eating whatever he wanted, being as loud as he wanted, and then on his way out the door, delivering a condensed version of his script in the time it took to put on his shoes. As I hurried him out the house for not following my rules, he would still be lecturing me over his shoulder and sprinting away before I could respond. I did not know how orchestrated this pattern of behavior was for him until after a dramatic episode occurred.

He had been visiting earlier that day and left one of his public library books with his little brother, a gesture of love to make his younger sibling happy. He must have told his father this fact, and came frantically to my door a few hours later, forcing his way past me and up the stairs, with his shoes still on. I tried to stop him, wanting to enforce another boundary put in place about respecting my house, and if shoes on the carpet would never fly at his father's house, why should he think it is okay at mine?

Being a sweet and gentle boy all his life, he fought off my halting embrace, started yelling as though he was in great distress, and began crying out of frustration while he searched for the book. After retrieving it, he fled out the door to a waiting vehicle being driven by the man who was driving my son to this madness.

This is when the kindness approach began. No more pressuring rules, arguments, boundaries, or expectations. He needed kindness from me. Nothing else would ever match the pressure he was feeling on the other side of his life. So, I listened to his rants, silently rejecting his script in my head while he delivered it faithfully. I reframed any negative comments he made around his siblings or changed the subject to model where a healthy conversation could go… and I kept at that for over three years.

He responded with almost complete disconnect from us. Starting university out of the country increased the physical and emotional distance between us. It was clear he had no desire for a relationship with me, which also severed a relationship with his siblings.

Two years of silence ended on one of his Christmas breaks. While visiting with his almost-adult sister, he agreed to come say hello to me. He entered the house he swore he would never go into and made polite conversation with me and new hubby. He also accepted an invite to have a private tea with me. We ended up talking for hours.

He was troubled, because he did not feel like he knew me. He wanted to hear about my childhood, any fun college days, what the beginning years of marriage with his father were like, and he looked at me through the same eyes as he did when he was young. Warm, curious eyes that sparkled as he talked about scientific theory for hours. I had no hope of comprehending his theories, even when he was 7, but nevertheless, he would talk, and I would eagerly listen.

I am not exaggerating the hours spent listening to him talk about science. Our homeschooling day never really ended. The conversation would just continue, as did the exploration of his little mind—into the kitchen, into the laundry room, into whatever room my chores took me to next.

Those memories are sacred.

Remembering that special time we spent together when he was young, was painful in comparison to the thousands of days we lost through broken connection—yet something else was showing up along with the pain.

Encouragement.

I believed we had an unbreakable bond created in those moments of simplicity, those moments of a mom listening to her son—so with great rejoicing, I felt this part of my boy coming back!

But then his gaze shifted. He looked at me with eyes more familiar to his father's than to the son I knew, suddenly appearing jaded and suspicious of every word I spoke.

This was not an attempt to reconcile. It was an explanation of why he could not have me in his life. At 20 years old, he still felt forced to choose.

My heart dropped to the floor in disappointment. Instead of coming closer together, he was telling me I would not be invited to his graduation, wedding, or any other significant moment in his life, out of respect for his father.

I peered into his conflicted eyes and softly said, *I understand.*

Even more than that...

I agree.

No one should take happiness away from him on any celebratory day. I loved him too much to ever ask him to feel like he was choosing between having his father or his mother attend.

That may have been the biggest 'kindness' moment in our history, certainly my biggest and hardest effort to stay true to my intention. I guess it would be easy to be kind to the people who are being kind to us, but when the hurts keep coming, how do you keep the kindness flowing?

I did not hear from him for another two years.

Yesterday… I booked my flight to attend his university graduation!

MIRACLES HAPPEN!!

Was it kindness that took hold of him finally? Maybe maturity strengthened him against being manipulated any longer. Or maybe it was both. Whatever led him to ultimately decide I could and should be part of his life again, it may not have happened if my kindness had not been consistent.

There were lots of wrongs for many years, and I am still getting it wrong. I fight on the same hills over and over—feeling hopeless while trying to find more hope and desperately seeking remedies to heartbreaks not healing—not ending. Perhaps it was these battles that made me desperate enough to try kindness.

This week, I came face to face with myself: A girl who fakes it for a crowd, a woman who can pretend she is empathetic, a mom who can disguise her selfishness, a wife who can avoid uncomfortable feelings, and I think I need… to do better.

Like I said last week, kindness is kicking my butt!

Even so, I am not giving up.

I believe there is a version of myself that feels, thinks, sees, talks, and breathes kindness for YOU.

> When given the choice between being right and being kind,
> choose to be kind.
> ~ Dr. Wayne Dyer

Week Fifteen

THE FAMILY SPOON

Mum was a foodie, before being a foodie was a thing. She loved trying new recipes and quietly beamed when serving a new dish. She was also very secretive about certain recipes and ingredients, so if you are hoping I might finally reveal the mystery of that-one-dish-you-wish-you-had-the-recipe-for-but-never-got-from-her, I am going to disappoint you. Mum did not give me those recipes, either!

On occasion, I have curated exquisite meals from my kitchen pantry. But when questioned on how such deliciousness came to be, rather than reveal it was a 100 percent fluke occurrence that I have no way of replicating, I bashfully say, *It's a secret family recipe.* If Mum was faced with the same question, she would nod and smile like she was agreeing to share, and then hope the person would forget they asked.

Mum caught me writing out one of her recipes for a church lady that left our house without getting her request in hand, and later asked me to get it for her. Thinking nothing of it, I hunted for the famous carrot and cauliflower dish Mum made for special meals, unaware that this lady had been asking Mum for months. Mum's smile was a mix of delighted pride and mischief, as she calmly told me not to give anyone her recipes, explaining that in doing so, it would stop them from being special.

Top secret recipes... Mum had her eccentricity.

It seems fitting to use a kitchen spoon as my icon this week. It is from the dinnerware set my family used while growing up; Quite fitting in a week that is focused on family or 'US'. The tip of this spoon is chipped in a circular pattern, like someone may have taken a bite out of it. How this happened, is a true mystery. It is a very sturdy spoon, born of the era when everything was made to outlive humans. It is certainly a chip and not simply a worn-out patch, as the notch is significantly grooved and not smooth. I am left to imagine what could have made a gap like that in a solid steel spoon. I conjure up images of it being used to leverage the opening of a bottle lid or potentially used incorrectly as a tool for random home repairs.

No matter how this fragment occurred, it makes the spoon even more dear to me. Because of this quirk, I can recognize it easily mixed amongst other spoons in a drawer. I like being able to spot things I love and know they are mine. If it were sitting on a flea market table *(Week Six)* or lost for years, I could confidently and boldly reclaim it.

It is the spoon my big brother and I used to stir cookie dough when we were old enough to follow a recipe independently. Mum held this spoon countless times, stirring up deliciousness for a family she loved. This spoon is a run of the mill, 1970s, factory-made product, and in its time, was probably not expensive to buy. Yet, no one else has a spoon like this spoon.

I think this is like family. We all have people in our lives who we are related to, we live with, we struggle with, or try to completely avoid—but like it or not, they belong to us—they are family.

My family is not special, and by *that* I mean, we do not have any particular status or fame, wealth or skills—but what we do have, are recognizable dents. This is not a bad thing.

How else would I be able to find my way through stormy and dark nights of the soul—nights when I cannot even recognize myself, let alone decipher the path ahead. Somehow, something familiar appears before me, pulling me closer to safety and comfort; My uniquely dented family. No matter how crazy the chips and cracks make me feel, I know they give me an identity, a clarity, and an assurance that it is okay living with imperfection.

Having said that, I understand there are families with complicated histories who have experienced generations of conflict and pain. I want to be sensitive to those who may have been deeply hurt by the ones who are supposed to love them best. In these instances, I would say that 'spoon' would be severely twisted, not just marred a little, and therefore you would have a different approach and perspective to who your 'US' is. Relationships are so beautiful because we can decide who we consider 'family'. We can give that honor to folks who are willing to show up in our pain, or who we allow to support us. These kinds of folks try like champions to reduce pain and create wellness for the ones they love.

Now back to my dented spoon—it gets the job done despite its marred shape. It causes no harm with its imperfection. I chose to squirrel this spoon away along with other important household items, in the likelihood of a sudden exodus being necessary from my former house. This spoon was good enough to make it out of that 'fire' intact—not perfect—but chosen.

That sums up my family, too. Imperfect and chosen. Now on to the business of being kind with US.

KINDNESS WITH US

Kindness is getting easier!

I think I found a grip this week, or rather, something to grasp onto as I consider how to fully embody kindness. It started with an apology.

A few months ago, a friend and I were on an early morning walk. We talked about some of her blended family concerns, and since her situation was more recent than mine, I felt experienced enough to offer some advice. With older kids involved, she was finding it hard to strike a balance of what behavior she should ignore and what was worth hashing out.

I opened my mouth, spurted out confident words from a toe-the-line parenting playbook, believing with all my heart that she should put the brakes on her adult stepdaughter who was taking advantage of her generosity. Sounds like I was protecting my friend, right? Giving her assurance that it was all in her hands to control. So, why do I owe my friend an apology?

My adult daughter recently returned home, taking shelter with us while she plans and saves for her next steps forward. It is such a blessing to have her within touching distance, unlike the half-a-world-away distance we knew for the previous two years. Even though she is as close as the next room, in the busy of daily life, it still takes an effort to make meaningful connection time happen. Combine that with the fact she was happily living independently for two years, and—well—there have been some bumps.

In fact, the same kinds of bumps my friend described to me on our walk. On the one hand, it is comforting to know we are not alone, that others are experiencing the same struggles. I am slightly relieved to know this issue may not be a dreaded defect in our family unit. But on the other hand, it was disappointing, because I was hit in the face by my own snap judgments when discussing the same thing later with hubby.

He had taken a similar stance I took with my friend, and I took a point of view not only contrary to him, but contrary to myself only a few weeks prior.

While some might consider this my prerogative, to change my mind on a whim, I feel it may be out of alignment with this fifty-two-week adventure, and certainly feels like it may jeopardize relationships within my family.

Yikes! The mission is to live, love, think, and act boldly in every area of my life. Building a strong family framework takes too much time to carelessly tear it down with quick, proud words.

So, I shut my mouth for a couple of days. *This is not so easy. I like to talk.*

I was helped by hubby being out of town and his ear not available to stretch, but I also realized that not enough time had been devoted to considering what I truly thought. In a year of choosing constant reflection, my base operating mode seems to be blurting stuff out without reflecting first. I really, really need to shut my mouth more!

Why?

Quiet—It nudges at what is important and I begin to examine priorities again—like in Week Four. *Start paying attention, AJ!*

For many years, my priority has been to build a home full of love and acceptance, a place where kids want to bring their friends, and will trust to bring their children when that time comes. Sometimes amid piled-high plates of busy and piled-up rooms of heartbreak, I forget this priority and instead focus on rules, expectations, and consequences. I do not think this is necessarily wrong, because I know it is a response to feeling out of control. And some days, I know these rules exist so I can merely survive.

As I reflect on the *implementation* of that priority, I notice our children are not bringing their friends over. I am noticing we seem to have a low tolerance for mess, disorder, and general lack of control. Our acceptance levels are deeply in question due to empty beds that once held sons. Am I so surrounded by a dense fog of "I know best" that I miss the glimmers of light leading toward a better sense of priority?

Time to get some priorities straight. Does having a clean house matter more than having a full house? I cannot get back time with my kids at home, as teens, as adults, or at any other stages that have passed. If mess and clutter are a bi-product of a house well-loved in, then that is where I want to live.

Next, my quiet examination continued with a reflection on how much personality exists within a family setting. We have no shortage of personalities in this diverse, dynamic, blended, and blotched group of people I call family. Each personality clambers for acceptance, wanting to be comfortable in whatever way suits them, and only sporadically cognizant of whether any clashes are occurring. I am not convinced that maturity alleviates the clashing, as I am well into my 40s and still have trouble adapting to humans.

As much as possible, I tried to view our family through an unbiased lens, without the hurt feelings, and without the historical nonsense that jades my perception of who we are when together. I found that looking at each person and situation with a blank page in mind seems to smooth the way for whatever bumps are on the agenda for the day. If all I see when I gaze upon my family, are the wrongs of yesterday, I hold us all hostage today.

We are not free if our past choices haunt us from the moment we awake. I would call that emotional punishment—punitive measures placed on us by others or we place on ourselves. I think people who feel punished can clash without significant reason, because conflict is their norm. If that is true, their clashing is likely unintentional.

Chemistry classes lasted less than a week during my high school education, but I have come to learn how some elements combine well and mix effortlessly without hostility. Like:

Hydrogen & Oxygen—Peanut Butter & Honey—Wine & Cheese

Some elements refuse to mix and will keep separating no matter how many times you stir them. Some combinations erode whatever is around them. And some things, when put together... blow up!

Oil & Vinegar—Oxygen & Iron—Mentos & Coca-Cola

They do not conflict intentionally. This just is. There is no fault.

Perhaps, if we are open to it, there is a way to mix incompatible people to avoid creating fireworks, unless that is the sort of action we are pursuing! One son sought those kinds of thrills by tormented his sister until she was ready to explode. He would then run away laughing in delight—but also scared out of his wits, knowing the wrath he was about to endure.

Stirring the pot was his adolescent way of making contact, proving some of his behavior was intended. At other times, he seemed helpless to control his actions, responding violently to whatever was hurting him. In a mediatory-mom moment, he confessed how he loved his sister deeply; Even though he said the opposite to her many times and would vehemently deny it if I told her it was true.

SIGH.

Oddly enough, she is the only family member he talks to now, which might suggest there IS balance to be found in the diverse nature of our multifaceted selves.

Personalities can be considered gifts we receive every day. They are a celebration of who we are, what we bring, and who we can become. When we mix all our juicy bits together, it might be the best gift of all.

My thoughts on priority and personality must somehow come together for this week. What possibilities appear in this unlimited definition of "Kindness with US"? I am hoping a strong shot of espresso brings some speedy clarity while we get back to that apology...

I started to think about how things could have played out differently during that conversation with my friend, which included examining some aspects of priorities and personalities before opening my mouth. Inside my most loving and positive imagination, I could see the situation changing, making a difference without even acting on it yet. Just dreaming of how the issue could be overcome was lifting the weight of it from my heart.

Coincidentally, work recently had us complete a professional communication course, "Crucial Conversations", where the authors use several steps to avoid getting stuck in a conversation that will likely not end positively. One of those steps is to avoid the 'or' in a situation.

For example, I am on a healthy life overhaul—*aka, a diet*—and if I tell myself I can only have this OR that, I feel deprived and crave the thing I did not choose. But if I figure out a way to have this AND that, by cutting both in half or alternating between the two things, I have satisfied all my wants and will likely continue to eat better, for longer.

With people, when I stop thinking relationships need to be this way OR that way, I start finding a middle ground where everyone feels heard and valued. I need to see that it is possible to have very diverse components within relationships. For the first few years, this was my biggest hurdle with hubby when we had a disagreement. I held a historical belief that any disagreement with a spouse would end in pain or shame. With a lot of patience and love from him, I learned it was safe to disagree with hubby.

It was more than safe—it was welcomed!

Hubby helped me redefine the standards of a healthy argument, without losing an intimate connection to a loving spouse. Redefining this concept is a long-term process, which means I have many setbacks, but what a beautiful, calming, powerful freedom! What else is possible?

Priorities—Personalities—Possibilities.

These are my best guesses for how kindness works with US.

Week Sixteen

LAYING DOWN THE LAW

Fantastic News! Here is an update on my lifestyle change:

I snuggled into a favorite pair of Guess jeans today—not my skinny ones, but nevertheless—progress is happening. I am still not comfortable wearing a tighter shirt with the jeans, so I keep plugging away at the treadmill, yoga, and yesterday's treat: Zumba!

The instructor might have thought I was slightly deranged, grinning throughout the session with my whole face, as I tried to keep up with her uber-Latino moves and energy. When I got lost, I made up my own tangos and twists, which I am sure burned more calories than if I had stopped to try and catch up to the patterned routine.

Aaah-riii-baaaah!

For this final week of focusing on kindness, I am starting with a definition I heard from some church preaching. I have not said too much about church so far, or how that part of my life goes, but I hope to delve into its impact on my healing a little farther down this writing road.

The message I heard this Sunday was simple: "Why settle to do only what good laws require, when you can take on the greater *spirit* of the law?"

It sounds like different levels are possible when following rules, similar to kindness having layers in Weeks Thirteen and Fourteen.

I had a chance to discuss with some friends what we thought the spirit of the law meant. We came up with some altruistic, utopic definitions of how our motivations for abiding by a rule might determine if we have taken on the spirit of it or were just doing what we were told.

This made we wonder where else in my life I am simply doing what I am told. What things are adding hidden stress and potentially only being done to meet the following criteria:

- Keep up Appearances
- Avoid Penalties
- Make Money

In other words, where in my life do I uphold the standard, but do not truly buy in?

Are any of these things stressing you right now?

I currently have about nineteen burdensome obligations sitting inside the catalog of my brain, and it feels heavy. Doing what I am told, or what I feel like I have no choice *but* to do, is smothering my thoughts and cramping my enthusiasm for living. What if I were to abandon any thoughts beginning with "I have to", "I ought to", or "I am supposed to", and chose words like "I get to", "I want to", and "I am happy to" instead?

Helping me focus this week is a bracelet Mum bought for me when I was maybe 9 or 10 years old. It is a thick silver chain surrounded by twelve charms. One charm is a cute little bible, which looks hand carved from mother of pearl or ivory. Ten of the charms have the laws of Moses written on them *(aka the Ten Commandments)*. The last charm is shaped like a heart and has such small writing on it that I am guessing it symbolizes keeping these laws within your heart.

This bracelet turned out to be significant in terms of discovering whether I am simply doing what I am told or giving everything I have to give; All my guts, all my heart, all my mind, and all my strength. There is a word in Hebrew that describes this kind of effort, this kind of heart action and it came up in the same message at church this week: 'Hesed'.

Hesed means 'the Loving-Kindness of God'. It is not just kindness, which I have suggested in Week Fourteen can be mistaken for being nice. This word means a powerful, loyal love or mercy and is always used as an action to show what is in someone's heart. It is not something simply felt, nor a passing mood or emotion.

HESED stays. Endures. Overcomes. I like this word.

Like a superhero bandeau, I feel twice as powerful, twice as smart, and twice as fast, wearing this bracelet. My fingers fly effortlessly across the keyboard while wearing this icon!

Maybe it's because it is shiny, maybe because it jingles, and maybe because it promotes ancient advice on its surfaces, but I feel as though Hesed is enveloping me in a bear hug of blessing. Hesed is preparing me to bring kindness into my community and world.

If I get lost in old patterns of behavior, I will remember my Zumba lesson and just keep moving along until I get back into sync. After all, it is my life-dance, and I am the one who gets to adjust the choreography to whatever music is playing. So, if you feel the same way, let's get started. Let's get DANCING!

KINDNESS WITH THEM

What I thought was going to be a week of Zumba-like life moments, turned out to be more of a swaying, smooth, waltz-type of reflection. It could have something to do with taking a trip back to my beloved little town, home to many precious people who helped grow me. Also, Hesed showed up through another church message (*YouTube links at end of chapter, if you want to hear the messages in their entirety*).

Okay, 'Loving Kindness'—time to get real. I did not know how deep this topic would reach, or that my kindness intentions would fall into the realm of the divine, yet this is the direction I was strongly, and clearly, led.

Changing my language from feeling obligated to act in a certain fashion, to describing it instead as an opportunity or privilege, made a positive difference in how I thought. Instead of looking at the action itself, I focused on the way I thought about the action. Let me explain…

Currently, there are nine people *(nine is not a random number)* with whom I wanted to connect over the course of this week. I feel these folks need some kindness for a variety of reasons and diverse needs. Some connections are physically draining. Some are emotionally difficult. Some are time consuming. And some needs are so tricky that it takes all my wits to convince the person to accept a little TLC, but I cannot get to them all.

I want to!

I run around like I am driven by an invisible whip; Squeezing in another coffee date, frantic to complete the next detail or fulfill another favor, while commanding myself to maintain or increase this relentless pace, while more souls pour into my scope of care. What begins as an honest outpouring of compassionate desire to lighten someone else's load turns into a crushing personal loss of oxygen.

Hubby tries to settle me down when my eyes circle inside their sockets, when I cannot remember where I put the car keys or ask him the same question four times without remembering his answer. He reminds me to slow down, that I need a break, that he is a friend who needs me too—and that friends sometimes sit and watch NFL games together.

Simple? Yes.

Enjoy football? No.

Meet you on the couch? I'll make the popcorn.

Cramming as much life into every minute possible is exhausting. It makes me question whether I should care about others so much. This in turn causes a flood of guilt, prompting me to start the next desperate phase to be everything to everybody.

This is my life… swamped and losing most of my sanity into the lives of others. Hubby and I have coped through this cycle before, but it wears US down.

I think something is different now. This year, I have a broader perspective of the kindness I show myself and others. Same burdens, same whip, same drive to do it all, but I am okay. Hubby is okay. What is the difference?

I decided to savor each connection by scheduling a pre-determined allotment of time, *including rest-time,* to maintain my energy and focus.

Since I am traditionally not great at keeping a schedule, I made another decision: To believe that small acts of kindness always fit perfectly into the bigger picture.

I am not big. I do not have big acts of service to offer. I think I am running around like a crazy person in order to prove I have value on this earth—that I have purpose. Acting in faith means my purpose is already established. I am exactly where I should be, with the talents and skills I need, to accomplish the work set out for me.

And *that* is BIG. Finding this new way of thinking about my role in the universe may be the axis of how I manage burnout and carry on with kindness toward people who have no way of ever serving me back. Maybe that is all I needed to find this week. What a beautiful reframe for staying in this nutty serve-circuit, remembering that my needs are part of the circuit, too.

No special skills required. No degrees or diplomas necessary. Only loving kindness, the strongest, most gentle message we can send to a hurting world.

So, I will keep pouring myself into the lives of others. Not a reckless pour that sacrifices all of ME, but a swaying pendulum pour, swinging side to side—filling everything as it dances to a lilting rhythm of a gentle waltz.

Mum taught me rhythm as a child, when practicing for music lessons—1, 2, 3—1, 2, 3—heavy, light, light—heavy light, light.

Work—rest, rest.

Run—rest, rest.

Fill—rest, rest.

Love—rest, rest.

Thank you, kindness. You have given me purpose.

AJ

Here are some reflective quotes on kindness:

To serve, you only need a heart full of grace and a soul generated by love.
~ Martin Luther King

How wonderful it is that nobody need wait a single moment
to improve the world.
~ Anne Frank

I think a hero is any person really intent on making this a better place.
~ Maya Angelou

The best way to find yourself is to lose yourself in the service of others.
~ Mahatma Gandhi

How do you define Kindness?

Links to Messages: https://www. youtube. com/watch? v=_QriMS3vOeQ
https://www. youtube. com/watch? v=DevMg0f5kBc
https://www. youtube. com/watch? v=X_FGafpuqUE
or Check out "Commons Church"

CHAPTER FIVE

CURIOSITY

Blessed are the CURIOUS
For they shall have Adventures!
~ Lovelle Drachman

Week Seventeen

BAD REPUTATIONS

This is going to be fun. Being curious has a bit of a baaaad reputation, so my goal in the next four weeks is to dispel the darker side of curiosity and find a bright, dazzling upside, which could be a crucial ingredient to igniting my heart with joy and hope. After all, curiosity suggests a beginning of something and if that is the case, I get to decide what that 'something' could be.

Exciting!

Here are some questions that have been tickling my imagination for a few days, while I have been focusing on being "Curious with ME":

Can we blame curiosity for when things go wrong?

Does curiosity get us into trouble?

Did curiosity really kill the cat?

These sprung to mind after a quick google search of curiosity quotes. There were plenty from Albert Einstein, inspiring and fun—witty with simple brilliance. There were alarming quotes from sources I assume were created from ultra-fundamentalist-Christian type points of view, where curiosity is likened to many evils in this world, but not quite the direction I am leaning in my search of what true curiosity means for ME.

Why is curiosity a topic worth exploring for my life? That is a very curious question!

When choosing the topics for this book, there were initially a plethora of options. In order to decide which ones would make the final cut, they had to audition their merit on the imaginary stage in my mind. Thirteen qualities rose above the rest by making me believe I could not live well without them.

As I move through each topic, I am convinced these were the perfect roads for me to discover, which makes me curious about how these thirteen characteristics stood out initially. Was it something from within my spirit? My soul? My analytical and highly mathematical mind? *Not a chance.* This IS curious work, to say the least.

My icon for the week is a theatrical mask Mum bought me as a gift, once she conceded to my drama and performance dreams not diminishing. This pretty mask hung on my college apartment wall for a few years, reminding me of lessons learned through the mandatory 'masque' training I eagerly engaged in during acting classes.

I felt more comfortable acting on stage behind a mask, than without one. It was easier to adopt unfamiliar character traits. This theatrical artform is truly grounded in curiosity, allowing anyone to apply a mask and become something else for a little while.

Exciting indeed!

Choose your own ICON for Curiosity:

CURIOSITY WITH ME

I have enjoyed this first week of curiosity. It made me feel smart, like fitting a puzzle piece into place after trying many mysteriously similar spots. There are puzzling mysteries in our vast universe, which I will leave to the scientifically curious people, so I can concentrate on more personal mysteries, like:

- Who do I want to be when I grow up? (*Assuming that may still happen sometime in my fifth decade*)
- What do I want to accomplish with my life?

One might concede that curiosity could have been the sole reason I started down this fifty-two-week path, potentially nominating it as the core of why this book exists.

The thing that stood out the most this week was how being curious with my thoughts and actions led to fewer judgments and less internal discord. I was more accepting of the present, instead of nagging myself about what I should have done, should have said, or should have thought. Constant internal judgements drain my energy and are brutal on my self-esteem.

So, I reprogrammed my nagging into an impartial question: *Why do I talk, think, or act in this particular way?*

Here is a small example:

Thought: Shoot! Forgot to start supper before going to work. Poor hubby will have to come home and make it after his long day.

AJ: Why did I forget to start supper? What happened instead?

Thought: I went for a run, packed my lunch, got ready for work, drove out of town to take a single mom out for lunch, then drove to the opposite side of the city to get to work. Is that everything? Oh yes, had a chat with one of our teenagers who would be spending the rest of their day alone.

AJ: Wow! I was busy, no wonder supper did not get started.

Thought: Call hubby and prepare him for eating a few minutes later than usual.

Hubby's response: Roger that.

AJ: Taa-Daah!

This would normally have sounded like 'failure'—not having finished an intention I verbalized while planning the day before. I would have agonized over letting down people who count on me most and told myself all kinds of lies connected to my value as a human.

I feel it is important to fulfill my commitments and be responsible to the ones I love in a manner that does not sacrifice *their* needs for the sake of *my* needs but finding a formula to successfully navigate that, is the tricky part. I think the answer lies in attempting to balance my *physical, mental,* and *spiritual* abilities. These seem to be pillars in determining if I can take on someone's needs *(or my own, for that matter).*

But those pillars cannot bear the brunt of the constant beat-downs of negatively charged self-judgments. I cannot deliver my best energy when I feel awful about myself. I do not rise to any occasion by flogging myself for defects. No—I simply get pounded further into heart-hardening turf, slammed into a quagmire of self-defeat, stuck deep in a historical abyss of *"you are **never** good enough,"* with no bottom to be found.

This must change. 'Stuck' is not a place where living happens. It is a trap invented to ignore challenges or remain blind to what is real.

Stepping up to take that risk, is curiosity. It does not quiver in the presence of regular fears, because it is not focusing on that. Instead, it looks beyond what seems real to discover another dimension—another reality. A place where quagmires are turned into beautiful gardens of endless possibility, simply by asking a different question.

Curiosity blasts criticism out of my emotional existence when I become an explorer of my motivations, actions, and beliefs. I am lighter for it. I am freer. I am exactly who I was before the question—yet, I feel stronger—because I asked why.

Fill your heart with awestruck wonder for yourself this week. Explore it all!

Week Eighteen

BOSTON, OR BUST!

In this second week of curiosity, I am looking at the people closest to me to figure out how to best be curious about them. I will be observing their words and actions, but will tread carefully around their motivations or thoughts, knowing that I cannot predict those, or assume they are like my own. Hubby reminds me of this concept, as it is often necessary.

But before I get right into it, let me share this hot news! I just returned from Boston, visiting that lovely son who will be graduating from university in a few months. I decided to go for a quick visit and to get to know him better before seeing him in a cap and gown. It was unbelievable!

Not only is he an interesting grown man, but he is also the same quirky kid I knew at 13, when we last lived together in a family setting. It would be inadequate to describe our last living arrangement as unhealthy, so without jumping completely away from my focus for the week, I will be alluding to some things that contributed to the twisted bits in our relationship. He is my icon this week. A fitting reminder from Mum that life trumps death, every time.

One of my favorite memories of the trip was visiting the campus 'mega-library'. Its grand and historic Ivy league arches increased my intelligence just by passing through them. The columns of ornate granite looked more like a castle than a place to do homework. Inside were giant rooms adorned in awe-inspiring eighteenth-century décor. One room had double swinging doors with circular windows that appeared to be portholes into another realm—another time. It made me feel like Alice in Wonderland, pondering what else I might possibly see when gazing through *(or better yet)*, when opening this door to whatever intrigue awaits.

Sounds like curiosity at work... but back to my son...

From the time he was about 4 or 5 years old, his father would smack my sons hand out of mine if he was holding it. When he wanted to stand close to me, walk close to me, talk close to me, be *anywhere* close to me, his father would physically push him away, calling him a mama's boy. Since his father was often not interested in being in the same room with his children, my son still had several chances to slide up next to me to talk about planets and solar systems.

When son was a baby, his father would make cameo parenting appearances to tell me I was not holding him right, not feeding him right, not speaking to him right, not mothering right—no wonder our mother-son relationship has been strained. There are layers upon layers of mistrust and manipulation laid down in the foundation between us. He likely does not technically remember this as part of our historic reality, but my guess is that he can remember it emotionally.

This is an unexplained kind of feeling; A ghostlike thought that whispers from your memory. If you could recognize it, you may not understand why it is there. It is like instinct, or an inner voice that seeps under a backdoor of your conscience, altering your ability to balance truth and reality.

After separating from his father, this kind of poisonous sentiment prevailed through infrequent mother-son conversations. My son seemed stuck in this place of unexplained feelings, fueled by lies that discouraged any positive interactions. Upon returning from any encounters with me, his father demanded a full report and review of what was said or had transpired. In those eight years, it was difficult to see past my son's hurtful behavior, and my own heartbreak, to understand the tortured teen in front of me.

I knew he believed with all his might that he was doing and saying the 'right' things. His unrecognizable mother appeared to be shattering, with wanton disregard, the values he was taught to respect. My task during this troubling time was to remain open to him as a person, by setting firm boundaries within a new set of values I was creating. I failed many times by defending myself with obvious justifications of why I was divorcing his father.

This is where the work starts for me: A long time ago—way before Boston.

CURIOSITY WITH YOU

More curiosity would have helped me during this time of estrangement from my son. I think it could have helped me listen to him more and ask more questions about what he thought, making it safer for him to explain his doubts and anger. Even if we still ultimately ended up on opposing sides of this forced family feud, I feel our relationship may have taken less time to repair.

I looked at my son this week, hoping for our hardest days to be behind us, and trying my best to stay on the side of curiosity. I realized there were many reasons that seemed to stop me from being curious about him. Here are the top five:

#5—I label myself as the most interesting person in a room; The one with crazy stories and a dynamic past, so naturally people would want to hear my angles, my views, my chaotic strategies… Am I right?

*Get over yourself, AJ! Make **him** the most interesting person in our conversation.* He did not disappoint. I had no idea he secretly desired to become a cowboy version of James Bond! Way cooler than his wacky Ma's tired tales of woe and glory.

#4—Assumptions are deadly to curiosity *(especially the uninformed kind)*. Just because I have been alive longer than him, does not make me an expert about him. He is different now than nine years ago, and he will be different again at graduation. Curiosity does not stop to assume. It keeps going and growing alongside the people we are curious about.

#3—I have no patience! *(Right back to Week One)* I want to know that I know, whatever there is to know about you, and I want to know it now! Waiting to hear what is actually true for you takes so much time. I would rather find a shortcut, jump to a quick end, to be done and move on to something more interesting—like what *I* think *(yup, back to ME)* rather than take time to truly understand *your* why. Knowing your *what*, is quicker than your *why*, and I can still pat myself on the back for thinking I am getting to know you.

#2—I am afraid!

Not in an "*Oh look, there's a T-rex behind us!*" kind of way, but…

What if you say something that makes me uncomfortable?

What if I realize how boring I am in comparison to you??

What if you are not curious back about me and it hurts my feelings???

I can only assume this fear is a leftover form of some teenage angst, neither terribly attractive nor flattering for an adult gal such as myself.

Now, for the #1 thing that stops me from being curious with YOU...

I want to be known.

I want to be understood, to talk until someone truly gets me, to be central in a quest to find what really makes me tick. You cannot know me unless I tell you all about me, and I am desperate for that to happen.

Curiosity showed me that I tend to hog the spotlight—I assume to know stuff—I am impatient—I fear being hurt—and I am selfish.

As a grown woman, with some of my children already adults, it might be time to ditch these immature tendencies. Time for a new motivation that asks 'why' and a new reason to step out of the spotlight to see who else is shining.

I am happy to report that my son shines! We all shine. Curiosity showed me how much.

Mum would have taken her time to know this grandson, getting into his scientific mind to find as many fascinating details as possible.

This week has done me a very good turn. By delving into the endless hallways of my son's very curious mind, I was lifted far above the limited horizon I created for our relationship. It is a weightless feeling, to discover something amazing about another person's life. Life is more interesting without being tricked by assumptions or fear. Curiosity is good.

Weeks Nineteen and Twenty

CURIOSITY MOSH UP

These two weeks are getting moshed together. Time is flying by without offering me a chance to finish writing about it. So, I am blending curiosity with US *and* THEM as a focus on family and friends as well as my larger surrounding community.

I started writing this post more than a week ago. I was upbeat and full of enthusiasm, as per the usual current pulsing through my fingers each week, as I type out what pours from my heart.

Curiosity began as promisingly weightless, comparable to stumbling upon a hidden treasure map and following its clues with joyous confidence in what mystery awaits in completing an unexpected venture. I considered five factors that stopped me from immersing myself in the magical process of discovering someone else's brilliance. The last two weeks have been beautifully curious with a comfortable balance of seeking and reflecting.

Do you sense a 'but' coming on? There is one, so I should introduce my icon first.

It has a tarnished shine, an odd shape and has been this way ever since I can remember. It also does not easily identify itself for the function it serves.

I put it on display to help remind me to be curious, but it is not the way Mum used it while it was in her possession. Do you have a guess?

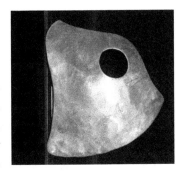

When choosing this icon, I thought it would match the intrigue and optimism generated from the incredible time I spent with my son two weeks ago. I began writing about a memory that fascinated me, and one he brought up during our visit. Time and trauma have plagued my recall, making many good memories fade while leaving the sick and sore memories so fresh I can taste them.

My intention was to describe what raising a very curious child was like, with his awestruck wonderment of anything scientific, his fascination with structures, and the glorious mystery of undiscovered space. His natural curiosity led us to many books, many inquisitive investigations, and the pursuit of a never-ending thirst for knowledge. He lost himself for hours on quiet missions to know it all. If there were a perfect example of being curious, this boy of mine *(about to be an ivy-league graduate)* would be it.

But I scrapped my draft when something old and tarnished crept into the picture that could not be ignored. Something already unearthed in previous diggings into US during the weeks of patience and kindness, but I could not address.

Suddenly, instead of a weightless and clear curiosity focus, I became clouded with mounting heaviness, forcing me to stop writing and pay attention to what was happening to US. I wish I could fully divulge all the details, or at least hint at some nuances leading to my halt, but it is not my story to tell.

These past couple of weeks have required me to honor the people I love by holding back publicly AND privately regarding a challenge that has been dealt into our hand, been chosen for US, and so far, has US not rising to the occasion.

You might be thinking—Miss 'Posi-Tiva' has finally dropped 'the act' because nobody can be that positive, for that long. Finally, AJ has joined reality. What a refreshing change.

For many weeks—months, in fact, I have rolled through topics and reflections, handling obstacles well, feeling settled and 'soul-full'. Some of the hurdles have been massively rooted by past trauma and current heartaches, reaching further than any depth I have scrutinized comfortably up to this point, and yet still seem to result in abounding strength and unadulterated hope—I have been in the ZONE!

Being there, is sweet. It has embraced me in a way I have not felt before. Like a long-awaited hug from someone I thought I may never see again, no words can express how much love and acceptance I have experienced after deciding to take on this fifty-two-week adventure. Not only do I feel more connected to a mum who has not been physically present in my life for over twenty-four years, but I have grown more grounded as ME, gentler with YOU, more gracious to US, and more genuine with THEM. Sounds great, right?

Maybe too great—not that I follow a 'too good to be true' kind of philosophy, but I have witnessed the universe open its cosmic power to auto-align situations in my life that have swung to either side of the spectrum between good and not-so-good.

"Being real IS balance."

So, why am I surprised that something tough has emerged—something that brought me into the *"Wanna fight about it?"* trenches—something that tests all my positive spins and 'think good-ery', and finds me standing firm on a platform of doubt, anger, near-sightedness, arrogance, and intolerance? Sleep comes at the price of pillow-soaking tears, and when those are gone, a dry-eyed numbness does not allow for sleep at all.

Please—do not feel sorry for me. This challenge chose US, so I know it is FOR us. Hard as it is to accept, I know we are going to be better for it, that we will grow and mature through it, and this is the ONLY thing keeping me sane right now.

As we tackle awkward family conversations that completely fail due to hidden agendas, incomplete thoughts, and unstoppable bursts of emotion—as we sputter through the tiniest of interactions—I decide to pause.

Curiosity has a dark side. Perhaps I need to re-evaluate my previous conclusion. Maybe it really did kill the cat.

Now, I am not giving up, not putting my hands in the air, and saying, *"Oh well, nothing can be done... Dead end here!"* Quite the opposite, which is why I find myself fighting in the trenches—not exactly how I would like to deal with this, or any other conflict for that matter, but a battle does occasionally befit my passion for living well.

Once I noticed myself, putting up my dukes and fighting unsuccessfully out of our unpleasant corner, I condemned myself for that tactic and quickly chose another: RETREAT!!

It's a tough thing to retreat from your family and community when getting away is physically impossible. The only thing left is to put up an emotional barrier.

Just need some ME time... pul-eeeeease!

The relief of ditching a disaster feels so perfect... for about fifteen seconds. My retreats seem to have tag-along visitors though, like guilt. Guilt loves a good retreat party and invites more hurtful friends like shame and dishonesty to come along for the fun. Self-righteousness always shows up late, cranking up the personal pity tunes, and getting a real party rhythm rocking. No shortage of bitterness and pride at this rave. They flow copiously, while resentment fervently dances as far away from connection, intimacy and vulnerability as it can.

This has been the 'party' in my head, heart, and house this week.

Curiosity has had me asking questions like *"How come...? Why not...? What if...?"* But these have not proved helpful in dispelling our darkening world. Confusing shadows cast mirages of trouble ahead, lying in wait to pounce. I hesitantly turn corners, fumbling blind against unknown walls, in search of a way out. I can sense fear blocking my belief in finding an exit for US, this being more complex than most of our past struggles. Time improves nothing. Silence assures no rescue is coming.

Light from our original entry point to this looming tunnel, has long since faded, leaving no option for retracing the way we came. Things are in motion that cannot be undone, nor do I necessarily believe they should be undone. I just know we need to move from here—but to where?

The Beginning.

Who do I want to be?

Can my life be something more?

Will I rise when life pushes me down?

Hi.

I'm AJ.

I am on a fifty-two-week discovery of finding my BEST self.

Nice to meet you...

Nothing can dim the light that shines from within.
~ Maya Angelou

20 WEEK CHECK-IN:

January – April 2016

After the stress subsided from giving testimony to save my career, the waiting for the verdict began. Four months may seem like a short time in comparison to the dragged-out years this complaint has taken, but that is how long I was told it might take. Maybe longer. So, I wait. And continue to build up more work endurance while waiting for my brain to heal from the persistent symptoms of a concussed head.

I have taken on the task of changing my nutritional lifestyle, which makes me grumpy for many days, but slowly I begin to see a difference in my energy. After a month, I can exercise again! Hallelujah! Things are looking up...

And then this breaking news. Unplanned, and without a partner in the picture, our daughter reveals that she is pregnant. I am steady and soft in my reaction, knowing this *is exactly the kind of thing I told my kids they could tell me—no matter what—and she has done just that. So, I assure her there is no judgment here. There is no pressure. Only love—and support—and reassurance that, **wherever** she lands, we are there with her.*

This is a raw and emotional time for all of us. Not being able to talk about this with anyone until her decision is made, hubby and I quietly converse with each other. When she is not at work, she stays in the dark of her room. Tired, angry, and seemingly unappreciative of the home open to her without question—without a price tag—without an expiry date. I am waiting again. Maybe tomorrow will be better.

Our youngest teens have turned 16. One is here to celebrate, and one is still out of our reach. An extended family tradition got uprooted, which felt like rejection for us, when it meant an annual visit would not take place. My love and respect for family stops me from giving further details but I remain hopeful of moving toward a future without resentment.

And lastly, I have been getting phone calls from a number that I do not recognize, and they do not leave a message...

How are *you* doing?
(*Take a moment for your own Week Twenty reflection, if it serves you*)

CHAPTER SIX

GRACIOUSNESS

No matter the road,
Grace is the detour.
~ AJ

Week Twenty-One

GRACIOUSNESS GETS GRITTY

Hello, my friends!

It is time for a new topic! Graciousness. Curiosity was a bit of an odd, yet formidable, topic and perhaps deserving of more contemplation after these fifty-two weeks are complete.

I chose the topic of graciousness as an alternative to *humility* when narrowing down the final thirteen. I was not able to shake the baggage connected to that word 'humility' and started to work through this historical trigger in Week Seven, but it seems to be popping up again. So, here we go…

During my growing years, I was taught that being humble was a spiritually worthy pursuit and might enhance your chances of earning a heavenly kind of reward. Then, throughout my warped first marriage, I was taunted with the concept of humility, which was used like a weapon against me whenever my thinking did not match my spouse's. There was no such thing as a simple difference of opinion. If I disagreed, I was rebuked for not having a humble spirit toward the person God had given an ultimate veto power. I was to submit in all things without question.

This conditioning led me to agree with him outwardly, keeping my mouth shut and feign the humility required to keep danger at bay. And then there were times I could not keep it contained and had to voice my opinion; Fears of saying something oppositional were outweighed by a greater need to express my deeply, personal view. These expressions were never a benefit. No intimacy or understanding was gained. Only perpetual mocking or scorn, and one more example of my tainted character for him to rub in my face. My thoughts eventually became irrelevant to me. I ceased having my own opinions, deferring to his in conversations, and in my own mind, in order to decrease chaotic episodes.

This survivor approach made me feel like I was handling it—like I was managing him. Habitually, I convinced people who discovered our dysfunction of how virtuous his motives were in straightening out my haughty, flawed ego. I defended his refusal to let me wear makeup and jewelry. I stayed away from public places to avoid the temptations of vanity and pride. This was how humility became a four-letter word in my life.

Almost a year after the birth of my third baby, my hair was a mess. Also refused haircuts, I had not had a trim for over a year. Hormonal surges during pregnancy had made some patches thick and long, but once the hormones had stopped pumping through my cells, my hair started to fall out in other places.

It reminded me of the matted lumps we once cut off our beloved farm dog, Grover, after a particularly rambunctious summer of trouncing through back woods and underbrush. Brushing his copper mane proved useless, due to large, clinging clumps of fur and thistle twigs. This would be the only time Mum allowed her 'good' scissors to be used on something not related to sewing, as they cleanly and efficiently clipped away the offensive furballs. Grover would self-consciously walk away from his trim, tail between his legs, probably feeling naked, but getting over his unflattering mane quickly. Not me. I did not get over it.

In fact, it bothered me so much that I did a crazy thing. I asked 'husband-boss' for money to get a haircut. It was real desperation, making that request, without a reasonable expectation of success AND the likelihood of conflict ensuing, but I needed it! He scoffed, told me my hair was fine, and that humble Christian women do not need haircuts. They live natural, just as God intended.

So, my natural, ratty hair would continue, matching the other unkempt, fuzzy areas of my body that had not seen the edge of a blade for years. My legs were so hairy that my own kids would stare, not being able to tell where my legs started, and my fur-lined slippers ended. I think my oldest boy called me wolf legs for a little while.

Equally horrifying was the condition of my armpits—a jungle on their own—and a shock to those who observed this marked departure in my grooming routine.

This was a far cry from the lady my mum raised me to become. Mum had great style. She had a certain flare, taking care to look sharp—perfectly filed nails, dressed for success, and ALWAYS sporting a quality haircut.

What a fright my hair would be to her in that condition. While a pre-teen, she enrolled me in a course that educated young ladies on how to care for their hair and skin, with remedies you could make at home. I chose one of those 'recipes' as my icon this week.

Egg whites—Olive Oil—Honey—Vinegar—Lemon juice

Can you guess what product these ingredients make, bedsides a yummy salad dressing?

Hair conditioner. Looks like my tresses will be getting a nice treat this week. Mum would approve. Not only did her hair look healthy and shiny, she never left the house without styling it—not even when she was on the way out to the garden to work up a sweat.

She never skimped on quality when it came to her style. Mum was a true, classy lady, and never gave up hope that I would find my way past blue jeans and high-top sneakers. I had a string of 'plaid' items hanging untouched in my closet due to her efforts, but no matter what variety of clothing the plaid embodied, I could not let go of my Levi's and Nike's. Inheriting all her clothes may have been reason enough to incorporate her classic style, but I felt like a 5-year-old playing dress up, and donning her clothing usually ended in tears. So, her entire closet joined the company of my lonely plaid clothes.

Then I got married. Jeans apparently were too fancy for attaining true humility. Oversized, hand-me-down sweatpants from husband-boss, were acceptable and wearing anything else, caused an unpleasant scene.

Sloppy clothes—slagging hair—shaggy body—no wonder I was bothered enough to ask. Poor Mum was probably stirring in her grave for me!

I was not asking for an extravagant salon affair. Cut and go. Simple and cheap.

Twelve-dollars cheap!

It was the wrong tactic to act like I wanted something, so of course his answer was "NO".

My insides were seething. I put baby down for a nap and filled a bath for the older munchkins. Mixed with the sound of toddlers happily playing with bubbles and sponges, I took clippers in hand, reached for a big clump of wiry hair, and shaved a strip as close to my head as the blades would go—right down the center of my skull. No going back after that, so I kept stripping away at it, until my nasty hair filled a plastic bread bag, and my head was bald—bald—bald.

Triumphantly, I marched into his office, plunked the bag of hair onto his desk, and muttered something about not needing the $12 anymore. He could hardly breathe from shock. Was he more stunned from my defiance, or how ugly I was without hair? Regardless, I turned my back when he questioned my sanity, left the room to take a shower, and bawled—bawled—bawled.

Choose your own ICON for Graciousness:

GRACIOUS WITH ME

"Grace + Gratitude = GRIT"

Living without a crown of hair on my head was a most humiliating experience. Not only because of judgmental stares from strangers but also because an unknown, unworthy image was reflected in the mirror. Who had I become?

I already knew by this point that I needed to escape the madness of my marriage, but I was stuck without means, stuck by loyalty to vows, and stuck by his spiritual propaganda holding me enslaved as though my soul depended on it. Stuck.

So now it makes sense… why I could not choose humility as a topic, even if I see the value of practicing it. I learned more than enough about the 'shoulds' and 'shoudn'ts' of humility, to almost choke it out of existence for me, at least until I realized something stronger was possible. When I allow myself to chuckle during rough patches, it grows. When I stop taking myself so seriously, it blossoms. When I choose to be less affected by hurtful actions, it releases seeds. And when I truly mean it and say to people, *there is nothing to forgive*, it multiplies into a full garden. I am somehow stumbling upon grace.

Not the Grace Kelly kind of etiquette Mum would have loved to see blossom in her tomboy daughter. Something more.

For me, graciousness transcends courtesy and elegance. It is a generosity of the heart that cannot help but give, because it recognizes how generously it has received, and therefore, simply must share. To do otherwise would be dishonorable and missing the point altogether. I do not want to miss this point.

Grace does not compete with humility. Grace does not show up because I deserve it. Grace understands the struggle in relinquishing my will for another persons needs. Grace patiently waits while I am trying to be something I am not. Grace reminds ME to try again, because mistakes are not final. Grace gently holds my purest intentions and whispers them throughout chaos and heartache.

Beautiful grace. It is here and always has been. It arrived like a gift and 'stuck' with me—held me—cheered me—re-built ME.

Amazing grace!

Week Twenty-Two

GNARLY GRACE

"If grace is more than simply how to be humble—there be a storm comin'!"

SWIRLING—swirling...

I guess I knew there would be tough bits during these fifty-two weeks. My oldest scars are hard to approach with softness, harder to examine without getting lost in their ugliness, and hardest to erase from existence, if this be my goal.

Just so happens, that is *not* my goal. Today, I am still on track to gaze directly at my hurtful past, go eye to eye with battles lost, pushing through any stiff or rough areas in my life that are stagnate, and hoping growth might be stimulated, if given a chance.

This reminds me of the efforts Mum put into our large garden on the farm. She and my dad worked hard to prepare a soil that would accept a variety of seeds, worked harder keeping weeds and slugs at bay, giving fledgling sprouts a chance to grow strong, and worked hardest to harvest and preserve a bounty of produce in sufficient quantity to feed our family through the winter, but this required more than hard work.

Dreaming, imagining, planning, and resting were also part of this healthy annual cycle and always included a celebration to share the fruits of their labor with extended family and friends.

TWISTING—twisting...

Many opportunities to extend myself graciously toward my immediate relationships have popped up. These were unexpected chances to test if grace could be generated from mere humans or if it only exists somewhere in the heavens.

For this occasionally grounded girl, last week was a good reminder that true grace cannot be earned or deserved. Grace is a gift born from loving sacrifices, to which I may never attain an ability to understand completely. If grace cannot be bought, sold, manipulated, or illegitimately manufactured, then I would like to immediately petition myself to stop running after approval, to stop clambering for acceptance, and stop desperately clinging to sentiments of people's praise. I chase grace, throwing myself into a panic at the slightest glimpse of disapproval.

A glance from a colleague, a remark from hubby, a gesture from one of my kids, and I convince myself to instantaneously adjust, conform, align, obey... and do it with a sweet, loving smile on my face. What kind of gnarly grace is this? A dangling carrot of worthiness attached to making everyone happy. I storm breathlessly toward an end that does not come and has not ever shown up despite my constant efforts.

Because I have no photos or implements from that farm garden to use as an icon this week, I have chosen a green head scarf Mum would wear to keep her hair at bay when we spent all day in the garden. This is a perfect icon to help me roll up my sleeves and dig into more grace.

"A storm proves the strength of our anchor."

GRACIOUS WITH YOU

I have a small confession to make, and think it has something to do with grace. There is a screenplay version of my life running parallel to my actual life. Drawn to the dramatics, I often pretend to be a film character while performing routine functions. Inventing complex plots and subplots, building tension and character depth, saying lines with precise attention, blocking my movements and bowing for the applause of an appreciative audience when I accept my Oscar awards. In my *mind*, I am kind of a big star!

Often, I cast myself as a hero or brave underdog, mimicking great film characters like Scarlett O'Hara, from *Gone with the Wind*; Holly Golightly, from *Breakfast at Tiffany's*; Inigo Montoya, from *The Princess Bride* ... Every line, look, and hook is memorized to entertain whoever might be watching—even if it is only me, watching myself in a passing mirror or reflective pane of glass.

Now that's a great confession! These characters are magnetic for their noble pride, unfailing hope, eternal optimism, and unwavering strength. I feel as though I am always preparing for a leading role in the adventure-comedy of my life, yet somehow never quite get the part. When I strip away this romantic notion, removing the fake characters and unrealistic scenes, I fall short.

For a while, my actual life looked like a B-rated movie of the week. Based on a true story, but viewer discretion was definitely advised! Life was not glamorous, not good, and ultimately not a pretense that was possible to maintain. So where does this lead?

Back toward the farm garden ...

CHURNING—churning...

Both feet are dangling from my high-perched tree-branch spot, watching the garden work going on below, smelling grass clippings from a freshly trimmed lawn, and a sense of wonderment of being held secure above the ground. Birds were aloft, insects crawling close, leaves rustling free, clouds curiously floating—all drawing my imagination to a heightened awareness of now—of *this*—of *life*.

Last week, grace got a little gritty, so perhaps this week, I need to descend from my treetop view and get my hands dirty.

"Growing begins in the dark."

I am timeless in this tree. Being lofty feels nice. It looks messy down there in the dirt.

The seeds are gently calling me—small seeds of grace beckoning me to organize and plant—promising a good future, if I live here—and work now.

I am content in this tree. Everything stops still. The wonder and awe of everything—and nothing—is up here.

The seeds persist in calling out—growing is a priority—doing my part—working together—the ground waits for an answer.

I can be anyone I want to be up here. Here, I am unconquerable!

The seeds insist—come down—do the work—one row at a time—you are not alone.

As the Hollywood screenplay fades, my dangling feet reach toward the earth. No more chasing down phantom shadows of acceptance. I need to sink into the shaking soil that livens with a fresh tilling. There is surrender alongside the tension of standing near the edge of an unpredictable storm.

I curl up into a tiny seed of possibility, vulnerable to winds of change and pelted by rains of displacement. I am disheveled. I may drown. I stretch toward the dark, searching for an anchor, and dive into the dirt.

Here... I can either wait or grow.

Which will I choose? It feels like a perfect time to hunker down and wait out this personal tornado. Our family issues abound, meaning my close relationships are regularly strained with high demands for my energy and time. *I want to be in my tree!*

"This tornado loves you."

Something is stirring—breaking. The squalor is moving, and suddenly...

There. Is. Calm.

It is the eye. An intermission. Everything not sturdy has been carried away. The sun is shining, the ground is moist, and nutrient-rich soils surrounds me.

Plant now. Let grace take hold. Now, is wonder. The worry can wait.

Hope.

Trust.

Stretch as far as tired, stiffened limbs will allow.

ROOTING—rooting...

No longer a stray seed, or a disengaged child swinging from memories. Many examples of grace have held and supported me, but I can no longer let YOU do all the work of grace. Your seeds of grace have sprouted and spread within ME and I am ready to grow beyond myself now.

I can hold YOU up. The storm has stripped away unhelpful habits, strengthened my core and dispelled my fears. I am free to live and give in grace, just as it was lived and given to me.

How does grace show up in the toughest of times? It digs down deep, embraces the storm and hangs on like hell!

Week Twenty-Three

WEEDING THROUGH GRACE

"Let the weeds and wheat grow together until harvest," said Jesus, when telling a story about farm workers who asked their boss if they should pull out the weeds that were growing in a freshly planted wheat field.

For this week, I have a proverbial weed-whacker ready to mow down anything that remotely resembles a weed—not exactly in keeping with the wisdom quoted above, but an *honest* look at how my seeds of grace have sprouted this week. Graciousness with US has gone a bit sideways!

When I plant seeds in actual dirt, I am careful to line them up in rows, making it easier to distinguish a seedling from 'weedling'. This maximizes my limited gardening skills and makes things look nicer at the same time. This does not eliminate me pondering what is growing—friend or foe—but it helps. Perhaps if I had been out of my childhood treetop more, and down at ground level working by Mum's side, I would have absorbed a some of her green thumb skills.

Again, I wish I had preserved a gardening tool from the old farm. Not to do actual gardening, but to use as my icon this week. Perhaps by the end of the week I will have a suitable alternate icon, but, in the meantime, I remember something Mum said about the fungi she studied in university. "Don't be scared of picking the *wrong* mushroom; Just look for the *right* one."

A perfect setup for the epic battle of grace between US this week. There is no surprise ending. No final twist. The story is still unravelling, so here is what I can share:

I challenged myself last week to be rooted during rising and subsiding storm blasts, which I did… about 50 percent of the time. That means something else happened for an equal majority of my week. I will call it stubbornness. There may be another, more accurate but less amicable, way of describing my behavior, but I shall stay with a positive framing of it for now.

Stubbornness is easily mistaken as a feeling of being very rooted and strong. Sometimes, I am graciously holding strong, while windy rains pelt my forgiving face and I await the chance to engage positively again. Sometimes, I am held together by threads of stubborn resistance, where I ignore anything hurtful and await my chance to avoid people and retreat. In both cases, a big smile might be on my face, but snarled up under my surface, grace and stubbornness are coiled up into tight, solid masses.

My intention was to plant seeds of grace and grow more of it, not to figure out how to co-exist with grace's nemesis! Always diving right in—here we go!

GRACIOUS WITH US

One of my historical strategies for creating a bit more grace within my interactions is through something I call 'the gimme'. The gimme is for moments I do not feel like serving someone with an action I might have easily performed in the past.

Usually, this is reserved for when I am in a bad mood, or tired, or lazy… or have said yes to everyone else in the world and now my family is asking, and I would be a terrible person to say no—so I reach for a gimme.

This led me to this week's icon, a gifted pearl necklace from Mum when I was about 15 or 16 years old. Had I known the superstition surrounding pearls, which are my birthstone and likely why she thought them an appropriate accessory, I may not have been so happy to wear them. For unwed girls, they are said to create tears, so only married ladies were to wear them as adornment. I know there are 59 medium sized pearls on this strand—nothing compared to the ocean of tears I have cried thus far… but back to the gimmes.

Gimmes also apply when people have hurt me in an uncharacteristic way. Most times, these blips slide off my reaction scale into emotional oblivion. With enough repetition, these gimmes build up into a heap of emotional triggers that begin to form barriers within formerly open relationships—reason enough to conquer true graciousness and not just hand out freebies that eventually have an emotional cost.

Temporarily, gimmes calm my mind and settle my spirits. Over time, a pile of unfinished business lies deeply buried among emotional memories accumulating in my core. Seems I tuck away, hang onto and hide, more than just physical stuff. I hoard negative interactions, too.

If I go to that place, that stale file room, that dark closet of unforgiven, unforgotten, unresolved moments, grace is eerily absent.

Yes, this is where I am heading. A place of unsettled dreams and haunting emotional upsets. A place I like to forget exists or underestimate its depth. At the surface, I can gimme, gimme, gimme like a champion, pat myself on the back, and carry on as though it should not be any other way. But I know better. I know an old children's rhyme about gimmes and how they never get.

This is how I feel—that I will not *get*!

I don't get why family relationships erupt into conflict or rebellion.

I don't get how friends that seem close today, disappear tomorrow.

I don't get what people mean when they say 'time heals everything' *(because I see a lot of old, miserable folks who have had plenty of years to heal).*

If life is like a garden and I see green, sprouting things that could be weeds, I am urged to decide.

If I pull the sprout up, nasty stuff cannot take root. This may rip out the intended plants, leaving very little to harvest, and little to show for my efforts.

If I leave all that is sprouting, it could hinder the quality of my harvest, the good plants being choked out of necessary sun and water by intermingled tares and thistles. This is also lost potential.

What of the sage advice I shared earlier? Letting it all grow up together until harvest? How can I apply this to grace?

Perhaps there is a simple solution. All along, I believed it was my duty to become the best gardener possible. It was my job to solve the mystery of what was useful in my life, and what was not. What to pull out and what to leave. This keeps me in a place of never getting it. After years of sorting through this life, I still cannot distinguish what will turn into something healthy and wonderful, and what will slowly choke out everything growing around it.

What if I shift my identity to something else? What if it is not my responsibility to decide initially what goes and what stays? Maybe I need to be okay with dandelions growing up alongside strawberries, because…

I am not the gardener.

I think I work in the dirt (*and might even BE the dirt*), and can learn basic growth patterns that result in successful planting strategies, but will I ever be the master designer of this jungle called life?

No.

That is beyond my abilities.

I do not understand the wisdom of letting everything grow together. My vision is limited by pride and perspective. My mind does not easily fathom a grander plan could be in motion. In this week of determining how to grow grace within my family—grace for US—I am at a loss to identify what is good or bad—toxic or healthy—meaning I am left with one conclusion:

I think we are just supposed to grow.

If weeds are naturally amongst us, perhaps all we can do is know they are present. Prying into and ripping apart all the suspected toxins might jeopardize the arrival of goodness. Weeds might just be a normal part of a growing, imperfect family. If I accept this as true, maybe gimmes will not become an overwhelming burden, and I can look beyond our entangled root systems, allowing grace to do what grace does best.

Such simplicity. Grow.

WE grow with—grow despite—grow alongside—and grow amongst… the weeds.

Week Twenty-Four

GRACE GETS OUT OF THE WAY

I talk to myself a lot.

Sometimes it is a silent scream, sometimes it is a quiet whisper, and occasionally it is a bold, out-loud pep talk to bolster my confidence or resolve in whatever direction needs going. I sometimes remind myself to evoke the raw power of pure love, likened to a superpower that waits at the ready for a hero in need.

Driven. Strong. Capable. Fearless.

I wonder if Mum ever imagined herself this way. I am guessing not, since she raised me to be humble—grounded. I was admonished for any grandiose pursuits that might potentially veer me from the safety of a tested route. Maybe this was typical of Mum's generation, which I appreciate for giving me its best, but I desire a different path. I like to test cultural and religious boundaries, especially if they withhold the very thing that culture, religion, and race is in greatest need of: Love, acceptance, and grace.

Ahhhh… grace. A pretty little butterfly, fluttering in mid-air, appearing like it might be possible to capture with bare hands and simple efforts, but it is not so.

Finding graciousness is proving to be a very big job. So big, that I find myself using powerful self-talk minute by minute!

Being planted on a gritty edge while digging into graciousness with THEM is truly surprising. Grace has been pushing me into a corner for the past three weeks. It has knocked me down, dragged me around, put me back on my feet again, and then does it all over again.

There is an old saying that adequately frames my current condition:

When the Going gets TOUGH
The Tough get GOING

Mum adhered to this philosophy. I witnessed her tough out personal heartbreaks, parenting showdowns, marital discord, and did not hear her complain. I did not feel her misplaced wrath, nor did I recognize whether she was processing prolonged issues. It seems she took stock of the cards in her hand, faced whatever force was upon her, and kept plugging away until the trouble had passed.

Rare were moments she physically appeared overcome or distraught with emotions. Even more rare were times she admitted to feeling hurt or having scars. I guess this is the stuff that 'gets going' when an 'easy' button is not available. She would have appreciated the modern version of that saying, its origins nodding to her British heritage:

Keep Calm and Carry On

She might have hung this slogan in her administration office, as a daily mantra for her stressful duties. I admired her leadership in our little community and liked listening to her talk to residents of our town while waiting for her to drive me home after school. She kept me entertained with the electric photocopier if she had to work later than expected. This machine was far more exciting to operate than the crank-handle model employed at the high school where Dad taught. And if she was really late, twenty-five cents could buy my happiness, as I skipped to the grocery store three doors down from her office.

For my icon this week, I will be reminded of her trailblazing character by wearing a jacket she once referred to as her "power jacket". Not only did she describe it as having a powerful *fit*, but it was also one of her power *colors*, a deep navy blue. This is how seriously she took her career and made every attempt to set an appropriate stage to accomplish her goals; Thinking, dressing, and acting the part of an inspired individual and leader. *Bulky 80s shoulder pads, welcome back!*

Mum worked long hours for a modest salary. She chauffeured us kids, volunteered in the community, and provided many musical and sporting opportunities for my brother and me. Mum never got a manicure, a pedicure, or any other spa-like pampering experience. I did not hear her complain about getting older or express a hankering to go on a diet.

These are intriguing facts, when strung all together. This may be a good place to start Week Twenty-Four.

Being depleted of chances to chase my fun, or deprived of a weekly allotment of personal pampering, lends itself to a feeling of being overwhelmed by career and parenting duties. As a result, I have sought out escape from my family as though desperately starved, my hair on fire, running without destination, adopting unhealthy habits—all to fill mysterious holes in an already jam-packed life, all very unsuccessfully.

The fact that I would not dream of doing more than my forty hours of work in a week without getting paid double time, is ONE clear indicator of how my world is different from Mum's. Thank goodness my chosen career has an equitable salary scale. One of the reasons I can do my job with passion is knowing I net the same amount as my male counterparts and earn enough to support my children. Mum would be proud of that!

But the biggest shift in the span of our lifetimes is how I perceive fulfillment compared to Mum. I am very interested in where grace will lead, if I point myself down that road. Here goes!

Mum wanted me to choose nursing as a career, which I thought had something to do with how she assessed my ability to care for others or my natural bedside mannerisms. But what if her main motivation was actually power? Get a career—wear a uniform—be a powerful force in the world. I may not have become a nurse, but I certainly fulfilled the career and uniformed parts of that equation.

This notion of power has me thinking about my younger son. After he ran away, I lamented about it with an empathetic cousin. She gently reminding me about the mischief I concocted as a child. Shenanigans and drama were also my forte, so having a son who matched my 'dukes-up' personality should not be a surprise. My wild, determined spirit gave birth to *another* wild, determined spirit.

Perhaps Mum saw this same energy in me and imagined *(as I have for my son)* what focus might best harness an unruly, yet bottomless heart. And if I am still finding my way, twenty-five adult years later, how do I expect him to have arrived into stability after only five teenage years? This comforts me.

Now, what of grace? I have gone to great lengths to describe the power I saw in my mum, have previously discussed my own strengths that have brought me through difficulties, and have likened myself to my teenage son, because these are things graciousness has been placing on my heart.

Somehow grace seems to be connected to power, and when I look at what our world is facing—violent extremist attacks, unjust allocation of rights, imbalance of wealth, gender intolerance, and a myriad of other quandaries—I must ask ... is graciousness taking me somewhere politically, culturally, or economically unpopular?

We shall see.

GRACIOUS WITH THEM

"GRACE. The Game Changer."

It was just spring break for us, so we headed to our favorite warm climate hideaway for a week of family fun. Every morning, I happily woke early, which is a thing that only happens on vacation—the *happy* part, not the early part—to go walking or running alongside chirping birds and the rising sunshine. I commonly observe hummingbirds in this area, who have been like cheering companions since starting this writing.

It now seems fitting to finish off the topic of graciousness by sharing the story of how hummingbirds came to be pivotal in my quest to heal and why they landed on the cover of this book.

After I realized I was one year away from being the same age Mum was when she died, I started contemplating how I might honor her life, and my own, during this year. As a visual and audio-styled learner, I went to the outdoors, taking in nature's chorus of sounds to imagine what pathway would point me in an inspiring direction. While this aided in a flood of peaceful, restorative energy, I was not getting any closer to figuring out what to do with my year.

With the prompting of a little voice somewhere inside of me, I had already begun writing about my harsh past, believing it would help express the emotional pain that needed addressing. I shared some chapters with a few close friends and was encouraged to keep at it because it was good. As I wrote, it felt very good.

I was not sure if I could delve into the memories that had yet to be uncovered, even six years after being released from my painful captivity. Slowly, with each keystroke, my wounds dissolved into words. Sentences poured out of me as I became the author of my story—my life. This... is power.

Taking fourteen years of physical, sexual, spiritual, emotional, and psychological abuse *(a time I felt I had no power)* and turning the tables to take undeniable control over what I allow to define me—well, it has been transformative.

Fast forward to waiting for an idea to take hold for this important year of honoring Mum. In the waiting, two things happened:

A dear friend, who knows I have been writing, suggests I blog and share my experiences with others. Duly noted.

And I have a dream.

An actual dream. In bed, while I was sleeping—not to be confused with a wide-awake daydream. It was a short vignette of a hummingbird, pretty and dazzling, fluttering over my head as if attempting to communicate with me. It then hovered closer to my face, which made me worry whether it was a friendly approach or a possible attack!

I have not known hummingbirds to get aggressive with humans, yet I felt troubled by this visitor. It was more than invading my personal bubble. It was right up in my face.

I gently tried to swoosh this little companion away, not certain of its intention, nor comfortable with its jittery fluctuations in speed and direction. It was not dissuaded from getting closer. It continued to hover, flitting in front of my eyes, as if to ensure I had indeed noticed it. I retreated, backing away to avoid any further contact, hoping to be left alone, and wishing this bird would go annoy someone else.

But my hummingbird friend was not going anywhere. It followed, no matter which direction or evasive maneuvers I made. It was not leaving me, and then the dream abruptly ended.

Okay—this is perhaps not a terribly insightful dream. No booming voices telling me what to do, no arrows pointing out a clear direction, no choirs singing, no lightning bolts dropping from the sky. Just a bird bugging me.

But what made this dream rare was remembering it when I woke up. When this happens, I must mull the dream over and try to get a better idea of what is going on inside my mysterious head. So, I looked up some possible symbolism for hummingbirds.

Their characteristics are symbolic of resilience, adaptability, optimism, and having a free-flowing spirit.

Since that dream, hummingbirds have been showing up all around me. Sometimes in the morning while I run, afternoons when I write, or in the evening when I am having a glass of wine on the deck. They urge me on, remind me of my focus, and put a smile on my face. I am grateful for their kind service to me.

But these friends were absent this week of spring break. Many other little birds were flying around, which I convinced myself could be hummingbirds but there really is no mistaking the unique flight patterns of my special, feathered soul mates. None to be seen! *Have they abandoned me?*

At first, I was worried something might have happened to their habitat, causing them to seek shelter elsewhere. Then I thought—maybe it was my current flavor of writing and the birds did not appreciate graciousness sounding so raw and edgy—instead of the anticipated joyous, smooth, poetic, fluffy, and light tones.

Grace is tough! Weeds are tough! *C'mon, hummingbirds, don't leave me now!*

I have been working hard to find an understanding of how grace works with ME, with YOU, and with US. Now that I am slogging through how to be "Gracious with THEM", my thoughts are piling up in a big muddle. I am swamped with doubts, tangled-up in thorns, and getting stung by thistles of emotions. I have struggled with this more than any topic so far, stumbling over shortcomings I see in myself while trying to live out—breathe in—and give away grace.

Graciousness is taking me down!

If the hummingbirds are gone, and my focus thus faded, it might be time to rethink my goals and gears.

For the last while, I have been in one of three gears:

- Get *to* it!
- Get *through* it!!
- Get *over* it!!!

These gears require an assertive, empowered mentality. It feels mandatory to have this kind of mindset, but there is a cost. Powering through big issues tends to limit my acknowledgment of the smaller details and important reasons for setting a goal in the first place.

So, how do I wrap up a month of grace?

On the last day of our trip, I decided to run backwards down a long hill, reading recently how it can be good for your muscles. I knew the hill well, so it seemed safe enough to try. I started slow. It was making me dizzy to see my feet moving along the ground in this manner, so I thought to lift my gaze higher, to see if that helped to regain my balance.

And there—where sunlight was meeting dewy leaves and branches of flora—was a friend.

It was hovering back and forth over a giant blossoming shrub. It moved in such a way that it looked to be drawing a smiling mouth shape in mid-air. Over and up one way, then back down—then over and up the other way. With its quick, flitting motion, I could see a quivering smile start to form against the shrub greenery. I laughed and thanked my feathery angel, who once again delivered striking clarity.

The lightning bolt message is this: Being driven, focused, passionate, and capable of doing many creative and generous things, is not a formula for producing graciousness. Certainly, I must keep striving to churn out my best work, follow my most fantastic dreams, and keep my eyes on spectacular motives, but this will never be the point.

Mostly, my eyes stay fixed on where I want to go, what I want to manifest, how to achieve my goals, and realize my dreams. I am not looking back to what carnage might be left behind in my wake. I fear the result of unlocking my intent focus from the direction of my desires. Yet, that is what happened this week. I turned my gaze from where I was going to where I had been, and it all became a little clearer.

Grace is about looking for the people who are waiting to be seen and hoping to be heard, and waiting on a platform to use their skills, their abilities, and their leadership. I cannot blindly rocket toward my goals, in top gear, without potentially leaving others to drown. Graciousness means looking back at the waves my passion creates, slowing my churning motors, and quieting the din long enough to allow someone else to emerge—to shine.

So, let THEM shine—and smile. There is plenty of grace for us ALL.

AJ

Where in your life do you want to plant more grace?

CHAPTER SEVEN

GRATITUDE

Piglet noticed that even though he had a very small heart,
it could hold a rather large amount of gratitude.
~ A. A. Milne

Week Twenty-Five

GRATITUDE GETS GOING

It is a new week, a new beginning, and new TOPIC!

This is a busy topic. Many writers, poets, songwriters, and social media mega-stars have explored and explained it. You only need google the word to find out what I mean:

- Let yourself be seen. Love with your whole heart. Practice gratitude. Lean into joy. Believe you are enough. ~ Brene Brown
- Gratitude opens the door to… the power, the wisdom, the creativity of the universe. You open the door through gratitude. ~ Deepak Chopra
- In all things, give thanks. ~ Apostle Paul
- When you meet obstacles with gratitude, your perception starts to shift, resistance loses its power, and grace finds a home within you. ~ Oprah Winfrey
- When we express our gratitude, we must never forget that the highest appreciation is not to utter words, but to live by them. ~ JFK

All great offerings of insight to begin a month of reflecting on how to be more grateful, but I will start, as always, by looking at "Gratitude for ME".

There are many buzz words that accompany gratitude—manifest, create, cultivate, grow, practice, journal—but my favorite would have to be 'invest'. I like thinking that, if I pay enough attention to something, give it plenty of energy and love, there will be a return of my investment. If that strikes a chord of 'what's in it for me', let's adjust that slightly and say: "What's in it for ME"—a subtle, but measured, difference.

I wrote about what is 'for' me during my very first week of patience. If I had to sum up the experiences I think are *for* me, it would be a broad, sweeping answer: *Everything* is FOR me. The pleasant, the uncomfortable, the familiar, the strange, the smooth, the awkward, the easy, the difficult—everything is meant for refining my edges and bringing me closer to my goal of living out my best life NOW.

After a grueling focus on graciousness, it is probably well timed to turn my thoughts to gratitude. It took me a few extra weeks to take in all that grace had to teach, which I believe is essential if we are to adopt a new perspective. I am cautioning myself to take that time. Yes, there are deadlines and expectations, and good for us if we make and meet those, but life should not be rushed when getting to the good stuff!

Here is the plan—a challenge for this first week of gratitude:

Making a list of three things that I am grateful for, each day of this week.

Easy, right? Here is the catch: The items on the list must be about ME. Three things—for seven days—meaning twenty-one grateful thoughts about myself. *Ya-huh!*

To help me do this, and for my icon this week, I am using a journal Mum was given while she was sick. Her thoughts were clouded, and she had a hard time remembering things after her unsuccessful brain surgery. To combat this condition, she used a school-style notebook to jot down important things, like names of people who visited her, odd jobs for my dad to do at home, and retail items she regretted not buying and wanted someone to pick up. She may have been sick, but her love of shopping was completely intact.

She also wanted to thank people whom she felt helped maintain her dignity during her illness, by finding clothes to disguise the forty pounds she gained on steroids, or scarves to cover her shaved head, or for engaging in meaningful conversations with her after she could no longer work in her proud career. These scattered thoughts made their way into random pages of her scribbler, probably never to be looked at again, but she could rest knowing they were expressed.

A friend gifted her a new journal, inscribing a dedication on the front page to an "admired, strong friend", but the rest of the journal remained blank. Mum's cancer was aggressive. She was gone before we had time to adjust to her illness. My brother has the scribbler now, and I have Mum's empty journal. It lives with every other diary and notebook I wrote in since I was 12 years old.

When I flip through some of my oldest journals, I chuckle about the content that often played out there—usually chronic friend drama or chasing boys—but one journal entry when I was about 14, says this:

Resolution

My New Year's Resolution is to have fun with the time on hand. Not let others control my emotions. I do hope to grow... a better and stronger ME!
AJ

Ah-hah! This started a long ago—signing off as AJ *and* looking for that best ME. This sojourn has been brewing inside me for almost twenty-five years! I need a minute to let that sink in... What a joy it is to resume this pursuit from my youthful heart.

My favorite notebook is a handwritten history of each of my children, their birth stats, first events, personalities, and how they interpreted their new world. Most importantly, it reminds me of how very much I loved watching them grow. I am so thankful to have this written down, as I have already started to forget which child did what, and when.

Now, back to my challenge... I think it is time to fill up Mum's blank journal, to honor her gratitude for the beauty and kindness around her, even while being swallowed by death.

Starting today, it will hold the first week of gratitude I have for myself, maybe including things like appearance, or attributes, and any other itty-bitty things that make me self-conscious. I will have one rule: No repeats. Each item must be something real and different each day.

So, grab a scribbler, sticky note, paper wad, journal, napkin, tree bark—and let's get grateful!

Choose your own ICON for Gratitude:

GRATITUDE FOR ME

I have noticed a consistent voice popping up each time I take pen in hand to write out three mentions of gratitude for myself each day. This voice sounds a lot like Mum's. Through my youth, she disapproved of talking better of one's self, in keeping with what I assumed was her conservative, traditional upbringing. She would quickly correct me for anything that sounded like bragging or looked like I was drawing too much attention to myself. Her stern glance appeared often when I expressed any creative dreams. Not surprisingly, it was seldom I heard a compliment from her. I am guessing those two concepts, compliments and bragging, were interchangeable in her role of shaping the growth of my young ego.

Sometimes, I would mischievously prey on this tendency of hers, and intentionally brag about a topic that would certainly get her swift admonition, then release the biggest grin as her reaction came rolling out. Sometimes, I would get upset and try to defend my choice of words or actions—possibly with steam coming out of my ears. She did not fall for my argument bait, leaving me to walk away in a huff, with no smirk on my face. Sometimes, I would get quiet, feel shame, burn with embarrassment, and harbor resentment toward this lady who seemed to not approve of me.

This is a different side of Mum—a side I have written about in those many journals and notebooks but have not produced for mass consumption yet.

She was not perfect. Her fast deterioration did not allow time for us to resolve some of these hurts. Since she is not around to defend herself, I thought it respectful to present her best characteristics, and examine positive anecdotes. It is tricky to ignore the unexplained, unsettled, fixed points of reality that exist when you do not get time to know anything different about a person.

But these feelings of having unresolved hurts with Mum are simply that: Feelings.

If I really want to get to what is true, I think I need a different lens; One that looks for moments where Mum saw who I was and loved me anyway.

For most of my life, Mum did not use affirming words. This was not her love language. Somehow, she managed to resign herself to accept my creative pursuits but was not happy about it. Relieved, yes, that I was engaged in anything post-secondary, but wistfully hoping there might still be a chance of that nursing degree and not a Theatre Arts Diploma.

I was finishing my first year of a two-year program when news of Mum's cancer came. It was not a nervous breakdown, a diagnosis from my non-medical knowledge that deduced her stressful, busy life had finally caught up to her. Cancer was the ultimate showstopper, a plot twist unexpectedly interrupting Act II of her life, just as it was beginning.

Mum rarely attended competitions or events where I was performing, the exception being piano recitals where both my brother and other students displayed the product of their practice. I was not a disciplined participant, so had little to offer in terms of impressing a piano-recital audience, but I liked performing—period.

Dad was often on stage with me, sharing this love of entertaining people, so feeling acceptance from him was never an issue. But Mum? Well, Mum would drive me to any venue, drop me and a cheque for the given amount, then pick me up after her shopping or errands were complete. Maybe if she saw what I could do, heard me amongst other singers, witnessed me grow in an art I was lapping up with every ounce of energy, she would become an endorser.

Nope.

It took cancer to do that.

After the doctors tried to remove her brain tumor, and attempts to regain enough strength to walk failed, she was confined to a wheelchair. Dad pushed her to my last performance of the year, where they seated her on the actual stage floor, there being no designated wheelchair access in theatres at that time.

It was an interactive musical, *The Mystery of Edwin Drood*, where characters roam through the intimate setting, and engage the audience in period-style banter. I played the formidable and bawdy character of Princess Puffer, an opium-parlor

Madame, who delivers a vengeful lament song, about a girl spiraling to ruin after a man has shamefully abandoned her. Very good drama, indeed.

1991 Getting padded up for my 'princess' character

During the performance, Mum, who thought she was whispering, would lean over to Dad and glow about my performance. She proudly exclaimed for the whole theatre to hear, who her daughter was: Me. This happened every time I went on stage. My fellow performers, who knew she was ill, helped me concentrate through this potential embarrassment, and we carried on as though it was not disruptive to our performance.

At one point, her wig got too itchy, so she whipped it off her head, gave her scalp a solid going over with her fingernails, all the while providing ample commentary about how gooooood it felt. When she placed her wig back on, it was slightly off kilter, making it look like she might be part of the comedy routines we were performing. I watched this hilarious scene unfold from backstage, folding over with silent laughter to avoid further distraction of the close audience. I wiped away ridiculous tears, trying not to smudge my intentionally smudged stage makeup, and collected myself each time I had to walk back on stage to act.

This was her final assessment of ME.

Great. Talented. Worthy. And she was Proud.

So why does her voice continue to confuse and frustrate ME?

If I cannot find a way to give more weight to her final affirmations rather than to her initial inability to voice positive feedback toward me, I do not think I will be able to believe my own voice.

When I stop and get quiet about the stuff I should be thankful for about me, I need to believe it, or it means nothing. It will just be an exercise of discipline and creativity, something that will sound good and appease my sense of accomplishment, but without really doing 'the work'. It will just be an easy button.

So far, I have not wiggled around the hard stuff, looking for an escape. No, I am firmly planted in discomfort. I am testing all my resistance to change, turning corner after corner of old thinking and believing, all in an effort to arrive somewhere—anywhere but where nothing ever changes.

"The last key often opens the lock."

When I was thinking of what I am thankful for about ME, especially in terms of appearance and attributes, I cannot help but think of Mum. She is in my mirror. Her voice whispers in my thoughts, challenges my direction, questions my actions, points out my weakness, and dismisses my strengths.

But a shift occurred while I was writing ME-related gratitude's this week. I started off flatly listing three factual details about myself, boring and safe. Then I started to add adjectives, describing how I felt about certain attributes. As I did this, another voice inside got stronger, sweeter—gentler—more accepting.

So, which voice wins?

The one that hurts or the one that helps? One that lays rotting in my stagnant past or one that does not care if a wig gets whipped off in public, but is simply grateful to be around for the experience?

Those who know and love me best cannot always give me this helpful voice. They—like Mum—are not saints. Where will this voice come from?

ME.

I decide what voice will lead.

Appreciation can make a day, even change a life.
Your willingness to put it into words is all that is necessary.
~ Margaret Cousins

For the first time, I put into words the greatest appreciations I have for myself. Filtering these words through discerning ears and a grateful heart, I have come to see myself, as Mum did, as the diverse, dynamic, frantic, and fanciful creature that I am. That is a very freeing, very helpful voice to hear.

If anyone struggles with a voice that tells them they are not accepted, here is some encouragement:

When people face mortality, or give themselves permission to express unvoiced regrets, wishes, dreams, and blessings—whatever they expressed before, changes.

I believe Mum would have wanted better words to be the foundation of my identity, no matter what other contrary messages I may have perceived from her. She would want me to know for certain: *I am worthy. I am enough. I have endless abilities. My spirit is unconquerable. I am unequivocally flawed, but that pales in comparison to how much I am unconditionally loved.*

I am just sure of it.

Week Twenty-Six

HALFWAY THERE

Wow! This week marks the halfway point to the goal of discovering a better way to do life!

Last week was the challenge to write three things I loved about myself each day. One week did not seem like enough, so I decided to keep adding to my list for the rest of the month. I might just fill up that little notebook of Mum's and take up someone else's challenge from a book I read a few years ago.

Ann Voskamp is a gifted and moving writer who pours out words from her heart. In her book, *One Thousand Gifts,* she shares pivotal spiritual breakthroughs, and champions small adjustments made, to find joy during painful periods of life. Her book was a godsend for me during an incredibly rough patch with depression and despair. With descriptive and poignant vignettes to seek out gratitude, I was directed toward how to live through loss, and even better, how to be thankful for your sorrows. *(Okay, I am still working on that sorrows bit)*, but even the fact that I can see this as a possibility now, means I could end up getting there one day!

But being *that* thankful scared me. As a result, I did not take up the challenge she issued for readers to compile a gratitude journal of a thousand entries.

A thousand is a lot! Even without a deadline, this number seemed quite intimidating. High-quantity outcomes scare me. Remember the pep talk I had to give myself at the beginning of this fifty-two-week campaign?

Now, here it is—a whizzing, warped-speed arrival at twenty-six weeks. Amazing! This might be an appropriate time to take some reflective breaths and allow some space for the lessons learned to seep a little deeper into who I am becoming.

To do that, I have a quick update on the hummingbird situation:

It occurred to me that I was potentially forcing an interaction with my animal totems by choosing the same paths where I had encountered them before. Seems reasonable to gravitate toward the familiar, especially if good things are happening there. Seeing a hummingbird feels good, so why would I choose a different road to travel? Because somewhere deep inside, there is also a frantic, desperate little girl who is hunting for that feeling, hoping it proves she is okay.

So, I chase down the same alleyways, pretending to have empty expectations, while hiding my singular intent: GET my blessing! I am either immature or crazy *(probably both)* to be repeating this tactic as a should-know-better adult. There may be some balance necessary between hunting for my best life and living it.

This is how I anticipate gratitude showing up. I am going to try to stay thankful in the now, for my people here, dedicating the next week to "Gratitude for YOU".

I am going to try and tackle each day and decision without considering how to guarantee a specific outcome. Forcing has not worked to attract hummingbirds. After twenty-six weeks of searching for solid answers and actions that lead to a life well lived, forcing does not appear to work with life either.

For an icon this week, I have chosen a dainty, pristine hammer from Mum's personal tool chest which I saw her use to tack upholstery and frame pictures. Since the smaller size allowed her to get into places where a bigger hammer would fail, it is a helpful reminder to watch for the subtle habits of gratitude.

GRATITUDE FOR YOU

While pondering the concept of what a best life could be, I am very aware of a strong trigger associated with the word 'best'. It comes from old, dysfunctional years where it was my duty, under the direction of a relentless husband, to be better than everyone else. I had to eat better food, use a better vocabulary, pray better prayers, exercise harder, be smarter, and act better than everyone else. He also asked me to be better than all his ex-girlfriends put together, constantly letting me know if I was measuring up to their best qualities—but what qualified as best?

Whatever *he* thought best.

It took several years to realize that I could not achieve this 'better' level, as his standard kept rising. Arguing that I had already met his established expectations only caused his standards to drastically increase, so I endured his rants while carrying on with my busy mommy duties.

For fourteen years I chased his impossible standards, which for a grown woman with a healthy enough upbringing, was tough to adopt. Modelling this for my kids to learn and then begin their own frantic pursuits of disapproval... well, it will be harder for them to eventually recover. They believe a sick version of the truth is reality. A twisted, controlling, feigned religious existence was apparently, best.

This reflection from my painful past acts like a sounding board for me now; Helping to process where I have been, where I am going, and where I NEVER want to be again. I see how magnetic repetitive behaviors can become. I can easily spin into a '*Groundhog Day*' looped thinking, desperate for hummingbirds or despairing over wasted time.

I accept there is a benefit in repeating healthy habits, but simple repetition does not take me the whole distance. If my only strategy is to repeat an established norm, I run the risk of forcing every outcome and losing the ability to see beyond that habit. I am apt to blindly follow routine because it is easier than jumping into something new—a possible explanation of why fourteen years of control and violence felt normal.

'Grateful' does not express how thankful I am to be free from blind obedience and hostile manipulation, but the minds of four incredibly gifted children, are not free.

Progress is happening, as they work hard to integrate a gentler, more loving reality into their outlook. I sense that a haunting voice remains inside them. One that screams accusations of not being good, not being worthy, and never being enough. How they deal with those untrue allegations, varies with their personalities.

One is driven to greater and grander life accomplishments, chasing the standard over happiness. One opposes societal norms, doing the opposite of what is considered a good idea. One runs from love and support, finding comfort in extreme conflict. One pretends bad things do not exist and ignores anything upsetting.

Are they wrong?

No. It is their direction—their hummingbirds to chase.

As they grow and mature, their direction will change. The voice they allow to win will change. I can only whisper softly into their ears, "*It is okay. YOU are okay.*"

And okay is enough.

Because I have decided to keep journaling my gratitude for a month, I set a goal this week to write a descriptive entry on every person within my immediate circle. I recorded how much I appreciate their conversations, spirit, characteristics, and efforts. Now, I plan to share parts of my entries with each of them, which feels a bit terrifying with teens, but one day they will appreciate it. Hubby is getting his entry instead of a birthday card this year. Lucky him!

It is a little weird, thinking about a right time to spurt out some grateful words, but then I remembered what twenty-six weeks has taught me: Do not force it. Live it.

Live thankful.

> **"If you are wondering whether the time has come,**
> **The answer is, yes."**

Weeks Twenty-Seven and Twenty-Eight

HOW TO THANK YOUR MOTHER

TODAY:

Iron shirts, hem pants, book hotel, make two important phone calls, get passport photo, repair chip in windshield, make supper, go to doctor's appt with daughter, go to couples appt w/hubby, go for a run, day five of my thirty-day squat challenge, apply for a raffle permit for daughters choir committee, change Christmas frame *(yes, five months after Christmas)*, send my dad a birthday card *(which turned into a birthday email, when I could not print some photos I wanted to send)*, and blog…

This is a list of things I made for myself to do, on my first day off in a month where I actually stayed home! I am not complaining. It has been a great privilege to gallivant, to and fro about the earth with hubby, with girlfriends, and with my children, but I also enjoy spending days at home. However, it is more pleasant to be in my comfy zone when the to-do list is not quite so long!

Most of this list was accomplished, by some small miracle. They were shamefully overdue, which instigated the reason I made a list at all, so it seems prudent to change TODAY's list, to THIS WEEK's, and maybe go to bed on time tonight— after picking up daughter from soccer practice. *Is it too much to ask for a second miracle today?*

> The average mom makes 19710 meals before a child turns 18.
> *So, for me, that's 19710 x 5… No wonder I am tired!*

Are you having one of those lives? Are you so busy taking care of everyone and everything, you have not had the time to read an entire book in a while or sat down to sort through the 4,257 photos on your iPhone… or maybe you are so exhausted, the only extra thing you can bear to attempt is simply finishing this topic—well, I have good news. This is the shortest chapter!

Remember giving ourselves permission to take this at our own pace, and not feel pressure to race through all the topics, as though getting to the end was the only necessary outcome? I am putting that into practice this week, by combining two weeks together again and choosing 'one icon to rule them all' *(apologies to the non-Tolkien fans, who are now inspired to read the "Lord of The Rings" series, so they get that inference).*

The epic icon that will represent this joint venture will be a Hallmark datebook Mum started before she was married, recording all the birthdays and anniversaries of family and friends. It is such a beautiful treasure; I may have to do a spin-off project when all the weeks are complete and dare myself to send a greeting card to every person in her book. Looks to be about fifty cards, or one per week. *Hmmm… that may need some mulling over...*

GRATEFUL FOR US AND THEM

We just celebrated Mother's Day, which is fitting enough for the topic of being grateful for US, but that is not the direction I am heading, yet. Some questions have come out of my journaling this week, so please, indulge this first one without too much introduction:

If you could go back in time and thank anyone in the world for something they did, who would it be?

Mine would have to be Abraham Lincoln, for abolishing slavery in the USA. Whatever his true motivations were, it was the unpopular and right thing to do. A close second would be that darling Mother Theresa, for her willingness to use God's strength and love to care for the sick and forgotten.

A strange third place goes to my elementary-school principal, Mr. L., because my life would not be the same without a specific piece of advice he gave, after being sent repeatedly to his office in grade three for getting into scraps with the boys. *GRRRR… I was an angry 8-year-old!*

He said to me, "The only time you need to fight is when you are backed into a corner and there is no other option."

Thank you for that, kind sir, and for your patience when saying it.

I used this advice often during my dynamic first marriage, sometimes to come out swinging and sometimes to escape. It *also* made me a nicer person. So, to all you teachers out there, wondering where your sage advice to students ends up, the answer is… in a book about forty years later!

My title to introduce Weeks Twenty-Seven and Eight, 'How to Thank Your Mother', aligns with finally being able to publicly celebrate the fact that I am soon going to be a grandmother! *Holy crackers and cheese…*

I remember searching my daughter's face for a clue on how to feel when she told me the news, but I was also playing musical chairs in my mind, realizing I was sitting where Mum was hoping to be before she died.

This is it! I have now reached Mum's ideal of what a fulfilled life would entail. A grandkid is on the way.

Do I feel ready? No.

Am I the one who needs to feel ready? Not really.

Do I feel the immediate urge to dye my hair? YES, absolutely!

For a few weeks after, I asked random people what would be the worst news they could get from their young adult daughters?

Everybody *(except one)* said, "being pregnant".

Really? That is the worst?

It is a harmless, eeensy, teeensy bay-beey! Babies are super cute and cuddly, give unconditional love, and enter your heart with a one-way ticket. Why wouldn't everybody want to have a whole batch of them?

With four of my own biological offspring and one extra as a bonus, one might argue that I did have a whole batch, which also means—I know how demanding the job of 'Mom' can be. This explains why my reaction to becoming a grandma was not instant elation. Stuff had to be processed. What is the plan? What are her needs? What options need exploring? What can I do to help? What, what, what…?

Now, to paint the whole picture, you must understand that *(not to name names)* there are a few 'A' type personalities in my house. Ambiguity is not popular. WE like to decide, declare, and do around here. The hardest thing to hear is, "I don't know."

YIKES!

How about now? Do ya know yet? What about riii-ght now? O-kaaaaay—and now?

My bottom line, while tottering on this scale of decision making, was to preserve relationships at all cost. Without a doubt, I want *my* baby to know that her actions do not condition my love. She is accepted and fiercely loved. I will fight and defend her honor and rights with all that I have. My loyalty never goes away, never quits, and never dies—even if I am dead. Anything can be overcome; We just need to stay connected.

I am certainly not perfect when executing this plan, especially when disagreements arise over logistics, but that does not stop me from getting up each day, wading into the muck, and uncomfortably finding a place to breathe, while I listen to those who need to speak. I am not backed into a corner with this; There is no fight, here. There is only a launching pad of possibility.

I do not know what lies ahead for this new life that is coming. What I do know is this: I can influence how easy it is to *transition* into the future her choices will bring. If there were ever a time I can lean into my best discovered parenting wisdom, it would be now.

> **"Our children are not ours. They belong to Breath.**
> **It calls them into being.**
> **Hold them… love them… give them all you can, and then… let them go.**
> **Thank Time. Thank Love.**
> **You got to be part of the miracle."**

~ Inspired by Kahlil Gibran, *On Children*

When I think about how much Mum influenced our family's identity, with her work, her values and ethics, it is no wonder I have come to admire her, flaws and all. She was just beginning the transition of letting me and my brother move on to our adult lives, so I do not have an example to draw on for how to do it with my own kids; Perhaps another good reason to be on this quest.

The time she had with us must have been enough to grow two adults who became love champions with our own families. My brother and I would both give our last ounce of energy, our last bites and breath, for the sake of the people we love. I cannot think of a better force to let loose into our communities and into this world. We choose people over money and do not pretend to be perfect.

This is how we thank our mothers. All the mothers. We acknowledge their sacrifice in holding on to us like crazy, then finding the grace and balance, to lovingly let us go. Again, I will not predict how this change will occur with all my children, some being harder to release when I can see them hurting and in need of help. Some have chosen to take the transition out of my hands and become adults without me—certainly a different kind of challenge.

Still, I am grateful for whatever time I had to hold them and…I am grateful for the chance to be around to let them go.

AJ

Ready to COMMIT to making a Gratitude List?

What will you use to record it?

How will you celebrate once completed?

CHAPTER EIGHT

HUMOR

Be SILLY
Be HONEST
Be KIND
~ Ralph Waldo Emerson

Week Twenty-Nine

LAUGH YOUR WAY TO A BETTER DAY

A young boy accompanied his dad to work one day. The father took great pride in showing his son the heavy equipment he operated for his earth-moving company. A backhoe, a bulldozer, and several dump trucks were just a few of the marvels the wide-eyed lad was excited to watch on a busy construction site. With great curiosity, the boys' ears perked up at the sounds the machines made as they moved effortlessly forward and back, the repetitive beeps and hums, warning those nearby of the direction these monsters were maneuvering to next.

After a while, the boy became hungry and asked to go to the grocery-store deli for his favorite treat. The father agreed and off they went to fill his little belly. When they arrived at the store, the boy noticed a very round lady awkwardly pushing a heavy cart. His father told him it was not polite to stare, so the little boy turned his head but kept his eyes carefully on this interesting sight. As luck would have it, this large lady was heading toward the deli as well, making it very difficult for this obedient son to pretend he was not still looking—not while walking right behind her!

Suddenly, the back-door alarm of the store went off, alerting staff and customers alike. BEEP. BEEP. BEEP. The little boy jumped quickly out of the way and yelled to his dad, "Look out, Dad! She's backing up!"

This is the only joke I ever heard Mum tell and a fitting way to start the new topic: HUMOR.

I am looking for humor in everything, as it has been a lifeline to me.

Mum's life was already past the point of saving when she started telling people this joke. Sometimes she would shorten it, wanting to get to the punch line quicker so she could finally laugh. Sometimes, she was laughing so hard by the middle of the joke that she could hardly finish. Because the tumor was pressing against her brain and crippling everything on her left side, her face looked a bit odd when she laughed or smiled.

Seeing the droopy left side of her mouth not able to keep up with her expressive and exuberant right side, combined with her bald head and puffy cheeks—well, if you didn't laugh at what her joke delivery looked like, you just might cry.

Before Mum's surgery, she had a very quiet sense of humor. My icon this week is an example of something she found funny. I have had it since I was a teenager and use it regularly, especially for rough mornings.

This mug has survived many moves, a fire (*a term I use instead of explaining to the children why they have none of their baby albums, books, or favorite things, which were left behind while fleeing with only the clothes on our backs*), a flood (*another term I use, this one to define a period of time when I was either intoxicated or hungover, and throwing away everything that remotely reminded me of my nasty past*), and a few almost serious purges of hoarded items. All that and yet the mug remains!

The other side reads: "I'm at my very BEST in the morning."

HUMOR WITH ME

Humor was a big reason I kept this mug, but there are many more moments in my life where I need to thank Humor for showing up:

- Almost getting me expelled from bible college after a prank in the dean's dorm went terribly wrong...
- Giving me a chance to apologize for being grumpy without saying that boring clichéd phrase "*I'm sorry...*"
- Getting me through a painfully long divorce, without committing murder...
- Allowing me to tolerate a moderately annoying, indoor, untrained, pet tortoise—also without committing murder...

These, and many other life circumstances, may not have ended so positively were it not for laughing myself silly with friends or family AND fiercely muttering to myself outside the earshot of others. It is my therapy. Perhaps it was Mum's, too. I often caught her talking with herself, which I immediately teased her about without mercy. She would take my ribbing with grace, a small smirk hidden in her buried chin, as she turned away to laugh at her own quirkiness.

The days leading up to Mum's funeral were sunny and hot, sizzling with promise of more glorious summer days to come. June is a month I historically anticipate, as it brings prospects of camping, beaches, and fire pits, but not that June. I was numb—cold.

After funeral services and interment rituals were finished, friends made their way over to visit and sit silently together. Sun poured through sheer curtains Mum had hung to filter, but not block, the rays entering through south-facing windows. Her brown reclining chair sat empty, her coral-colored afghan still laying rumpled from the last time she'd flung it off during a medicine induced hot flash.

Her stylish personality still tangible around the room, amongst furnishings and fixtures that carefully made their way into her intentionally designed living space. I remember hearing muffled voices say, "We don't know what to say; We just thought we should come." And that seemed to feel good. I felt loved but could not respond. My feelings had been cut off that day.

I am still unclear why I was so determined to not cry at my own mother's funeral. Maybe I thought it was my new role to stand strong for our family. Dad was ripped up. My brother was slipping away. Who would hold us together when the one who did that was down in the ground? Who would make it okay?

I stood stoic, not a tear in my eye to mark that public day. Wave after wave of grievers approached, sobbing their sympathies, overcome in sorrow of a 'too soon' death. I held them. My shoulder dried their tears. They… were sorry. I… was silent.

How brave those friends were, coming to sit with an unresponsive hostess. Eyes open, but not focused on anything, all senses frozen with no thaw in sight, until something catches my eye. A flicker. There is movement coming from the kitchen.

Do I leave my stupor to identify what this is? I slowly pull my focus toward a kitchen filled with early-evening light, where Mum's twin sister has been putting out food for visitors. She is looking right at me, desperately signaling for my attention, while also trying to not look like she wants my attention. Once my gaze settles on her face, I realize that she is starting to laugh. She holds up her two fingers, upside down and wide apart, and with as much emphasis as she can soundlessly muster, she puts her fingers back together while directing them towards me.

I do not 'pick up' what she is 'putting down'.

She tries again, eyes bigger this time and darting toward my legs, fingers slamming together now, to make her point. My brain slowly turned the information over… together… me… legs—OH! Put my legs together?!

Wearing a pleated skirt, with my knees unconsciously falling to either side, was apparently quite a view from the sightlines of the kitchen. Aunty looked so pleased when I got the correct answer in our little charades game and kept chuckling to herself as she turned back to her busyness—just like Mum. I could not help but grin.

This broke my emotional prison, as I began to laugh along with my aunty, who taught me something important that day. I could intensely miss someone I loved and still smile. You can appropriately grieve someone and still laugh. You can try to block out painful loss by prohibiting your sadness, but it will block every other emotion along with it.

When I go to funerals now, I try to share a fond memory or funny anecdote with the loved ones. I hope it reminds them to feel and remember happy times, to laugh and love in the hope of a future that will get brighter, once grief and loss finish their course. I think if my mum could have talked on her last day, she just might have told that joke again—and again—and again, so her dying breath could be a mighty exhalation of joy.

I want humor to fill my last breath and lots of other breaths in the meantime.

Choose your own ICON for Humor:

Week Thirty

THE ORIGINAL SILVER LINING

"Humor with YOU" is no joke!

I have buttons. Red—HOT—buttons. After learning from my sympathetic elementary-school principal that punching people was not a viable option for responding to triggers, I needed a new strategy. This is exactly the kind of discussion I currently engage in for my career, with school-aged students—young hot heads, quiet bystanders, and kind-hearted youth, all of whom need permission and options to manage conflict.

This kind of conversation was not available when I was in my formative years, so it might have been luck that directed me toward something less explosive, when my license to clobber annoying people was taken away. I was to recognize my feelings and do something else about them—my flushed face and a tongue begging to lash out were indicators that it was time to walk myself directly to the principal's office.

Unfortunately, that strategy was only effective during school hours, but I still ended up adopting a 'walk away' technique for other anger-filled occasions, like:

- When I was 11, and the baseball coach told me I could not play with the team anymore, I turned on my heels, mitt in hand, and stomped two miles down the gravel road toward home. Apparently, looking like a girl was a problem on a boy's ball team, and it did not matter how many hits or outs I accumulated over lesser skilled players; I was never going to have the 'right' equipment. Grrrr...

- At 15, I was with friends having a bonfire at a nearby lake. A standard campground outhouse served as the only facilities available in this remote, valley location. When I used this 'facility', a couple of friends thought it funny to tip this stinky old structure over, slightly jamming the door, and leaving me stuck sideways until I could wedge my way through to what I hoped would be a solid piece of ground. A long walk, up a steeply inclined road, was duly needed. GRRRR...

- Fast forward to 18, when I listened to a friend express one too many antagonistic comments about my spiritual views. Again, my feet pivoted swiftly away, to get swallowed up amongst crowds, rides, and vendors of the fairgrounds we were visiting. We stayed apart for hours before bumping back into one another again. Roooaar...

- At 22, a few weeks after Mum died, I needed to have some fun, so I invited myself along with the boys on a night my boyfriend was to be their designated driver. He acted like I did not exist, ignored me when I talked, and avoided my eye contact, so I walked away without saying good-bye. Taking a few of his friends with me, we gobbled up some 'tasty' convenience-store hotdogs, laughing all the way, which was exactly what I needed. My boyfriend and I did not speak again, not even to break up. GRRRR-ROOOAAR!

Looks like anger is no joke, but what does this have to do with humor? Time for the good stuff!

HUMOR WITH YOU

"When life hands you lemons…
Call me.
We'll make pie!"

One of my favorite walking-away-mad memories started with sitting at our round kitchen table after supper one night. Mum was not there, so the odds were stacked against me, two against one *(my dad and brother vs. me)*. They were teasing me, trying to get under my skin *(not hard to do)*, and I was getting frustrated by their remarks. To make things worse, they were laughing at how upset I was becoming.

I pushed my chair back from the table, made a dramatic exit, huffing and puffing, and looking for a door to blow down. I could still hear them snickering after I headed down the hallway, when I realized my reaction had been a bit exaggerated.

I entered my room, banged some drawers and kicked some stuff around while looking for a certain object to help exact my revenge upon them. Once found, I came barreling back out, screaming at the top of my lungs about how *"sick and tired"* I was *"of not being taken seriously!"*

They fell silent when they heard me coming, maybe bracing for the wrath they were about to endure, but both fell from their chairs in laughter when they saw me—donning Groucho Marx glasses and moustache—hands on hips and striking a feigned pose of disgust, trying to hold back my own escaping giggles.

That walk ended quickly but taught me something important about myself.

I may be hot-headed, but I am not pig-headed. There is some reasoning in my mad tyranny.

As quickly as I get cranked up, I can bring it back down. This is my dance. This is my week.

Up and down—fast curves—a quick dip—loop de loop—and shake a tail feather.

I was under the impression that humor would easily fluctuate between things being funny or entertaining, but this has not been the case. Why should I be surprised that another topic is taking on a completely different tone than I anticipated?

Here comes the curveball: I often lament about the estranged son who ran away and cut off all communication from us. If you thought the announcement of my soon-to-be grandma role was shocking, you better sit down.

That boy walked through our door this week!

YUP!

I was not dreaming or hallucinating, and I am not even making it up to tell a good story. It is simply true. I have the knives to prove it—which is why he wanted to connect. He was looking for clients for a newfound networking endeavor: Selling kitchen knives.

My eyes saw him last in prison garb. Today he wore a suit. My ears last heard him bark obscenities at me. Today he spoke eloquent, professionally scripted words. My hands last tried to help him while he stayed at a youth shelter, resulting in the mysterious smashing of my car window, and sitting on shards of glass on the ride home. Today he respectfully asks for my assistance.

Is what I am hearing and seeing now enough to erase these unpleasant memories and start fresh with new ones? Even if the sensations of phantom slivers in my derriere have ceased, it still does not stop random pieces of glass popping out of nooks and crannies whenever my car hits a bumpy patch of pavement.

So—he calls—and asks to pick up a connection, because he has found the start of a decent life direction. He is not hopped up on drugs or anger and needs my help. My outside voice says, *Yes!*

My inside voice says, *HOLY BLEEP-ITY BLEEP!*

How will I act? What will I say? What is he going to say? I drove myself bonkers 'what if'-ing every possible scenario. Dizzy from over-thinking, I finally gave up in a goo of emotion and let it all go.

It would *be*... what it would *be*.

Satisfied with that summary, my thoughts turned to how I might enrich his experience of re-entering the same door through which he'd fled years ago.

I must bake up some love!

Aromatic, fresh cinnamon buns would welcome him back home. As he emerged through the door of our arranged meeting place, nervously determined and with a bag full of knives, I thought: *What... could possibly go wrong?*

For the next seven hours, we talked knives, food, dreams, and even visited with a friends' family for another knife demonstration. And we laughed. Really laughed.

I felt proud. He survived. He is trying to thrive.

I do not know this 18-year-old soul, who looks and sounds vaguely like a boy I once knew, but I was happy to be near him. I relished his enjoyment of being fed, was ecstatic he accepted the quilt I handcrafted when I needed a way to feel connected to him, and felt honored he asked to be driven home to his apartment.

My mind says he will not call again for some time, that he got what he came for: Some healthy knife sales and referrals for more business.

And… that is okay.

When he is ready to truly reflect on our relationship, I pray he remembers seeing soft eyes and an open heart.

That will be a great day of laughing, joy of all joys, and the glimmering silver lining that gets me through dark days.

Humor keeps my joy muscles strong and ready to work…

Keeps my hope gauge from falling below empty…

Keeps me from walking away forever…

Keeps me sane…

I simply must keep trying to look for the silver lining—'til all the clouds roll away and I see YOU again.

30 WEEK CHECK-IN:

May – August 2016

She has decided to be a mom. There is relief in knowing a decision is made, but a whole new set of worries are upon us. What does that look like? What role do we have? How do we balance everyone else's needs and comfort as we prepare to increase the population within our walls? There is conflict in how our space is divided. Because our hearts have been broken several times by kids leaving unexpectantly, we have coped by reserving their space until such time as it can be determined there is no longer a need. This may not make sense to anyone else, but hubby and I get it, and we honor it for each other.

After attending son's graduation, he returns to our home to work and save money before beginning a new adventure. I am over the moon for this connection and to have him so close. Unfortunately for him, he has an early morning collision, totaling the vehicle we bought for his younger sister, but thankfully crawls out of a steep ditch, unscathed.

The unknown phone number calls again, and to my surprise, it is the son who ran away years ago! He wants support for a business venture, and I am happy to oblige. No questions, no hesitations, just when and where can we meet. We see him three times while big brother is home, even joining us to celebrate his brother's graduation. I find the courage to offer him the quilt I made for him in the first year he left. Crafting it helped me remain close to him and gave my mind something positive to focus on, rather than the emptiness of a house less full. But, as quickly as he came back into our lives, he has slipped away again.

There is finally a decision for my 'trial', and it is not a good one. I am facing the task of bouncing back from the injustice I feel, to pour my outrage into something productive, and prove the judgement inaccurate by continuing to work in the most transparent and upright manner I can muster. Given the choice, I decided to pull away from the frontline, and work in a lower-profile position, where I have tackled the hardest thing I can imagine doing—working with information technology.

Starting to regret my grade eight decision to not take computers classes...

And my van died.

Week Thirty-One

LEARN, LAUGH, LEAD

English is weird.

There are many grammatical exceptions that make it a tricky secondary language to learn. The strangest thing about English for me, is the use—or misuse—of homographs.

Such as:

- The bandage was wound around the wound.
- The farm was used to produce produce.
- The dump had to refuse more refuse.
- The soldier decided to desert his dessert in the desert.

- Since there is no time like the present, she decided to present the present.
- I did not object to the object.
- They were too close to the door to close it.

I have mixed up homographs with homophones *(or is it homonyms)* as recently as deciding on a title for this chapter. The confusing culprits—lead, led, and lead—mean something quite different, when used in various context. Am I writing about a certain metal that is extracted from ore? Is this week's focus a past-tense action of who was in front of a parade? Or is my topic more about a direction someone decides to go, and others may follow?

A bit of googling revealed that the word 'led' is becoming obsolete and being morphed into its present-tense version, 'lead'. This seems more confusing—I lead the meeting yesterday about lead in the pipes, so you can lead today—word nerds like me, rejoice! This homonym is getting juicier!

The oddities of the English language do not stop at blending the meanings and pronunciations of identical words; They go much further. Here are some examples:

I before **E**... Except after **C**... or when your foreign neighbor Keith receives eight counterfeit beige sleighs from a feisty, well-caffeinated, weightlifter.

WEIRD!

With rules like these, I am surprised we learn to spell at all, although from my lead/led/lead example it could be argued that spelling skills are fading. Perhaps with the onset of spellcheck technology, alerts for grammar and auto-corrections, we will eliminate errors from our written language—or not. As much as software programming has advanced and thinks it has captured the accuracy of details, the amount of times I read documents with correctly spelled words that are erroneously used in context, is cringe-worthy, especially in my own writing! Baahh!!

In true renaissance style, I self-edit and proofread my work about twenty-three times, which I am told is quite taxing on deadlines. My dog-eared, soft-covered thesaurus sits handily beside my computer monitor. Yes, a thesaurus 'app' is available online, but I like thumbing through the pages. I like feeling the options oozing through my fingertips and chasing down the perfect word without burning my retinas with the blue monitor light.

As I have discovered at work, not everyone shares my zest for language and grammar, so I will move on to why I think this all connects to "Humor with US".

But first, my icon for this week:

It is a blank card Mum purchased while visiting her East Coast roots. Charlottetown was the home of one of her favorite characters, Anne of Green Gables. She chuckled quietly at the antics of this beloved and well-documented girl when it became a TV series, and she did not miss a single episode. This was one of the few ways Mum managed her stress. She often commented on Anne's grin, and I cannot help but wonder if she saw a bit of herself, or me, in this little face of innocent mischief.

HUMOR WITH US

Grammar reminds me there are lots of exceptions to good rules, which has helped shape my idea of humor with the ones who are closest to me.

When our son ran away five years ago, I wrote him a reasonable letter, explaining what coming back to our house would look like. He would need to pick up right where he left off; Still 'grounded', still expected to abide by house rules, but still deeply loved. I did not get to deliver this letter to him. His father waited in a running vehicle like a getaway driver, speeding away while I frantically pursued on foot, despairingly waving the letter above my head—a true Hollywood-style scene.

It took my son a couple of weeks before falling out of favor with his father, and a couple of months to wear out his welcome at random friends. For the next two years, the phone would ring at all hours of the night. It was not him calling, but rather concerned community members, city agencies, and the police. I would run to his side—hungry, lost, sick—but my sentiment stayed the same. *You are always welcome home, but the rules haven't changed.*

Phone calls turned into jail visits, jail visits turned into outbursts, outbursts turned into complete disconnect and stayed there for three years. Trying to keep what I thought were normal rules did not work. It did not pull our son back to us.

This week, we miraculously had him back for a second visit! His siblings and grandpa and grandma were lucky enough to join in, and hubby and I sat back in awe of what was transpiring before our eyes.

We cooked, they ate.

   We talked, they joked.

      We cleaned, they played.

         We watched, they connected.

            We cried, they laughed—wildly.

It was like watching the Turner Classic Movie channel. The image was a bit blurry; The sounds muffled a bit like the action was taking place just out of range, and the plot had a happy ending written all over it. True to a well-written script, I was lost in time and space, not sure of what was real, and never wanting any of it to end. Hearing them laugh, watching them interact, seeing this different person in the body of a boy I once knew—yet still know—was astounding and ever so humbling.

It was my proof that prayer works—that families overcome—that rules only work sometimes—that exceptions are necessary in order to keep loving.

I have many relationships that work on the premise of picking up where we left off, no matter how much time has passed. I am thinking this is not the case for a parent/child relationship that has been strained to the breaking point. It cannot be picked up where it was left off. It must move beyond the pain and sorrow of lost time and love. I can only pick up right where he is now.

This is US.

Hubby and I came to a halting realization, with the many stressors we are experiencing currently with our children: Whatever we consider and decide to act upon regarding our family, cannot divide relationships.

No, we do not want to walk on eggshells.

No, we do not want to be hurt.

No, we do not want to be taken advantage of... but the rules might look different, if it means saving relationships with our kids.

This is not a perfectly executed or balanced decision. We stumble over our pride, our rights, our sense of fairness, and our beliefs in how to guide our kids to a healthy sense of responsibility, while still managing to squeak out a snicker or two. We must laugh to remember our lives are in a forward motion. WE are building, strengthening, and trusting.

Laughter saves us from rigid rule keeping. It frees us to wander, to wonder and to accept the exceptions. It reminds us of love—that big, BIG kind of love that makes us braver than we believe, stronger than we seem, and smarter than we think—and reminds US to never let go.

Week Thirty-Two

HUMOR 101

The last installment on humor is here! Madness has ruled in my life for a few weeks, so I struggled to get this chapter exactly right. It is still not where I want it to be, but I suppose there must be a point where I proclaim that 'good' is good enough.

This is how I think I look when I write:

And this is how I actually look:

As I ponder how to wrap up the topic of humor—a.k.a. "Humor With THEM"—I cannot help but think of an event I attended with six thousand 11 and 12-year-old children.

This massive number of kids were gathered for a celebration marking a year of their community service. It takes all my colleagues, plus many corporate sponsors, to plan and execute this giant affair. Volunteers help to feed, entertain, and honor these responsible students, giving them a chance to enjoy one of the wonderful historical parks our city has to offer. Some of these students would not be able to afford an outing of this kind, but because of so many generous donations, these students enjoy a free, fun and full day of hardy party.

And party, they do!

Music pumps through large speakers while they wait for hotdogs and chips to be placed into their hungry hands, so *they* dance. Spontaneously forming a conga line (*minus the actual conga moves*), they hold onto each other's shoulders, weaving and chugging through throngs of kids, inspiring others to join and smiles to appear.

Familiar tunes get cranked up as the children's bellies fill with old-fashioned candy and soda pop, so *they* sing. On popular choruses, their voices rise above what is booming from speakers, and it seems to increase their fervor.

They are too excited to walk toward the free train rides or wait patiently in line to take a spin on the Ferris wheel, so *they* run. Spiking sugar levels spur them faster toward the next exhibit, the next thrill, wanting to eat up everything this day has to offer.

Even amidst the chaos, something lovely was happening in this crowd of children who were gathered together but did not know each other. They were united. Not coaxed, not rehearsed, not directed... they were sharing the moment corporately and personally, as evidenced by their wide grins and rolling laughter.

One of my favorite moments of the day was leading this energetic mass in singing our national anthem. Because my work allows me to attend various events at schools, I have often been privileged to hear choirs of youthful voices sing, bringing me to tears in a millisecond. There is just something about hearing those kids sing, especially on holidays where emotional sentiments are elevated *(gets me every time)*.

For this sunny and celebratory day, almost seven thousand voices rang out with such power and conviction that it was difficult to keep my throat from choking shut. I backed away from the podium mic to allow more of this wave of joy and spontaneous patriotism to flow from their lungs. I listened in awe, wishing their voices could flow into the hearts of our city, our country, and our world. Their conviction and unity sounded like a complete answer for tough political agendas and hard-hitting social issues. This is what unity sounds like—and acts like.

Why were these youths so ready to burst forth into their songs, dances, and games? I think it is a simple answer.

They were invited. Their needs were met. They were accepted.

I would go so far as to say—they were loved—in that agape, universally friendly, 'share a Coke and a smile' kind of way, which needs no words to express. It only requires the willingness to be vulnerable enough to care about others.

I wonder if current events like school and mosque shootings would still happen if these kinds of connections were adopted by more people in our world. I wonder if terrorist groups could convince even one recruit, if there were more generous, united songs on our planet. I wonder if this philosophy could decrease the divisiveness within my work team. These are heavy matters, not easily tackled globally considering differing values, culture, religion, or financial and political gains.

So... what could possibly help?

Immediately, I thought of the United Nations. Think what you will of their policies or effectiveness, it is hard to disagree with their intentions. I looked up if they had a youth contingency, and not only is there one, but there are many opportunities:

Youth for Human Rights

International Youth Foundation

International Youth Council

Rotary Youth Exchange

Fantastic options… if you can afford $1300-$3000 USD to attend international conferences—if you are between the ages of 16-28—and if you speak English. I would think these criteria would limit potential delegates, especially to kids growing up playing soccer in the dust with a coconut shell. Plus, I think the age range needs to be younger in order to preserve the participants willingness to dance, sing, and run unashamedly toward new ideas, places, and people.

So, I googled 'kids helping the world be a better place' and WOW!

Here is a taste of what I found: Youth tackling issues like hunger, poverty, literacy, health, environment, gender equality, social justice, universal education, racism, clean water…

Lists of their accomplishments go on and on.

This—from kids between the ages of 4-17. Their innocent observations see something broken and do something to fix it.

So, how will humor get wrapped up nicely in a frilly bow with sparklers on top?

HUMOR WITH THEM

Something that seems missing globally is an ability to laugh at ourselves. We admirably practice self-awareness, but when taken too seriously—when taken beyond the importance of humanity—when taken outside a context of how short our lives are and how immeasurably ignorant we are, seriousness can fail us. It *has* failed us.

This was never more evident to me than when passing by an artist's kiosk at an international fair this week. Included in his solicitation to draw caricatures of us, was a promise to make fun of me and hubby.

That was enough to hook hubby, so we sat down to patiently await the inspired product. As people passed, they inspected the canvas while chuckling—looking at us, and then back to an intent artist who was asking me to smile, which I took as a good sign—or so I thought.

Everyone who noticed the drawing being created could not help but stop to check us out, gauging for themselves the likeness captured by this artist's pen. All manner of people passed by, of different age ranges, genders, races, and cultures. Some gave us nods or winks. Some gave an encouraging thumbs up. Some spoke to each other in a different language, but no translation was necessary. They were getting a kick out of whatever was growing on that canvas!

A few ladies with broken English said it was beautiful and perfect, making me a bit worried, since I was a less-than-willing subject from the start. But watching people react was both entertaining and strangely comforting, as I sat nervously waiting for our true selves to be revealed.

Can you spot the difference?

When my initial horror wore off, a few seconds after viewing this work of 'art', I realized how randomly brilliant it was, why people found such joy in it, why it was perfect and beautiful—why I should laugh along with hubby and the rest of the strangers at the fair who saw our warbled dents and flaws and had a better day because of it.

Watching their faces brighten, their moods lighten, and their feet quicken made me realize we have an invitation to not take ourselves too seriously.

After four weeks of delving into humor, I can confirm the following:

- Laughter is Language
- Laughter is Medicine
- Humor invites US
- Humor unifies US

AJ

Where does joy show up consistently in your life?

Who adds humor to your day?

CHAPTER NINE

STRENGTH

You've always had the power, my dear.
You just had to learn it for yourself.
~ Glinda, *The Wizard of Oz*

Week Thirty-Three

ONE STRONG MAMA
___

It… is here!

Week Thirty-Three brings a NEW topic and a great moment in my writing timeline. It is my birthday, which is always an important part of the year. *Just ask hubby—he will confirm it's a really big deal!* This year is more than a number; This is THE birthday I turn the same age as Mum was when she died: 47

I want to hide. I want to cry. I want to rant at the heavens and beat my chest, not prepared to be this age, not ready to accept this reality, not willing to face a year I have been dreading for the last decade.

Yet, here it is.

So, I take myself by the scruff of the neck, force a steady blast of oxygen into heavy lungs, lift my chin to brace for this striking blow, and for a moment, I feel strong. Ready.

Ready for the next four weeks of looking at what it means to be strong.

As always, I begin this new topic by searching for the most intimate version of strength. The kind that is reserved for ME, for who I am now, and for who I want to become.

My icon for this week is a birthday card Mum had in her collection of cards. Her writing is not in it, the plastic sleeve is still intact, so I am left to guess its 'special daughter' description was meant for me. Its pale pink exterior and soft golden font are reminiscent of an era gone by, transporting me back to the last traces of time Mum and I spent together.

I do not remember receiving a birthday card from her that year, understandably forgotten in the bustle of her suddenly declining health. My twenty-second birthday was overshadowed by the approach of death. Between trying too hard to love my then boyfriend and losing the parent I had yet to appreciate, my birthday was of no consequence. Within two weeks of turning 22, Mum was gone—the boyfriend was gone—ending the glorious epoch of 'being 21' and beginning something new—the desert era.

I wandered for months.

Disoriented.

Starved.

Abandoned.

Unable to comprehend what direction pointed home. My once certain path now foreign and wild, hosts of scorched emotions dancing like tormented spirits around a disappearing flame of my once energized soul...

I was 22. I did not feel strong. I did not feel young. I did not feel.

Vulnerable to the trickery of a mirage-like savior appearing before my empty, aching eyes, I headed toward a marriage I thought would restore my former glory days.

It did not.

More hunger. More sadness. More agony—except for one thing.

Becoming a mother rushed life into my shrunken veins, opening my heart to embrace the sacrifice of death as a necessary balance for the great joy of life—the circle complete.

Death must come, so that life can be.

That mystical, life-transforming perspective held my imagination and hope for the next fifteen years without birthday or holiday celebrations. Mirage marriages come with a price.

Maybe it is the reason my hubby now takes such care to celebrate each of my birthdays. Trips, concerts, fine dining, fairs, theatre events, and always a specially wrapped gift or card. My wasted years have been restored and multiplied with joy—boundless joy—over and above all that the desert took from me.

STRENGTH WITH ME

Now, what about strength? I have heard many people use this word to describe me, so I must know something about it. Right?

"If God gives people what they can handle, I must be a bad-ass!"

HAH! I think when people tell me I am strong, it is usually in a moment I feel the weakest. Am I consistently being misread or is there something else going on? This seems to be a good place to start exploring.

One of the more recent times I recall being told I was strong was near the beginning of this year.

After coming back from a nine-month medical leave, a colleague called me strong. Maybe because I took on a new set of schools in an area that had been neglected for a while, meaning my first order of business would be to rebuild trust and relationships. Maybe I was considered strong because several relapses had forced me back into treatment and I had to advocate for a return to work process that was not detrimental to my healing. Maybe I looked strong because our team had lost and added personnel, so I was regarded as a junior member with seemingly invalid experience. Or maybe they saw strength because I swallowed my pride to accept new or changed procedures that moved away from our previously established protocols. *I mean really, I was only gone nine months. It should be the same job, right?*

My colleague's personal lives had also changed. Not that I am an avid office gossiper, but it is nice to know the bigger chunks in the personal lives of people with whom you spend many of your waking hours. Getting married, having babies, taking fabulous vacations, renovating or buying a house—those sorts of chunks.

I was saddened to hear a sweet, single mom, who works on a similar team as ours, had lost her 15-year-old son to suicide. She was off work for a time, so it had been a while since we bumped into each other. When a colleague told me the tragic news, I thought of sending her a sympathy card, so she knew I was thinking about her and her younger son; Both boys a common topic of discussion whenever we met. We would chuckle together about a story of something they said or did, things that make parents want to pull out their hair. She had worried for her sensitive boy who seemed to be negatively targeted at school.

Several times, I had reminded myself to *get to that card*—but had forgotten day after day, then week after week, until now—five months later.

I saw her coming down our long office hallway, mid-morning light from rooftop windows making it easy to recognize who was approaching. I had about twelve seconds—a relatively long time—to formulate what I would say and do while we walked toward each other. She looked deep in thought but jolted out of it when she recognized me.

Her usual chin-up, broad smile was replaced by a tilted half-smile as she said hello. I said her name, probably with more emphasis than necessary, and put my hand on her shoulder. She looked surprised, as there are few affectionate gestures offered from colleague to colleague in our tough profession. I am not sure if following that gesture with a hug or saying how sorry I was to hear this news started her tears, but they trickled immediately down her face. She looked drained—spent. More lines on her face, more creases in her expressions, evidence of her 'desert' days and tormented nights.

As she wiped away her tears, she explained that no one talks to her about him. She understood. They do not want to see her cry or make her feel bad, but that is not what she needs. She wants to talk about how much she misses him, how he made her laugh, how much potential he had to give, but she stays quiet—alone—to not make anyone else feel uncomfortable.

What is wrong with this picture?!?

A grief-stricken mother, at a workplace with responsible adults, doing her best to reassemble a shattered heart, and *she* is worried about *our* comfort?

This should not be her story. This should not be the suffocating atmosphere she must endure, while managing her grief. We chatted for about ten minutes, telling and re-telling our parental woes, frustrations, and fears, then parted to continue our scheduled days. She thanked me for remembering him, for talking about him, because she never wants to FORGET.

I get that. I still live that, even after 25 years. I do not want to forget Mum.

I want to remember Mum and laugh…and vent…and cry…and be okay knowing death has balanced the creative power of life.

Do I know it gets easier to accept? Yes.

Does my colleague know that? Not yet.

She thinks she is at her weakest. Driving herself crazy at home, vacant and emotionless at work, self-described as hollow inside—obliterated. She would not see herself on the strength squad.

But that is what I saw. She was waking up each day with a broken heart and choosing to breathe. She… is who I want to be—ONE STRONG MAMA.

> I thank whatever gods may be
> For my unconquerable soul.
> ~ William Ernest Henley, *Invictus*

Choose your own ICON for Strength:

Week Thirty-Four

STRONGER THAN YESTERDAY

Oh wow! There are only eighteen weeks left. We are cruising through the topics!

Currently, this is the second week of strength, with a focus on 'YOU'. Last week, I shared about a single mom losing her teenager to suicide, bringing awareness to how much burden parents place upon themselves and how our perspective can make it seem like we are not able to cope.

I suggested we are stronger than we feel and endure more than we could possibly imagine—and if I did not make it completely clear—I believe there is *always* someone else who has a far greater struggle than I would ever want bear.

I pick right up on that theme and forge into a week of considering what strength looks like for my closest relationships. To do this, I will be focusing on how my story has plunged me into deep recesses that felt as though they would not end. Hesitantly and carefully, I wade into these memory-filled waters, knowing what lurks there, knowing it is scary, but knowing it did not end ME.

Figuring out how I made it through is going to be my focus. I want to understand why love survived inside of me, how certain choices prevailed, and know beyond a shadow of a doubt how to strengthen my closest bonds with YOU.

I always considered myself physically strong, perhaps due to my tomboyish nature or my competitive approach to anything sport related. What I lacked in skill, I did my best to compensate for in power and determination, but genes also played a big role in any of my athletic successes. Mix that with feeling like a big fish in a small pond, and it is understandable why I pictured myself as large and mighty.

What I perceived as my physical strength shaped my identity as someone who could handle obstacles. I did not quit on the field, on the track, inside the rink, on the dance-studio floor, or around the ball diamond. When others stopped or grew weary, I was more inspired to keep going—to keep trying. Effort was my most accessible asset. A close second was my outgoing and unfiltered personality. I was an exciting mess of teenage confidence!

But the formidable layers of who I was, which took all my teenage years to build, were demolished within one day.

15 and Happy.   *17 and Sad.*

At 17 years old, it would have only been puppy love, but I lost the person I believed was my soulmate. Like other dreamy teenage girls, I went gaga over a cute boy who held my hand. We had liked each other for years but living in neighboring towns before being able to drive, made connections tricky.

Somehow, we serendipitously attended the same local events, knew when we were in each other's town, and unknowingly ended up at the same vacation resort for a week-long stint—he for hockey, and me for singing.

That was the first time we decided to become something solid, to not leave our encounters to chance, and to be more than convenient crushes. We always seemed to have a silent connection, a core understanding of who we were and what we wanted. We had big dreams, and maybe that is why it could not last. Shortly after our resort trip, he got drafted away to the WHL. We wrote, talked on the phone, but it was the last time I saw his face.

I did not need to be told the tragic news. I felt him all day. He was gone, but must have been hovering close, letting me know he was going. When I heard their travel bus had crashed, I spoke out loud to that spirit who was intently near. *"You better not have been playing cards at the back of the bus again."* That was the place I knew he always sat, and the spot later reported to have been the seats of the four casualties.

Of course, then I was certain. There was no doubt, but I went about my plans that evening, denying my intuition, justifying my silly gut instinct and convincing myself his light was too bright to be extinguished … and collapsing when told … that it had.

I cried for days. I had nothing of his to hold, only things of mine he had touched: A stuffed bear he teased me about carrying as a good-luck charm for track meets; My diamond ring prize he put on his finger after watching me sing for the Miss Lumberjack competition; The letters he wrote making plans to see each other when he got home...

I was dazed for months. Being in a small town, teachers knew my story, asking how I was doing when I made it to class, and ignoring the many classes I did not make. My grades were failing, so Mum prompted big brother to swoop in, helping me cram three months of information into two days' prep for exams.

Graduation loomed. My grad gown photos were depressing, eyes brimming with tears, face limp and numb, thinking of my 'should-be' grad date.

My recovery was slow. I created a shrine of newspaper clippings and photos, preserving these treasures in a sacred box that went everywhere with me.

I went off to college, incidental boyfriends came and went but I was still longing for the friend that understood me best. Travelling helped. Exposing my heart to beautiful places and positive people slowly thawed my frozen veins to believe love would be possible again—which landed me on the doorstep of turning 21—the golden year! I finally felt free of the sadness that had consumed me for the last three and a half years. Twenty-one was a year to sing—really sing!

I have often wondered what made 21 feel so remarkable. Maybe it is because most of my 17 to 20-year-old days felt lost and 'heartblank'.

Again, and again, throughout my stories, I become a shell of myself. WHY??

Because of YOU.

My closest relationships have manifested the worst, most painful, gut-wrenching hurts, that time has not eliminated. Mothers and boyfriends die. Fathers and brothers are absent. Husbands are cruel and abuse. Children lash out, blame, and run away. Self-image and identity get destroyed. Dreams are crushed—and all because I have YOU.

YOU weaken ME. *Yes, I just said that.*

YOU have many needs, and drama, and expect strong ME to handle everything. It is no wonder I go blank.

Empty. Dark. Silent.

THAT is where I go. Does that sound like strength?

STRENGTH WITH YOU

Here I am. Pushing for the maximum output again, for the ones I love—fulfilling their needs before mine.

I want to work, but YOU need a break. I want to write, but YOU need my attention. I want to chill, but YOU need excitement. I want to play, but YOU need my work. Repeat.

And, repeat.

Eventually, if I have not been able to find an organic trail leading away from this pattern or if there is a barrage of demands all at once, my emptiness turns ugly.

I have battled depression, come through an extended drinking binge, survived an unhealthy period of promiscuity, and hid every hurting part of me under a huge pile of denial—to feel okay. These are not strong moments. They are unforgiving, unrelenting, and emotionally stunted phases of heartblank.

True.

But...

It does not stop there. If it did... I would not be here.

Yes, I burn out. Yes, I get sucked dry. Yes, I reach out my hand for a solid lifeline that ends up pulling me back into the very mire I am fighting hard to exit. But that is where YOU are—IN the mire—and I cannot leave you there alone.

So, no matter how messy and mixed up things get, no matter how tired and angry I feel, no matter how imbalanced or lopsided relationships can be, I know it does not stop there.

My work is simply this: Lift YOU up... until you feel the sun warm your skin... until you get used to the view... until you can lift yourself... until you want to lift others... until you are ready to lift ME.

And so, we go. And go. And go.

The strongest thing I can do—to be stronger than I was yesterday—is to keep building YOU.

"It takes magnificent pressure to make diamonds.
That's why diamonds are magnificent.
YOU are a Diamond."

Week Thirty-Five

STRONG ROOTS

Knowing that so many of you are bravely on this adventure with me, sharing your insights, confirming your truth, and sending all your encouraging words of love, is *so* healing. Thank you, from every part of my heart, for arriving at Week Thirty-Five with me.

This week, the focus being "Strength with US", I want to tell you a little story about a plant. It is not an ordinary plant—actually, wait—it *is* ordinary. Totally ordinary. So ordinary, there could not possibly be anything more ordinary.

It has ordinary needs. Takes ordinary care. It had a life before ending up in my hands, twenty-four years ago, so it has been ordinary for many years. So why bother telling this ordinary-plant story? Because, Mum would like it. She surrounded herself with plants.

Before becoming a municipal administrator, she used her Bachelor of Science Degree in the botany department for our local university. She would often take me and my brother to her office, where she prepared petri dishes and tubes, fungi, spores, and other strange-looking roots inside odd-shaped receptacles.

She wore a long, white lab coat, looking smart and focused with her dark hair pulled back into a thick, low ponytail. She sat in a heavy, metal-framed, creaky chair on wheels. It could gain momentum quite easily, so my brother and I pushed each other along the smooth, polished, industrial flooring creating a racket of noisy fun. Mum would allow a few back and forth passes of this regular occurrence, before sitting us down with something quiet to do while she finished her tasks.

I did not hear Mum speak much about life, but I did hear her explain, in depth, about plants. What should be planted together, which perennials were hardy enough for our unpredictable winters, how to care for trees, when to trim, and when to transplant. If only I had enough sense to apply those principles in my life, it might have saved me from some big hurts and time on a therapist couch!

We had plants throughout our house while I was growing up, in different locations according to their specific lighting needs. Only one plant would not perform to Mum's standard, so she would take this hanging fern to the university greenhouse, deliver it to a man who was like a plant doctor, who would revive its droopy and browning leaves, so it could return home for another try at staying healthy. Mum did not give up on this plant.

But this is not the plant story I want to tell. This is my attempt to frame up how plants and growing things have been part of my experience. Sadly, with all this exposure to plant culture, I did not glean any kind of green thumb-ism at all. But—to honor her skill—I have tried to learn.

I have planted—*Nothing comes up…*

I have watered—*The weeds like that…*

I have fussed and pampered, and sprinkled sunny words of encouragement—*Almost had lettuce once, but a hailstorm wiped it all out…*

The failed onions seeds that I planted last year, volunteered this year, and somehow, we had fresh chives in May! Pure fluke. So, I am not gifted with anything green (*unless 'flower-ish' things growing out of the rock beds count*).

Mum's early death prevented me from picking up lots of helpful tips, like why you should not marry a man who is not your best friend. Yes, she said that once, along with some other sage points on who to look for in a soulmate, so that will be my icon this week. Please share these pointers to every teenager you know!

Your future spouse should:

Have sparkling eyes.

Wear clean shoes.

Treat their mama well.

Be your best friend.

STRENGTH WITH US

I did not remember Mum's excellent advice until I was already well into my first marriage, wedding jitters and promises of joy long gone, and hitched to a man who saw 'green' in a different way.

Green was for lining and increasing bank accounts, for which ALL had to be sacrificed. Trips, a second car, restaurants, fun, long-distance telephone calls, using the electric clothes dryer—everything was under scrutiny to pinch out another cent, another dollar.

In those days, stores often allowed refunds without needing a receipt. Many did not ask questions about why the items were being returned, maybe my burning embarrassment was evident. It was a way for him to punish me for desiring nice things, or for getting pregnant while trying not to, or for having people who cared enough to give gifts, or for being a disappointing wife. I was always in the wrong, so to make up for my failures, I did his bidding. Dirty work, if ever I did any.

One non-refundable present was a plant, inside a beautiful clay pot, which is where this plant story really begins. It saw some bad days. Drought. War. Famine. Neglect. There were days it did not look as though the plant would survive. Without any green sense, this plant struggled under my care. My ex would look scornfully at it, perhaps because he knew someone dear had given it, or perhaps because he disliked plants in general, but whatever his reasons, there was no love extended toward this plant.

Instead, he used it as a figurative litmus test on how our marriage was doing, vilifying me as a "parasite" who sucked the life out of everything around. I think his exact words were, "If this plant survives, our marriage will survive," but it was all up to me to make that happen.

He would not participate in any nurturing toward its healthy end, although he barked about how he knew better, saw better, and cared better than my thick head ever could. He insisted on everything looking perfect within his view. The house, kids, yard, vehicle, and that plant; All should be immaculate and pure, and I was on the hook to deliver that standard. He sought me out numerous times—using more steps than it would have taken for him to get to a tap and just water the bleeping plant himself—to tell me the plant needed attention!

So why, when I had one hour—just sixty minutes—to choose and remove my mum's antiques from that house of horrors, with a police escort to ensure the peace, and under the pressure of knowing I would never again see anything left behind—why did I take this plant?

Because it was a gift from beautiful people? Yes.

Because it was an innocent amongst a hostile feud? Yes.

Because deep down, I knew I had done everything I could to save it? Yes.

Because even before I was able to comprehend it, I must have known that it was not my fault. I was never supposed to take on that responsibility alone. That plant was given to two people who were meant to help it thrive. He saw the plant was in trouble. He watched it fade and go limp. He withheld what would have revived it to maintain his short-sighted, ego-centric principals—and still, the plant lived.

Barely.

Because I kept it alive. I sacrificed my dreams, my thoughts, my faith, my joy, my heart to keep us all living—and that was killing me.

I did it for fourteen years—stayed strong—holding on ferociously.

For vows

    For children

        For family

            For the pet fish

                For the innocent plant

                    For proving we were okay

Staying in this family disaster took STRENGTH. Lots and lots of it. Victims of domestic violence are not weak. We believe harder, love fiercer, and trust greater than imaginable, in someone that will never deserve it. I think that is why we were drawn to each other. One person feels they can offer healing, and other person wants to be healed, but each of them have no idea how.

Strength kicks it up another notch when letting go of this toxic kind of life; Leaving a person who would rather let everyone perish than change his ways, was the hardest and best thing I have ever done. Maybe I did learn from Mum after all. It was time for a transplant.

This ordinary plant reminds me I gave everything I could, except thankfully, my last breath. I am reminded that WE do not have to look perfect and we must not believe any lies pointed at US.

I may never be an amazing gardener. I may never actually reclaim the flower beds in the yard that have turned into a jungle. I may never be a perfect caregiver for my family either, but it does not matter. Time with family *matters*. Living in and embracing the beautiful chaos *matters*. It is accepting flawed days with flawed people who happily go to the water tap when they see a wilting petal.

In these past few weeks, family emotional demands have been off the charts from their normal cycles. What a difference it makes to share these burdens alongside a partner who can match my heart strides—whose eyes sparkle—whose shoes are always clean—who honors his mama like a queen and is absolutely my best friend. This US is getting there and still growing… STRONG.

AJ

What are your emotional strengths?

ENCOURAGEMENT

A candle loses nothing
By lighting another candle.
~ James Keller

Week Thirty-Six... and Thirty-Seven

STRENGTH FOR TODAY

I know, I know, we should *still* be in Chapter Nine—and Week Thirty-Six was supposed to be about "Strength with THEM", but something interesting happened. I realized that strength was morphing into a different topic: ENCOURAGEMENT. Since it just happened to be my next topic, I decided to tackle them both at the same time. Looks like Chapter Ten will be busting out of the pattern *(since they are not my strength, for the rest of the book, let's completely mess with the patterns)*, starting with: "Strength and Encouragement with THEM".

Morning by morning
New mercies I see.
Great is thy faithfulness
Lord unto me.
~ Thomas Obadiah Chisholm and William M. Runyan

This quote is from an old church hymn, written on a framed print Mum bought shortly before she died. I am using it as my icon to gather some momentum as I endeavor to marry the topics of strength and encouragement. I cannot remember if she had a chance to hang this picture on a wall before she died, but I do know it was tucked away so deeply, I had completely forgotten about it—until a day came that I needed it.

Stored in an old, weathered chest, safe from the destructive intentions of a person not willing to control himself, it was exactly the kind of inspiring message I could have used during years of isolation and abuse. When I rediscovered this print, inside crumpled newspapers and cedar chips, I was instantly jubilant. Another artifact MADE IT THROUGH THE FIRE!

"Lost in the fire." Remember? This is the term I used to explain why toys had vanished, why photos that once existed were no more, why bedtime books that swooped darling minds away into fantastic realms could no longer be read. All lost in the 'fire'.

My heart aches at the thought of this tangible evidence of a family not spared.

No matter how thin the threads of family ties may have been, there was still great pain in tearing apart that last surviving tenue of fiber. I avoided that kind of pain for years, choosing instead to cling desperately to an unhealthy relationship, scared to let go, not sure if the anguish of change was better than the agony of staying. It was tormenting and life draining to consider either course of action. I can look back now, ten years later, and clearly answer the following questions: Was it worth the distress? Did it make up for the version of 'family' that got lost? Was this heartbreak good?

Yes—to all the above.

Not easy, but good.

"We fight for things to stay the same AND we fight to make things change. Moving on is not easy."

I chose to live in the same neighborhood after splitting up, to limit some obvious shifts in the regular functioning of my kids' lives and allowing them to keep the same school, sports teams and friends. Optimum damage control was the mission. Did it work? Each child would have to answer that question, their experiences being very different, based on their ages and their personalities.

Older daughter was 11 and adopted a mom-type role, sometimes taking care of younger siblings while I continued shiftwork. Younger son, 9, saw himself as the protector and patriarch, being the only male in the house. And younger daughter, 6 and sweet, stayed innocently infantile, seemingly unmarred by any historical pain or transitional upset. This all sounds pretty good, right? Not bad results for kids brought through a fiery battle.

Their roles, adopted for survival, soon turned into personal wars. Battles for power ensued. The children and I were equally unaware of my authority as a parent, being stripped of that respect by their father. I had no idea what parenting platforms I should stand on. I only knew the ones I would never stand on again. How could I manage four kids who only followed directions to avoid suffering physical pain, who thought I was the biggest idiot on the planet, and had to reject me to please him?

Ten years has not been enough to recover from the effects of that family bankruptcy, BUT there is no longer a continuous ache throughout each day. Joy, peace, and breakthroughs consistently appear!

As my older daughter matured, she thoughtfully asked, "Did we have a fire?" To which I looked at her steadily and simply replied, *"Yes... a BIG fire."*

So, how does this relate to my outside connections and potentially bigger circles of influence? How do strength and encouragement creep into my community perspective when I consider what it takes to overcome significant loss?

Let me introduce you to Mad Marvin. This is not his actual name. I cannot tell you that, since he is a real colleague of mine. We have both been assigned new roles, which neither of us feel adequate to handle, with a floundering project that was started almost a decade ago. Is ten years coincidentally the same numbers of years since my divorce?

I think not.

From the moment I put eyes to Marvin, I knew he was mad. And from the first words out of his mouth, I knew why. He had no filter when sharing his anger and bitterness toward an organization he felt had punitively placed him in this undesirable, hidden corner of a lukewarm enterprise, to which he had no aptitude or interest. I felt exactly the same way but was determined to make this situation work. And, I decided to scoop Marvin up for the ride.

At first, I tried to reframe his negative comments into positive ones, suggesting this new role could be protective in nature and the outcome one of "champions".

Yes, that word came tumbling out of my mouth, like I was conducting a Superbowl rally! Do you think my contagious disease of enthusiasm infected him?

Nope. Mad Marvin does not want my Pollyanna propaganda. I think my optimism made him pout harder.

Strike One.

Next, I used every ounce of empathy I could muster. I wiped the smile off my face, and got low and intentional, much like an animal whisperer would when they want to gain the trust of an anxious dog or horse. I listened, nodded, agreed when appropriate, and offered my support.

This seemed to make him angrier. My empathy somehow gave his bitterness a green light.

Strike Two.

After talking to hubby, and getting his spin on Marvin's disposition, he suggested that maybe the organization was better off without an extremely mad person, so, I decided to test this theory by vigorously engaging my disenfranchised co-worker.

You might be thinking: *Of course, AJ is going to conclude this guy should be given a second/third/ninth chance to get through this eclipsed phase in his life and given grace while he figures things out.*

And yes, I will eventually land there—but it was tough!

He was helping me with a task I had very little guidance or clarity to accomplish, resulting in vague outcomes. I was ploughing through as diligently as possible. I hoped my drive and determination would model to Marvin the effort needed to resiliently bounce back when given a ridiculous I.T. assignment. He matched my passion by complaining about purpose and process, feigning work, and sending bogus data for me to log as accurate.

That ticked me off!

I do not like where I am or what I am doing, but if a portfolio has my name on it, I will not accept sabotage from a man-child temper tantrum happening six feet from my workstation! I started to check all his data myself, feeling upset about having to do his work as well as mine, while flickers of bitterness and distrust ignited against Marvin.

I wanted to shake him, smack him, clap in his face—SOMETHING to wake him up and get him producing. He was not churning out the work, and dare I say, was not churning out his life. He was in a canoe, with one paddle, stroking only on one side, splashing wildly in a desperate circle, getting nowhere.

Maybe he needs to just paddle. I have paddled. Hard. Against my ex, against myself, against guilt, against God, and anything else as though I needed to exhaust myself. When I had nothing left, I put the paddle down. Marvin is not ready to do that. He cannot hear my words or digest my empathy. This is his chosen strategy for survival.

It will serve him temporarily, then fade into the wake of whatever direction he chooses to steer himself, OR he may capsize from too much wallowing and then swim back to shore—or drown. Whichever way, it will be his choice.

I can choose to be my healthiest, most-aware self when I am around him—cheer him—accept him. My role is to be bigger and stronger than his current pain, ten years more experienced in the field of suffering to know better than judge him. True encouragement cannot come with any judgements, so I lay those down, just as I would appreciate others doing with my uncharacteristic behaviors a decade ago.

This is a new outlook on how to live well within a hurting and mad world. Check myself. Judge not. Give grace. Say kind things. Listen. Wait.

So, release your devils into an accepting paddle, Mad Marvin. Something will bring you back amongst your angels if you decide that is where you need to be.

Yes, there is much work to be done—for angry colleagues, for dynamic family antics, for our hurting world, but we have the strength to make little decisions that carry a big impact. Today is a good day to shine a light into another person's darkness, even if they retract from the glare. Once their eyes adjust, they may welcome the light again, maybe even shine some of their own.

Strength for today and bright hope for tomorrow…

"Refuse to sink."

Week Thirty-Eight

FAMILY CHEER DEPARTMENT

I want a refund!

For the past couple of months, it has been a privilege to have two of my adult children live at home. Their circumstances vary for why they have come, but the reasons do not matter. There will always be room at our inn.

We have had a full house before, have tested and stressed our family bonds, but this time is different. I think we have reached a whole new level of difficult emotional encounters and personality hurdles. So why I am standing in line at the complaint department demanding a refund?

Because, over the course of these few months, complaints have been slowly trickling into my conversations and expressions. Like a nagging drip, now turned into a downpour, I find myself spraying everyone around indiscriminately, even the kids, maybe hoping to somehow expose my hidden anxieties. This is disturbing.

It used to be an intentional standard of mine, not to talk about the struggles each child was going through with their siblings. I labelled that standard as "not my story to tell." When they eventually shared with each other, it gave them power to choose what to make known and what they wanted to keep private. I gave myself an extra pat on the back for being nothing like their father when it came to privacy *(as in, letting them have some)*.

While living with him, nothing was private. All conversations were monitored or had to be repeated, word for word. All thoughts were poked, probed, and prodded like an alien invasion, and all doors *(even for the bathroom)* were to remain open.

An underlying perception that someone was watching, listening, or could walk in at any moment pervaded our awareness.

Lack of privacy leaves a BIG hole in relationships, so that was an easy parenting platform to build up when I first began working on my foundation for single parenting. I felt certain that holding my children's confidence would score a solid 'A+' in my imaginary Parenting 101 Class. *High-five me!*

Maybe because the kids are all almost adults or have become more perceptive of when I am brushing topics away, but something started me blabbing! Blah, blah, blah about *this* kid to *that* kid and about *another* kid, and so on. The stories of five diverse kids with wonky backgrounds, tend to be quite rich and juicy—and ripe for gossip.

It never occurred to me that gossiping was possible within a close family circle. It took my 16-year-old daughter looking at me like I had three heads *(which happens daily)*, followed by her saying, "well—you are not being nice" to realize that my gossip was real. Full stop, AJ.

Me… not nice??? I think I have heard it all now! I am nice—VERY NICE, and just for the record, do not speak to your mother that way. Before all those words fell out of my mouth, she added a little eyebrow raise and bent her head down to look at me through the top of her eye sockets, and I knew she was right.

In a classic reversal of roles, my attitude was adjusted by a 16-year-old who never met my mum, yet somehow knew her default move whenever my childish behavior needed some work. Mum did not voice complaints about any family members. She did not gossip about our woes. I need to figure out what has happened to me—pronto!

It has been stressful supporting our 21-year-old daughter through her pregnancy. Time is quickening the day we will finally meet this new addition to our family, and I am still not sure if I am being much help. For a sense of what that looks like, she has publicly shared on her blog how hard it has been for her to maneuver through this life-altering event:

https://saltandlightt. wordpress. com/2016/07/05/were-all-eventually-going-to-be-okay/

Her story compels me to tears, as I know I have added to her confusion and heartbreak as she reluctantly redefines herself. Not perfect, that is me. That is all of us—and where Week Thirty-Eight starts.

ENCOURAGEMENT WITH US

Since I combined 2 weeks in the last chapter, *(strange how that keeps happening...)* this week is going to be the 2nd of focusing on encouragement. To really keep things lively, I am also going to work backwards from THEM *(last week)*, to US *(this week)*, then continue with YOU, and finally finish the topic of encouragement, with ME.

But let's get back to the complaints department to see if I can get a refund.

ME: *Yes, hello? I want to return these complaints!*

Department Manager: Hello, ma'am. What is the reason for your return?

ME: *Regret. Bags, and bags, and bags full of deep regrets.*

All my complaints were emotional purchases bought out of desperation. I was hurting and shopping for a quick solution—looking for that big 'fix-all', which led to impulsively buying a complete line of complaints. No forethought to their use, whether they would fit with the rest of my lifestyle, or if they were legitimate.

At first, I bought only one complaint. It felt smooth slipping off my tongue and released a slight hiss of pressure from wherever I was stuffing my feelings. But one was not enough. There was still a vat of pressure inside of me and a singular complaint seemed too weak, so therefore... *I must release more. Soooo much more!*

The more I bought, the more I needed. I thought I was a clever complainer, releasing my steam in an even, controlled manner. I was not like Mad Marvin at all, because I disguised my negativity in humorous comments or forced laughter after expressing my unpleasantness—pretending this was not how I seriously thought or felt. Not sure I convinced anyone, since my daughter was obviously not fooled.

Was it possible the exact characteristic I saw in my bitter, disenfranchised colleague was the challenge I was wrestling with now?

Could more layers to this onion be peeling away, in an eye-stinging effort to get my attention?

Did I succumb to projecting onto Marvin what I needed to work on inside myself?

Whew! So glad I decided not to judge him and instead see how grace was available. Maybe this is what my grace-work a couple weeks ago, was all about. Maybe, but

I am grateful to see grace waiting for me on the other side of this fumble toward having a more encouraging character.

So, what did I end up using for an icon this week? Well, it was a tough one, as nothing stood out as perfect, so I closed my eyes and picked. Here is what I came up with:

A retro green and white gingham cross-stitch tablecloth. Mum made this one for our round, dark oak kitchen table. She liked doing it so much, she made about a thousand more and gave them away to anyone with a pulse—to the best of my recollection.

But I digress…

Department Manager: Sorry, ma'am. There are NO refunds on complaints. YOU need the 'Repairs Department'.

Turns out, repairs cost more than the original complaint-purchase price. It means I owe a *schwack* of positive emotional deposits into the accounts of all my family members *(a debt that should be sweet to pay)*, so I started with hubby.

Oh yes, poor hubby! Great as I think he is, he was not spared my saucy slurs, which looked like cold shoulders and diverted eye contact. I got right to work, put love above pride, and remembered why he won the title of "best friend".

What happened? Another shock!

OK, its not really a shock. If hubby and I are good, generous, and accepting toward each other, there is less stress everywhere else in the family. Choosing ferocious love this minute, helps us all to live through the next minute. This does not sound particularly profound or new. It just sounds simple, and true, and exactly what I needed this week to stop complaining about inevitable flaws and keep encouraging our endearing and interesting little family.

It does not seem coincidental to have the word *courage* inside of encouragement. My strength and patience are working hard to make-up the emotional deposits I owe—ten deposits for every withdrawal of a complaint I thought or said—it may take me a few years to get out of the red.

Fun years, no doubt, that I look forward to cheering, living, and loving up.

Three cheers for being a normal, imperfect family!

And three billion cheers for all the US's out there.

Week Thirty-Nine

ENCOURAGEMENT ENDORSEMENT

Summer days—summer nights—where have you gone?

It was so effortless contemplating encouragement while relaxing on a deck chair, sleeping in late, with no agenda and no appointments. For ten days, I drifted away from anything that felt difficult or tricky, floating along on graceful waves toward Tranquility Town, a most desirable destination while on vacation/staycation.

Reading. Writing. Sunshine. Great Food. Great Company.

What a perfect environment for encouragement to flourish!

Well, it did flourish—until day eleven, when my foot met the gas pedal on the drive back to work. Arghhhh!!

WORK!

I am lucky to have a job, I tell myself.

Having a steady pay cheque affords my family so many opportunities, I remind myself.

This career helped save me from a disastrous relationship, I scold myself.

Get your cheer in gear!!

Nope. Not today.

Perhaps one of my gauges is out of order. The tank reads FULL, but there is no gumption today.

Resources depleted.

This cannot be! I just spend ten wonderful days in Cool Cucumber Land. How can I have nothing in my tank?

I had strength and hope to encourage THEM, grace enough to encourage US, and now on the week of trying to find what it means to encourage YOU, the reserves are dry, and I am parched.

Okay, FINE! No encouragement. I guess that means no writing for a while either, since my focus IS encouragement. I can skip the rest of this topic. *Who would notice?*

OR…

I could scam out some rickety wisdom stolen from another person's less complicated life. *Big exhale.*

It is a wacky, woolly ride, this fifty-two-week trek, full of big falls, huge surprises, awesome rewards, and heart-wrenching defeats—but it is real. Not stolen, not invented, and not giving up when things get bumpy. So, I put down my laptop and decided to breathe. I will not chase inspiration. If encouragement is to be found for YOU, there will have to be another way to find it.

Because right now, I am tired.

Tired of being upbeat all the time. Tired of trying to make lemonade out of life lemons that keep dropping from the sky. Tired of being so tired, I cannot remember where I put the squeezy thing to make refreshing summer drinks from sour, stinging fruits that show up announced and uninvited to my life party. So, I cross my arms, dig in my heels, skid to a halt, and look around—dazed—having no recollection of who or where I am, or how I got here.

That kind of tired.

So, I took a week off from writing, slid back into routine, and hoped to stumble upon a little encouragement. I was not too tired to pick out this week's icon, which seems unrelated to the topic, other than it makes me happy for two reasons:

The first reason is, Mum made this. It is one of several similar items that I managed to salvage from 'the fire', most of which I recently let go to be repurposed by a sweet niece who creates recycled masterpieces.

Check out her Facebook Page:

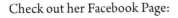
www. facebook. com/retronomics. recycology

Mum would have liked this 'recycology' stuff, so I momentarily suppressed my hoarding ways, and released a tight grip held on the drawers and shelves of an overcrowded basement closet.

I had already put away Mum's doilies, to modernize our cozy country-style home. This happened right around the same time I stopped wearing sweats pants out of the house. It was a *What Not to Wear* meets HGTV phase. I was surprised how easy it was to 'break up' with my sweats. I really wanted to burn them but knowing our city bylaws do not permit this kind of purging rage, I tossed them in the trash, along with any other clothes that did not make me feel fantastic. But could I toss something created by Mum's time and effort?

No way! So, on a shelf they sat, until niece came calling for them all—except one, which found a home in my fifty-two-week icon basket, and occasionally, gets a featured spot in our house.

The second reason I get happy when I see this doily is it reminds me to sit and craft for a while. It tangibly connects me to Mum, as my fingers can feel her love in every stitch. It may be why I am a lover of textiles. Nothing brings me more pleasure than running my fingertips along a rich, intricate weave of fibers or material. It is why online shopping can never be my thing. I need to touch stuff and hold it before deciding if it belongs with me. I feel Mum now, by touching what she touched. And according to my kids, I touch them a lot, too. This is how I discover and remember people—moments—and things.

ENCOURAGEMENT FOR YOU

Maybe my icon for this week is deeply related to encouragement, as it has helped me realize what it takes to be an encourager, which I assumed would be heavily verbal in nature; Always having a positive anecdote or reframing negativity out loud. With a tongue leaning fervently toward the bright side whenever given a chance. I use vocalizing, almost as comfortably as touch, to disguise any discomfort I experience when facing tough matters. This basically feels like a superpower—vanquishing all my fears, sorrows, and stress by obliterating anything negatively charged.

I love my superpower! In a weird *(but not creepy)* way, I think it loves me back.

NEWSFLASH:

Being eternally optimistic is exhausting! It takes high doses of adrenalin to keep pumping out good news. My cheeks hurt from smiling, my tongue swells from chattering rainbows, and my eyebrows spasm from constantly lifting my face into an arching exclamation mark that begins and ends all sentences... but, where was I?

Oh yes, my tank is empty, and I am not chasing encouragement. I am going back to work after ten days off, and I see it: Mad Marvin's empty office chair. We arrive at different start times, so I was not worried for his whereabouts initially. But as the day progressed, and his chair remained unoccupied, I finally had to ask about his status. A colleague said he had been told to find another assignment; There was no longer suitable work for him in our department.

My heart sank. We are drowning in work, desperate for able bodies and minds. Anyone with a heartbeat is gladly given a desk and some sticky notes. No, he was tossed like my sweats—given a clear, yet unspoken message: YOU do not fit. YOU do not belong. YOU fail.

My thoughts immediately raced to blaming myself for not staying a course of persistent Posi-tiva-Diva tactics. I had failed him by staying quiet, when I should have been shouting from our industrial, fluorescent, dropdown ceiling. My backside ached from kicking myself for not encouraging the 'caa-caa' out of him. I confessed my crimes to hubby that night and wondered why, after all this retrospective, introspective, proactive, intuitive work, I am still falling short on being a good person and doing a good thing?

I was down on myself. Really DOWN!

Now I was empty—and deflated—and disappointed. Did I mention tired...?

At work the following day, a chipper voice called out to me down the hallway, and I turned to see Marvin smiling and waving at me.

He can smile. *Who knew that was possible?*

He said he was back, would be working with us again, and apologized to me for his poor attitude and negative comments. He said he'd had an epiphany to do better. *Maybe he reads my blog...*

I shrugged my shoulders, tried to play cool while alluding to something about being a trooper, and we walked to our desks laughing like it had always been that way.

I have no clue if my interactions with him affected his changing tune, but maybe there is more to this 'quiet example' thing, modelling what I stand for instead of blurting it out constantly. And that is exactly the approach I used with all the YOU's in my world this week.

Words do not always fit. I cannot hug every problem away.

Showing up... is enough.

40 WEEK CHECK-IN:

September – December 2016

I feel like I have been in the middle of too many unspoken and exaggerated miscommunications between soon-to-be momma and hubby for the whole time she was pregnant. Undoubtedly, this has been a cause of great stress and discomfort in a place where new life is supposed to rain down joy and fresh starts.

But like it or not, ready or not, babies come in their own time and on their own terms. WE are so lucky for that! Here she is, everybody! An inspiration, a bright light, the sweetest cherub—thank you, Universe! Meet my brave and fierce granddaughter!

All our worries and fears melted away when she showed up. Of course. That is her job. To make us remember the delight and blessings of life. We want to be better humans

for her, giving all that we have—no holding back—so she can experience a world that invites her to explore all her stories. I am in love, love, LOVE!

We had to say good-bye to oldest son as he moves to another continent for a few years. This is a good goodbye, one that I do not mind saying. There are plans to meet up across the sea, and I can think of no better way to send off your child. Words said, hugs given, and bonds strong.

Then come the newborn baby sleepless nights. I may have crossed a line or two, but there were times I woke in the middle of the night, hearing the babe crying, and stumbled toward the sound in a zombie-like state, only to be told firmly to go to back to bed. Sometimes, I would let new momma keep sleeping by handling the early mornings waking's, but it was a steep learning curve for me. I eventually figured out my place. Apparently, I am NOT the momma, now.

Hubby and I are tense, again. We seem to have a very different approach for parenting little ones, and often disagree on what our daughter should do, which is a bit pointless, since WE are not her baby's parents. Hmmmm, I sense a pattern, here.

But what a comfort to hold this little babe. She is healing us in so many ways. Mum would have been delighted with this little person. I must cherish it for both of us.

I attempted to connect with my lost son again but keep falling into the trap of bringing up the past. Again, I brought another sibling into the mix, breaking a trust I pride myself on keeping. This turned an olive-branch offering into a big wedge, the last thing our severed relationship needed. Sigh. Back to square one.

Your Week Forty thoughts?

Week Forty

THE QUIET, THE COLD

Grammy's little writing buddy is helping today while her momma gets a much-needed rest. Later, she will also be my banana-bread-making buddy, and then a wonderful workout buddy, and finally, when Grampy gets home this evening, his NFL-watching buddy. She fits perfectly!

Who has time to write when all this granddaughter goodness is going on?

That could be my excuse for why this chapter has taken longer than usual to complete, but that would not be true. Struggling for inspiration and floundering for meaningful steps through this topic of "Encouragement with ME" felt a bit like self-inflicted torture, or like someone with intimate knowledge of my vulnerabilities was doing their best to rip me apart inside.

When I started this chapter—over three weeks ago—it was spilling generously out onto the page. Several themes showed up, opening multiple avenues to pursue, and then—it just stopped. I was unable (*or unwilling*) to finish, because everything pouring out of me was leading to one destination… and it was not pretty.

> *"To begin—easy.*
> *To keep going—tricky."*

Not pretty, nor acceptable, and not where I imagined myself to be going while searching for an anecdote describing how to find encouragement for myself.

My original assumption was this:

People are going to encourage ME, specifically the close, loved, wise, and open-hearted folks whom I have purposefully chosen to be near, who help me gain a better understanding of life, who hold me to a greater standard of truly living rather than just existing—those kinds of people. My Circle.

Sacred. Trusted.

Thank God. Really. I thank my Creator—it is finally my turn, I whisper to my tired, depleted self. Work has been stressful, home life has been bumpy, my volunteer commitments seem to multiply daily. I cannot *wait* to be encouraged!

I will be fed. I get to be held. I can rest. I kept waiting—watching for a clear indicator that my trouble-deflecting fists could come down, while listening for the roar of my cheering squad to kick in. If I am not lucky enough to escape the arena ring entirely, at least someone would be fighting in my corner for a change.

Crickets.

No blast from an advancing horn from my heart tribe.

No family to steady their eyes on my life.

Hubby and I were separately working on keeping our own heads above turbulent waters, secretly crossing our fingers to not be called upon to save the other.

Talk about living on the edge! I found myself going cold. My heart tightened, generosity in thoughts and speech thinned. Blame swirled constantly at the surface of my brain, banishing everyone to doom and pushing my fate down the highway toward martyrdom.

Here is the catch. My circle and family should not be responsible for me.

These thoughts—messages—labels—and coldness grow with fear and distrust. They freeze out what I need to hear the most. It spits out, on repeat, *I do not belong… I am not loved… I have no hope.*

I must be close to the summit of something great, which could explain the temperature. The cold taunts me to quit. Gnarling its teeth with intimidation, stalking across my path, preying on my people-nature, and creating phantom conflicts to keep me from warm connections. Anything, to distract me from the truth:

I am SAFE. I am HELD. I am LOVED.

To warm things up for this topic, I am choosing an icon that can wrap around me on days that feel comfortless. Mum's mitts were my favorite choice when heading to the ski-hill, or for spending winter days in the yard with my BFF, Grover, our Irish Setter/Golden Lab cross. He was a sweetheart of a pal and made every bad teenager day better. Since Grover is way more appealing to look at than a tanned pair of leather mitts, here is a fuzzy, old photo of my dearly loved friend.

ENCOURAGEMENT FOR ME

With a tank on empty and the yearly battle with winter temperatures underway, it is no wonder I am down. Who will encourage ME?

Well, someone came along who needed more encouragement than I did. In fact, she asked openly for it. I met her recently through a public event I was hosting. That harmless encounter turned into a challenge, or an encouragement duel *(perhaps to the death)*, as her terms seemed to reach beyond healthy relationship building.

Even though she was voicing the same thing I had silently been waiting for, I wanted to tune her out. I took stock of her approach—unrealistic, demanding, selfish—and then I really wanted my distance. I would never let ME get to that point.

Looking pathetic.

Begging for love.

Starving for validation.

And yet that was ME on the inside—both presently and historically.

Who was I to judge this person voicing her needs, when I could not verbalize my own?

So, I shamed myself into entering this lonely lady's world, certain my gigantic aorta could not fail.

Find the strength—and throw in some humor for good measure.

I invited her to my house to join a group that meets regularly for growth and connection. I believed a circle of trusted folks could help share the burden of caring for this friendless soul.

Nope.

We were not her cup of tea. Not relational enough, or authentic enough *(according to her forty-six-minute exposure to us)*. And more specifically, **I** was too fake.

WHAT!?

Fake! ME?

Listen lady, I am not fake! I BLOG!!

All my emotional triggers were set afire with indignation. Not because I am a rookie at accusations of being fake but because each time it happens, there is always more at play than a selfless comment meant to 'help AJ become a better person'; A welcome intention, were it so.

The first person to suggest I was 'hollow' was my college acting coach, who did not see past his own ego to understand why he could not pick away at mine. College was sandwiched in the years I was either losing Mum or had just lost her, so my emotions were shut down for survival. I was not about to turn them back on without guaranteed safety—something not promised in acting class.

My other accuser should not be hard to guess. Picking up where my acting coach left off, he accused me of being fake so often that I became immune to it. So, he upped his accusation and changed his description to "EVIL". After reading a book titled *People of the Lie,* by respected author M. Scott Peck, my ex galvanized 'fake and evil' as accurate characterizations of ME. Projection, at its finest.

I got quicker at recognizing when someone was putting their garbage into my back yard, complaining about the smell, then pointing their finger out to embarrass me into fixing it. But recognizing it did not make the garbage disappear.

I think I have two choices when facing people like this: Accept more piles of caa-caa into my life or pack up and move away.

If that sounds harsh, try breathing under a mountain of trash.

But back to being fake...

For a couple of moments (*ha ha, okay, it was a couple days*), I was disturbed, talking hubby's ear off until collapsing into bed without a true resolution within me. For the next few days, I wanted to blast my story to everyone at work, potentially debunking this incredulous tale, and be vindicated through someone else's eyes.

Nope.

Not the right place. Not the right time. Not the right people. So, I stayed quiet.

Smile. Laugh. Shrug. BREATHE.

Then I sensed it: A shift. It felt like encouragement!

Where did this come from? Was it a result of one of Mum's old adages—that whenever stuff got difficult, it would build character? Maybe.

But that did not quite fit. It went deeper. Something bigger and stronger was stirring in my core.

"The hero she had waited for was inside all along."

It gently flooded my body with comfort and power. Reminding ME that...

I have come far.

    I know who I am.

        I know where I want to be.

Breathe. You are doing fine.

This is the work. This is the dance. This is the stuff that makes ME.

I pray we all can see how far we have come, trusting the brightest version of ourselves has not yet arrived, but is most certainly, on the way.

AJ

Hardships often prepare ordinary people for an extraordinary destiny...

There are far BETTER things ahead than any we LEAVE.
~ C. S. Lewis

What would you say to encourage yourself? To encourage others?

When is intentional encouragement necessary?

CHAPTER ELEVEN

CLEVERNESS

The beautiful thing about learning
Is that no one can take it from you.
~ B.B. King

Week Forty-One

ME... SMART?

How does this new topic strike you?

Cleverness—or to put it another way—Being smart.

I am trying to recall my reasons for keeping cleverness as one of the thirteen virtues to be examined. I thought it held some significance for my healing but almost a year later, and following ten other intriguing chapters of focus, SMART sounds a little boring and maybe not worth the effort.

But then I remembered... 'smart' and I have history—a very long history that lands somewhere between feeling like a screamo-metal song and a softly whispered soundscape.

So, I stop, get settled, and begin to unpack why cleverness merits some attention.

Full confession: I have never felt truly intelligent at any time in my life.

Yes, I know feelings can be deceiving and are not always accurate or true, but still—there it is, my inaccurate confession that now must be managed.

This week's icon is a couple of things from Mum's academic portfolio. She continued to improve her skills and credentials right up until the time she took sick. I saved many framed examples of the certificates she achieved, which tie in perfectly with this week's focus.

Mum had a science degree. Clever Mumma.

Dad had an education degree. Clever Poppa.

Brother was top of his class and became an accountant. Clever Bro.

I should fall right in line behind all these smarty pants, right?

School was not a success for me, unless gym, band, French, and home economics count for something. I would never raise my hand in class to ask or answer a question, too afraid of being wrong or sounding like a dunce. So, I sat quiet—half engaged and half in a dream world. At best, I endured school until it was finally over, and I could pursue my real passion: Music.

Music was going to be the thing that would prove my math teacher wrong, when he said I would use the stuff he was teaching one day. Music, *not math*, would save me, so I put all my 'big dream' eggs into that one basket. There was only one, tiny flaw…

Mega Passion—Check.

Stage Presence—Double Check.

Creative Talent—Double, Double, Triple Check.

Technical Ability? *Well … that could be best described by sticking my tongue against my lips and blowing raspberries 'til next Christmas!*

I was only half a musician. I hustled my portion of talent, performing during and beyond Bible college. I travelled to be part of various creative projects, and finally landed in theatre school to secure that highly revered and somewhat evasive college diploma. And surprise, surprise—guess who attained the highest GPA in the class?

Interesting.

Mum was already gone by the time I graduated, but I knew how happy she was to see me step back into the role of student. She would have been proud to know I crushed college.

This started me thinking—maybe I do have a little cleverness in ME. Maybe 'smarts' are a little different in everyone—and maybe that is what Mum was trying to say all along.

But her quiet voice was replaced by a loud gong in the year following my successful college experience. Married, pregnant, and informed repetitively that my diploma had no credit.

WORTHLESS.

It did not hold the same value of a university degree, or better, a master's degree! Now *that* was something. Only the very clever could achieve that, and since I was too afraid to even consider university, I could never truly be on par with smart people. So, it only made sense that, since I did not understand higher levels of thinking, I should accept cooking and cleaning as my most suitable skills. Knowing how to sew was a bonus in rounding out my perfect portfolio as "house wench". He called me that so many times, the kids probably thought weddings are when you become husband and wench.

This attack against my intelligence continued and engrained within me a template that defaulted to someone else's thoughts, someone else's language, and someone else's beliefs.

Poor ME! I could not act, talk, or THINK without needing correction from a smarter person, who made a convincing argument how incredibly fortunate I was to have his pity and tolerance.

Grateful. That is what I was admonished to be: Grateful to him for keeping his vow, indebted to his generous oversight of my fatally flawed intellect.

This is the rut that held me firm for years.

But little moments would come. Small reminders sporadically replaced those manipulative lies with a fleeting but powerful truth: I was clever.

So clever that when each of us were given the same IQ test, administered by a professional peer of his, my ex and I scored almost identically. How could that be?

No university degree—growing up on a farm with cows and chickens—goofing off in the theatre arts scene... How was my IQ on equal footing to someone with a master's degree in English?

INTERESTING!

- When given the task of balancing bills and frugally managing every resource within the home, who paid for groceries, utilities, and gasoline on $87 a week?
- After being goaded into applying to be a police officer, then told I should give up because I could never actually accomplish it, who passed the rigorous exams and sailed through every obstacle?
- When taking the law enforcement domestic conflict training, who quietly followed the model by packing an emergency bag, eliminating that and other barriers which rob victims of chances to escape?

A clever lady, that's who!

CLEVERNESS WITH ME

If I look back at myself—who I was, what I did, and why I did it—I can see trends and blips emerging. Not all my patterns are healthy, but everything is suggesting something similar. Just as a heartbeat registers peaks and valleys on an ECG, I have moments that rise above the others and give true and unequivocal proof...

I am Strong.

Smart.

Whole.

WORTHY.

Lots of other nastiness and noises attempt to cover up these facts, so I must remind myself of the blips.

Seeking help after too many concussions, I watched the in-patients at the brain injury clinic struggle with worries and doubts of eventual recovery, and just knew that I had to get better, that I would fight harder than anyone to get back to my full capacity, and that I would follow all instructions to be well.

BLIP

Heeding the advice of a psychologist upon separation, and not entering another relationship for two years (*remembering the results of ignoring similar advice and getting married too soon after Mum died*), I was determined to learn from my experiences and give myself time to heal.

BLIP

Drowning in an assigned I.T. work role, I embraced an attitude of growth, welcoming the opportunity to learn and the potential doors it might open—doors that would likely not appear if I adopted bitterness.

BLIP

If I listen to my heart, I hear it pump—then rest—both equally important functions.

Life cannot be *life* without both.

PUMP. REST.

I have had my moments—my blips—and I have had blanks. I used to think the blanks were proof my blips did not exist, especially when the distance between blips was great, but the blips keep coming.

I set out to heal the ugliest hurts, to honor Mum's last year of life, by designing and filling a blog dedicated to writing.

PUMP.

When I listen to a friend—hold a baby granddaughter—go to bed early because life can wait until tomorrow...

REST.

> You have brains in your head, you have feet in your shoes,
> you can steer yourself any direction you choose.
> ~ Dr. Seuss

Choose your own ICON for Cleverness:

Week Forty-Two

YOU IS SMART!

Hello, ALL YOU Smarty Pants!

Yes, I mean YOU! If I am smart, YOU is smart.

Apparently, I am not the only one who has contended with this concept of not fitting the mold of traditional intelligence, and rightly so. This narrowly exclusive academic model has been centuries in the making, cementing itself into the western cultural mindset of our schools, businesses, and homes. But that is not what I think needs tackling this week, when the focus will be to sort out the meaning of "Cleverness with YOU".

Finding a suitable icon for this week was a bit hard, at least a tangible, photographable, visual one. Instead, what I hear rattling around in my head is a phrase Mum said whenever my mouth got too smart: "Don't get snarky, young lady".

'Being snarky'—also NOT what this week is focused on—although living with teenagers can seem like a bubbling, hot cauldron of snarky.

So, if I am not going to take on the slanted undercurrent of academia, or the general 'snarkyness' of teenagers, what *am* I going to do?

Pick up right where we left off last week: Witness to an emerging pattern of clever action versus purposeful stillness. If I am going to continue learning from experiences, I must remember pivotal moments and ignore the empty ones.

> Weak people revenge
> Strong people forgive
> Intelligent people ignore
> ~Albert Einstein

Now, I cannot confirm what Einstein meant when he was quoted as saying this, but it likely was not meant as a parenting tip. Then again, maybe it was; A quick google search of his personal life reveals he had a daughter who was barely mentioned, which could be an example of ignoring emotional discomfort. I am not certain ignoring uncomfortable situations is a great direction to head, recalling times I tried to escape from emotional discomfort and ended up prolonging the unpleasantness.

What I take from this clever man's quote is this: Actively try letting go of negative, empty, non-life-giving moments. Then, maybe figure out when, why, and what, to ignore. *That* would be a considerably smart achievement.

As I put this idea on a low simmer inside my brain, I realized there was another layer to this kind of awareness: Listening.

If last week was concentrated on active observation, this week seems to involve active listening as the key to being clever with the closest people around me.

First, I travelled back in time to see if my past could shed any light on this theory of listening.

Not listening was my specialty when it came to things Mum said. When I was about 15 years old, I tormented her when she reacted to me suggesting I would choose a black man to marry—about which previously I believed she felt nothing but acceptance—her circle of university colleagues being very diverse and regularly a part of our family social activities. I remember the gifts that were given to her from their cultural origins and can smell the interesting aromas we would experience when sharing meals in their homes.

Contrary to what she modelled, I think she might have been a bit racist, in keeping with the conservative views of her generation. The thought of having bi-racial grandbabies made her distraught. Citing religious and cultural differences as being too challenging, she expressed how confused the children would be about their identity—well, it was enough to send her into a right tizzy!

Amusing as it was to see my mother in a worked-up state, I was not actually serious about a plan to marry someone of a different culture—yet that is exactly what happened.

My children are beautiful beings, who seem quite certain of their identity. Their hurdles seem to rise from unique parts of their personalities or from the cruelty they witnessed and endured through formative years. I know Mum would have loved them, even if she may not have approved of my choice in partner, so I do not regret dismissing her caution.

When wonderful hubby and I were dating and contemplating whether blending our families was worth the price to be together, he met all of Mum's criteria from Week Thirty-Six and her 'nerd' advice from Week Twelve. Although I do not find hubby particularly nerdy, part of his nature is purposefully studious. In comparison to my artistic, creative nature, he leans toward the other side of that spectrum, which I happen to like very much in him.

As a best friend, he tests my blind spots and still manages to respect my power of choice and thought. He tested my ability to listen the day he disagreed with how I generally blamed my ex for all the wounds my heart had to endure during my first marriage. Now I was in a tizzy! How could he say or think such a thing, especially when he knew in detail the sickening years I had survived? This was starting to look like a relationship deal breaker.

Whether it was the trust already established with him, or his sensitive, informed logic, I listened. It turned over and through me, not letting me dismiss or ignore the truth rising from something scary.

I chose to be in pain.

I can remember the exact moment I decided for certain that an escape would be necessary to end my troubled relationship. And it took nine and a half more years before I ran out the door for the last time. I gave that marriage a solid effort. Hung in there for better days to come, to preserve the family unit, and to preserve the outer appearance of vows made before God. Being victimized seemed like a better choice than being responsible for breaking apart my family.

If you had asked me then whether I felt like a victim, I would have said, *"NO."*

I worked very hard to live as though nothing unpleasant had ever touched my life, but it was deeply entrenched in my emotional language and actions. My default identity was powerless, helpless, and therefore blameless to all the wrongs that were done to me and my children.

So, I listened—hard, but not to my nagging emotions that wanted to blame someone else. I wanted to hear something else for a change.

I wanted to truly understand, turn a corner, face myself and who I needed to be, on the inside and out.

"When pain is the teacher, a lesson learned is the cure."

Once I saw clearly how my own action, or inaction, contributed to my unhealthy environment, I could not have it both ways. It would have been easy to continue blaming an ass for ruining fourteen youthful years, but I would never have gotten over it.

I would never grow. I would never heal. I would always be a victim.

The reasons I stayed in that pain are undeniable, whether noble or not. But I had the power to choose. Then and now. Giving anyone else that power seals my identity.

A girl who chooses not to be herself.

No, thank you. If there is a choice, which I now know there is, then I must work to be free of this powerless mentality, every day. I must listen to the precious loved ones around me who know me best, who love and accept my edges, who point out when my identity is fading, and who respect the fire and frailty of my beating heart.

Clever AJ listens to YOU.

And with that, this week's icon emerges. A book of meditation given to my mum when she was sick. Gentle words of assurance and peace are held within its bindings. Pages to write and reflect, images that cheer… possibly the inspiration for the format and details of this book. No, I haven't invented a new wheel for emotional awareness. It was already there. My 'smartyness' just borrowed it. *Insert Kungfu fighting moves here.*

Hoooo-yah!

Week Forty-Three

WHALE SMARTS

Feeling clever? Have you ever tried to operate someone else's shower?

Hello, Week Forty-Three *(or is it Week Fifty-Nine... or Sixty-Four?)* If you are like me and have deliberated a bit longer than a week on some topics, I have good news.

Starting this week, I am going to count in 'whale' years. *YES.* Whale years are very long, and by that reckoning, I am actually ahead of schedule by about sixteen decades!

Coincidentally, although the name of this book is *Finding HER Stuff,* my original blog name *'Finding 52'* shares its name with another online entity, a whale-watching group of scientists who have conducted research on some unique and mysterious whales whose songs have been recorded at a higher than usual level: Fifty-two Hertz—hence the group's name.

> Whales do not sing because they have an answer,
> they sing because they have a song.
> ~ Gregory Colbert

I do not have a higher-than-average singing voice, quite the opposite, which might be the point at which this analogy breaks down, but here is what I know so far:

Whales sing—I sing.

Whales are social creatures—So am I!

Whales are known to attract the opposite sex with their voices—Me too… and sometimes, I do it on 'porpoise'.

Whales are monogamous. Despite what my ex has claimed, I am definitely in this category.

Whales have a lot of offspring and live in large groups. Did I mention my five kids?

And then there is whale time.

I think I have lived most of my life taking longer than the average person to arrive at appointed destinations. I wear a watch and try to respect its job of fitting things neatly into order, for me and the intersecting lives of others, so it truly brings no pleasure to have people waiting on me to arrive. Yet somehow, it is in my DNA: A fascinating, frustrating characteristic that has ebbed and flowed through all my breathing days. Slow, but eventually covering great distances—like my whale friends. So, if you are waiting on me to finish this fifty-two-week mission, anxious to see the end of your own exploration… take heart! We are getting there.

If I *was* counting in human years, this is the week I have officially arrived. **I have now lived longer than Mum.** And look, I am still here, dreaming up my best life.

WOOHOO!

So, I push on *(tardy, but spry)* through the last few topics, hoping to understand more pieces of the mystery that clutter my past, collide with the present, and create my future.

YOU is smart. That is where I left things last, convinced that I must quiet myself in order to listen to love and wisdom. To keep building upon that, I kept listening… and wondered how many things in my life would have turned out differently had I been clever enough to listen sooner.

Uncle 'M' said, "Sing country music. You could go far."

No thanks, Uncle. I am not a fan of the country scene.

But he was right. That genre was waiting for a big female artist boom, and it came… about the same time I would have completely paid any proper performing dues. Oh well. Blog and work night shift—*that* is my rock 'n' roll now.

Paul from the Bible said, "Love don't quit."

Okay, I may have slightly paraphrased that verse. The actual wording is "Love never fails." Had I really listened and discerned these three words, I might have understood earlier that if love is failing, it is not love. Fighting harder does not produce love. Love is, or is not. There is no trying to love someone. Lesson learned.

In my clearest moments, I know everything has come from and through what it must, in order to arrive exactly where it should. If I had a chance to return to the past and re-do something, but it did not come with a guarantee of keeping the people and parts of life I love now, I am quite certain I would not risk it. Although this kind of revelation confuses me, I would probably do it all *(yes, ALL)* over again—knowing it would hurt, knowing the cost—in order to preserve the precious, irreplaceable now.

That does not seem very clever! I mean, choosing to re-do the very stuff that has taken every ounce of my determination, focus, and love to overcome—COO-COO for coco puffs, right!? How could I willingly approach that kind of despair, where hope and joy are long-gone dead, and my only escape relies on fluky instinct?

Let's ask the whales…

Here is an excerpt from *Spiritanimal.info*:

"The whale spirit animal is the earth's record keeper for all time. As a totem, the whale teaches you about listening to your inner voice, understanding the impact your emotions have on your everyday life, and following your own truth."

Whales are also commonly associated with emotion, inner truth, and creativity. Additionally, they can be a symbol of holding wisdom, physical and emotional healing, valuing family and community, peaceful strength, and communication.

WOW, wow, WOW!

Now we are getting somewhere.

My icon this week must be Mum's Bible, where exists one of the oldest stories of WHALE vs HUMAN interactions. It relays an awesome tale of a man trying to escape God's plan for his life by running in the opposite direction God tells him to go. When he runs out of land, he boards a ship to further the distance from where he is meant to be.

This is when trouble hits. A terrible storm suddenly appears, threatening the lives of everyone aboard the vessel. The man eventually realizes it is his actions that have turned the weather deadly.

Here comes the good part: He convinces the captain to throw him overboard to appease the violent sea. Reluctant, but afraid of the ship capsizing, the captain tosses him into aggressive waves, to his certain death… but he does not die.

He is gulped up by a large fish, or whale, where he stays—not dead—just swishing around with other slimy, swallowed carcasses. After three days and nights of this dank and dreary experience, he is finally ready to go where God asks. The whale spits him out onto a beach, and he finishes his original quest.

So why do I care about whales and old bible stories, and what does it have to do with US being clever?

I can attest to running blindly in an opposite direction from where I probably should have gone.

I have tossed myself at the mercy of the sea, rolling under wave after wave of blaming self-defeat.

I have been swallowed up by a sickening black hole, been spat out on the shores of embarrassment, and wiped slime from my reclaimed soul to set my uncomfortable feet on a track toward renewal.

And then, just at the point where I could no longer remember the stench of the beast's belly, my hope restored, the darkness vanquished by flooding light, and my fear of rough waters abated; I found myself staring into the mouth of another whale.

This time, it was not sent for me. It swallowed my son.

Could I have done something different to change his course? Maybe a better question would be whether the man in the story could have been forced to do God's bidding?

The obvious answer sounds like "yes".

Any worthwhile god should be able to command obedience from one of their prophets. Likewise, a responsible parent should be able to control a wayward child.

But people are not puppets, with gods or parents pulling at the end of their strings, meaning that we all have choice.

I *could* have done many things to help create space for my boy to be safe and happy in our pre and post whale home—a failing he cited as the ultimate reason his young brain could not rationalize remaining with his family. His choice.

We all need choice, in order to be fully present, truly aware, and taking full ownership of our lives. Otherwise, we are completely helpless and need to blame someone else for our unhappiness.

This week has taught me that we all get swallowed at one time or another. Whether it is you or a family member getting slogged about, it is temporary. Whale time may seem like an eternity, but it ends when we are ready to move on to something more positive and more beneficial, something truer to who we are meant to be.

Whale time is not fatal. It brings peace, and freedom, and beauty, and everything that is loved in the now. So, would I do whale time again?

You bet!

When I extend patience and grace to a son thrashing about in a foul pit, it helps keep family a priority, even when some of US are running and sailing as far away as possible.

If blind suffering must be, it would be smart to get comfortable while waiting, remember the joy, and reflect on the sorrow.

Whale time is not wasted time, because I know where WE end up. I know restoration and getting spit-out onto new shores waits for US.

And that is good. And sweet. And clever. And TRUE.

> Let faith oust fact. Let fancy oust memory.
> I look DEEP down and I DO believe.
> ~ Herman Melville, *Moby Dick*

Week Forty-Four

CLEVER ENOUGH

Week Forty-Four is uncomfortable!

It keeps me up at night, will not let me sleep late on weekends, constricts at my collar, and kicks up a mean sweat.

Steady up, girl... I whisper affirmations that remind me... I am right where I am supposed to be for this week—this moment—for reasons the universe may never reveal. This is "Cleverness With THEM".

Remember that 'client' who was trying to get me fired? If not, head back to Week Twelve and the 30 Week Check-in.

I want to pick up on some unfinished business with this trial and verdict, nine years after the actual occurrence. The details of my policing role must remain a bit protected, as my organization and colleagues would expect me to honor and respect the privilege of knowing sensitive details of people's lives. However, it may be helpful to explain a bit about this situation, to better understand the lasting implications of this verdict on my career.

The file was a domestic related arrest, although the two parties involved were no longer living together. In the eyes of the law, once people have habituated together in a familial manner, or have had kids together, they are considered as 'domestic related'. This man and woman had an 18-month-old and were not amicable. I had taken a previous report from the woman several months prior, but she was not ready to *do* anything about the violence. I understood that. I did not push an agenda on her. I simply took the information, and as she was not in any immediate danger, I left her with resources and information on interpersonal violence and how to navigate bumpy child custody issues.

A year later she came to the office to report she had been beaten, the child being in his arms for some of it, and a body full of bruises. Police should do something about this, yes?

YES, that is the idea—protect those who need it, and so my partner and I went about finding and arresting the man responsible. He was uncooperative and using his rights not to say anything (*not even to indicate he understood what we were communicating*), so we had no choice but to go with her version of the event. He was charged, given an order to not go near her or his child for up to ten days, until a judge could hear both their stories and come up with a suitable way forward.

Ultimately, the crown prosecutor dropped the charges, which is common and completely within their scope to determine what cases will bear the weight of a trial, but in no way indicates the merit of the original arrest.

Many people who get arrested do not understand the duty of care for a police officer; The necessity to intervene sometimes before all the facts are known. Charging someone for an offence is different from *convicting* them. A judge does that. Police mitigate risk factors that stop or decrease potential harm to people and property. I was not issued a crystal ball or a wishing wand with my duty kit, so have relied on studying the habits of humans to predict risk and piece together puzzling events.

I acknowledged how he could have felt unfairly treated but affirmed throughout the 'trial' that my motives were based on safety—protection. I know he felt punished by being arrested and having to go through court processes, and this fed his nine-year war.

During his address to the 'judge', he maintained an emotionless state, straying from his robotic story only once to re-enact a quote he claimed to have come from me, delivered with a chilling and calculated emphasis: "You will never see your child, again!" He concluded by stating how my words and actions had unfolded a multitude of negative experiences for him.

Then he listened, the whole next day, to why I believed he simply had not understood my role or intentions in this complex situation, and that I most certainly did not say he would never see his child again. But again, I understand how it could FEEL that way.

I did my best to *show up* on these days.

Fully reflective.

Exaggeratingly empathetic.

Sometimes animated.

I did not put further emphasis on the lack of rationality for his string of logic, since I knew the perspective leading him there. His feelings were real. They just were not accurate.

Nevertheless, after it was all said and done, the upper echelons within my organization decided to agree with this complainer, and formally stated I was in the wrong.

WHAAAAT?! **I** screwed up? ME? You think **I** blew it!??

Oy Vey!

So, what happens when higher ranking officers judge other cops for things that happen routinely in the course of any investigation?

Was I fired? Nope—but it was an option.

Are there career repercussions? You bet! I cannot be promoted or competitive for another position for 5 years. And if you think it is kept a secret as to why I am not moving anywhere, well… let's just say gossip is alive and well in police culture. It is a real possibility that the rest of my career will be 'black-marked', even after the 5 years are complete.

Was I given a choice to fight back against great odds with another appeal? Yup. They even offered free legal representation—such a strange offer, after feeling like I was given up as a sacrifice.

Did I appeal? Nope.

It is over.

Wait—I decided not to fight? The Muhamad Ali fighter in me, warrior, kickass girl, backing down out of the ring entirely?

C'mon AJ, that doesn't sound like you. You gotta fight this one. You can beat this! What are these fifty-two-week ramblings doing to ME??

I think I am all about standing up to oppressive people, speaking out against wrongs afflicting the innocent, entering battle for noble causes—but does retreat ever fit into this mindset?

This week we honored the life of a great personality of our century. Let's check in with 'The Champ' to see what he has to say about our topic.

CLEVER WITH THEM

Muhamad Ali impacted our world in a manner few had been able to do before the onset of global social media. He had magnetic charisma, intelligent humor, unwavering values, and a mighty spirit that led him to defeat not only his boxing opponents but his own doubts. His career comprised of spontaneously dynamic interactions with reporters and fans. In true comic-book hero style, he had many friends as well as foes, and ongoing controversial moments in the spotlight. He is quoted as saying things like:

> Impossible is just a big word thrown around by small men
> who find it easier to live in the world they've been given
> than to explore the power they have to change it.
>
> Impossible is not a fact. It's an opinion.
> Impossible is not a declaration. It's a dare.
> Impossible is potential.

Impossible is temporary.
Impossible is nothing.

Many sport champions embody this same spirit.

Since 2016 marks the year Ali departed from our earth, it seems fitting to somehow pay tribute to his champion mentality in a year focused on how to become a better version of myself.

For this week, I cannot pretend Mum was a huge boxing fan, telling and retelling stories of great fights, or whether she thought Ali was the greatest boxer of all time. But I know she was a fighter for people she loved, had the spirit of a champion for her community, and planted trees and shrubs with a Zeus-type of effort, to make the heavenly gardens that exist today in that sleepy little town.

She may not have been as loud as Ali was when he fought against sporting odds, social popularity, and racial biases. Even when losing his boxing license for refusing to accept subscription to the US Army, he stayed true to his beliefs.

I never met Muhamad Ali, but maybe I did not need to—I had Mum.

I am the GREATEST!

Try screaming that to yourself every day. It is one of my favorite Ali quotes. It drips with the kind of celebration and freedom I would love to exude.

Confident. Expressive. Fierce.

Most days, I feel like this on the inside. I think I have seen myself as a fighter since grade three, when clobbering my way through every playground conflict was the status quo. My dukes flew freely before figuring out that I did not like spending time in the principal's office.

When I reflect on the ease in which I entered squabbles as a child, I must draw a connection to my ability to withstand fourteen years of domestic conflict. Struggle sits with me. I do not fear it. It does not predict my comfort. I can endure it draining my guts, zapping my heart, and fading my shine. But there is more to this equation.

How can Ali and my historic hostility help this week, as I wonder how to be clever with all those around me?

More quotes from the champ, of course!

> The fight is won or lost far away from witnesses
> Behind the lines, in the gym, and out there on the road
> Long before I dance under those lights.

This quote also applies to last week and reminds me that it does not matter what words I write, or if I technically win a public complaint. As I sit with my 'punishment' of being benched to a desk, I am either preparing to win, or losing the next fight.

I hate the bench! It is the worst. I am a competitor—a contributor.

But not now. Now I sit. Sit and wait.

Seen through a different lens, sitting could be labelled as protection and not punishment.

And that is where we come full circle. Me, this complaining man, Mad Marvin, my ex—we all act in accordance with what we see as fair, significant, necessary, and wise. We ALL arrive to our actions from this place.

> I hated every minute of training, but I said, 'Don't quit.
> Suffer now and live the rest of your life as a champion.

Oh. Did he say suffer? What about the butterfly and the bee...

Looks like there are more miles to go. More mountains to climb. More valleys to pass. More words to come...

> My real work started after my career in the ring was over.

Oh boy. The real work? I am a bit confused about what you mean, Ali... Is my real work beginning after I quit fighting?

> A man who views the world the same at 50 as he did at 20
> Has wasted 30 years of his life.

So, maybe I do not need to fight every battle that seeks me. Young AJ might have felt comfortable there. Old AJ feels different things now. Peaceful things. Things that discern between *doing* good and doing what *feels* good.

It did not 'feel good' to lose—to fail. In this, or any other scenario, losing is tough. Choosing to keep losing, is tougher.

This decision, however unpopular with my fighter instinct, was clear. A war I did not start must end now—because I say it will—because I think it is time—because my work is about to begin, and I need ALL my energy for that.

So, it is OVER, regardless of the victor.

To be clever with THEM, I need not care about an outward appearance of losing. All my other actions and words should be enough to prove how my truth unfolds—soldiering love—hooked on hope—mugging out dreams and trying to make it all count!

AJ

The secret of change is to focus all of your energy, not on fighting the old
But on building the new.
~Socrates

What do you love about yourself?
(*Brag a little, please!*)

If you lived out in confidence, believing your personality, experiences, empathy, and attitude were more than enough to tackle any experience, what would that look like?

If you had an obnoxious *nom de plume*, what would it be? (*Mine is Little Big Hot Mama, which is how I make the kids address me if they want requests granted.*)

CHAPTER TWELVE

GENEROSITY

True character is most accurately measured
By how you treat someone who can do 'nothing' for you.
~ Saint Teresa

Week Forty-Five

A PRISTINE PAGE

I cannot recall if I shared aloud my intention to slow things down for the month of December. I think hubby, and a few select insiders, heard this declaration. It was sincere, especially since my November was unusually full. I counted the days left before being able to breathe—to rest.

I imagined the sudden, cool air filling my anxious lungs with refreshing waves of calm—compared to the hot, hurried gulps of oxygen being desperately shuttled to frantic feet and weary arms.

In my best self-aware analysis, I knew what was needed: BALANCE—the kind of balance my previous forty-four weeks of concentrated reflection has revealed to be essential to living a great life.

Yet balance is escaping me.

No center.

I shake and wobble my way through objectives and deadlines, spewing out more results than initially planned, all under the massive mission of 'yes'—that magical, powerful word taking ordinary skills and abilities to their brink. Its natural nemesis, 'no', waiting to pull the proverbial pin if given a small window of opportunity that never comes, historically overshadowed by that hammed-up, crowd-pleaser, superstar—YES.

This is not the first time I have been in this shaky arena. In fact, I might be considered a professional yes-girl, born to do what others put off, eager to achieve more than your average bear, convinced all hours of each twenty-four must be compacted with productivity and social connectivity.

Little research has been conducted into the *quality* of this output, but I suspect there is a direct link from my actions to how I gauge my personal worth. However, knowing this does not prevent the imbalance from happening.

What am I missing?

Swing after swing, I am striking out on finding life balance. I am a kid on a teeter totter who cannot stop sliding from one end to the other, occasionally getting bumped into the air and sprawling to hang onto the center.

BALANCE.

This will be my mantra in the new year, and Week Forty-Five, as I figure out how to build "Generosity With ME".

Perhaps it is not good timing, thinking about ME during the holiday season when themes of benevolence are supposed to preclude any self-centered sentiment. I was hoping for an effortless and perfect release for my overextended brain and body.

As soon as December rolled in, it hit: A tsunami wave of sparkling ideas.

Who can I bless?

How would I do it?

What would it take?

When can it happen?

I would like to say I rode this gigantic wave with poise, agilely maneuvering through schedules and details to obtain the ultimate outcome of having everything perfectly wrapped and ready—bows, ribbons, lights, tree, treats, photos, cards, decorations, calendars, handmade gifts, letters, postage—all while staying within a carefully considered budget.

The budget was about the only thing that could boast a 100 percent success rate. Everything else was either not started or did not get accomplished. In the pre-Christmas pandemonium, I flung items and tasks around as if they might magically come together on their own.

Here are the casualties:

Candles still in bubble wrap, cookie tins empty, randomly placed ornaments set down all over the house waiting for divine decorating inspiration to fall like winter snow… Christmas cards are collecting dust waiting for my pen to scratch out some personalized greetings, our annual family puzzle *(this year's is a whopping 1000 pieces)* lies incomplete after 4 weeks of random attention… the poinsettia looks like it got poisoned and run over by a lawnmower… and our family photos—well, let's just say we went with a frantic, frazzled theme this year. I could go on, but should really attend to the unwrapped grandbaby cooing under the Christmas tree…

I wonder… Since budget management seems to be my most successful endeavor, could I create a *time* budget, or develop strategies to decline requests *(especially when they come from my own brain)*, and design an alarm or trigger to let me know when the allotted time is coming to an end. This idea had a tiny head-start from Week Sixteen.

Perhaps I could track my time stats for a while, to determine how long it takes to do the things that draw my attention. Consideration could be given to people with whom I share greater intimacy, depending on their current needs and whether it is a life-giving thing versus a life-sucking thing. Maybe I could concoct a non-emotional, mathematical equation that would decide what accurately fits into each day or week. Shoot! I promised my math teacher I would never use his numerical propaganda…

This would be a huge shift of perspective!

Instead of recklessly squishing in as much as possible, time could be carved out with care and efficiency. Sounds great in theory, but does not sound like ME.

Fact about AJ: There needs to be a very good reason for me to change a general operating mode. It might be a stubborn streak or possibly something on the spectrum of lazy—perhaps it borders on a fine line towards quirky, but whatever the cause, there is usually a significant lag in time between *knowing* I need to make a change and *making* it.

Even when the consequences are dire, it is tough to get out of a rut and initiate a change.

> You change your life, by changing your heart.
> ~ Max Lucado

GENEROSITY WITH ME

When I was young, a grade-two teacher made a note in my report card saying that I often forgot my shoes and came back late from recess—and nothing has changed. I chronically forget items I set my mind to remember and still come back from 'recess' late.

Always.

My busy-fun is too distracting, *which I sort of like,* so there really is no reason to change. *Sorry, family.*

In my first marriage—thirteen out of fourteen years of which were violent—it took *five* years for me to realize that I needed to leave and the other *nine* to do it. WOWSA!

What kind of time lag is that! Survival seems to be a good reason for change, yet it was a slow, reticent process.

Last year, I began a healthier eating program that I am still on today, keeping off weight that took many months to lose—my *physical* body proving to be slow to change as well. It is something I would have never decided to attempt but for a picture hubby snapped of my backside. *YIKES!* That photo was a *very* good reason to change. In reflection, losing weight was one of the most generous things I did for myself last year.

So, my abysmal failure to slow things down this month must stem from not having a good enough reason to do it, which leads me back to generosity.

I am fully prepared to say that, after a month of feeling out of whack, out of steam, and out of breath, I am officially the biggest Scrooge when it comes to being generous with myself.

My judgements are brutally harsh and ignore anything potentially positive.

My expectations are unrealistic, with stingy deadlines.

My demands exclude the overall wellness of their singular, primary subject: ME.

Sadly, I have not yet found an antidote to this disease of my life—this chronic ailment that absorbs all granules of time not nailed down or already filled with something else. Does this mean I have given up on finding a way to remedy this plight—that I am destined to accept this stingy outlook on myself?

It is tempting to give in, to excuse it away and accept the fact that this is me and I am not likely to change. Not in a spirit of defeat, but rather as a decision to tolerate my suffering...

Ahhhh... now this is familiar terrain: Enduring insufferable emotional conditions for the sake of the bed. Yes, THE bed—the one that people say is made and now must be laid in—quite possibly the worst advice to rattle through the hallways of my mind while wondering if I should be looking for an escape door, or perhaps a window—even a rickety airshaft would be welcome. Anything would be better than pretending to be strong enough to stay in my stagnant mess and accepting it as my punishment for being there in the first place.

Where did this faulty philosophy land me, besides almost in a psychiatric ward? Learning that it did not *serve* me and could not *save* me. It most certainly did not restore or grow ME.

So, what advice do I have for ME as I plunge into a new year, a pristine page, a fresh start toward achieving balance?

If I am lying in a bed of busy that leads to exhaustion, am afraid of appearing to be anything less than a superwoman and so keep relentlessly pushing to achieve more and BE more—STOP.

It's like an old nursery-rhyme adage I heard play repetitively on a cherished vinyl record as a child:

> Stop little pot, your boiling is done.
> There's quite enough porridge, for everyone!
> ~ Mother Goose

Boiling porridge, writing stories, rescuing boring weekends—whatever ends up swallowing the days I have left, I am going to try creating goals that require positive, healthy chunks of my energy. Hopefully this is an adequate strategy to limit my urges to randomly fill every space. I also commit to patiently observing any doubts or obstacles my slow-to-change mind brings up, trusting there are many ways to achieve success, even when I cannot accomplish wearing pants every day.

I have generously given myself these goals:

- Thirty days of yoga. Quiet and focused. It is simple breathing with movement and stretching for thirty consecutive days. Easy, right? I had to drag myself out of the door on Day One! I am three for three though, and heading out the door soon for Day Four...
- Another nutritional cleanse. Drink that water, purge those toxins, eat clean food, and regenerate tired cells. Last year it restored my fitness level to normal, so I cannot wait to see where it goes from here.
- Run—specifically, a half marathon—which has now morphed into three half marathons—a bi-product of challenging others to join you and they challenge you back!

With this in mind, my icon this week will be a sweater Mum commissioned to be knit for me when I was 16 or 17. I am quite sure she could have managed to knit it herself since she had the skill and tools necessary, but she was a career woman with her own kinds of time-budgeting challenges.

Knowing that someone else had formed this sweater did not make it any less meaningful when I received it. Mum thoughtfully designed its color and theme, even having it completed twice when one of the musical notes she requested was sewn on backwards. I too must learn this art of making room for others to be superhero sweater makers/bakers/chaperones/shuttle drivers/committee members and other such stuff that pulls me away from balance.

Breathe and Bend.

Fuel Up Right.

Burn Rubber—and Blog.

BALANCE.

> *"Most days I eat vegetables and exercise.*
> *Today, popcorn is for dinner and pants are optional.*
> *This is Balance."*

Choose your own ICON for Generosity:

Week Forty-Six

THE GENEROSITY GAP

Two weeks ago, while escaping our routine for a few days, hubby and I flew south for a warm, relaxing weekend. Happily, I drafted about a thousand words getting ready to share this week's "Generosity With YOU". Thinking I was well on my way to seamlessly build upon last week's concept of balance, I sat proudly at the front of the airplane *(a rare treat)*, laptop and spectacles out, tapping away at the keyboard while the rest of the passengers boarded.

I imagined them wondering if I was a bigshot CEO of some corporate empire, or maybe they thought I was a famous writer and dared not to ask what body of work I was currently authoring… or so the movie reel plays in my head.

Sadly, no one will ever read those inspired words. They were zapped into the cosmos, lost in +30,000-foot-high airwaves. So, I begin again—from scratch.

Sigh. *Chin up, girl. The healing is in the writing, not the words.*

Several years ago, I did a passions workshop—not *those* kinds of passions. It was an exercise in how to determine one's greatest interests and identify moments that hold ultimate joy. Not surprisingly, my top five interests had a mix of creative and social activities that serve up heaps of fulfillment in my life. The workshop helped me see how passions can grow or fade, and that what was important years ago may not be presently significant.

My most shocking example of this was my love for singing. That passion used to keep me up at night, envisioning my life as a rock star, touring, and recording, which I have done, but on a much smaller scale than what I had dreamed up. In the passions workshop, you are asked to go through a process of elimination, where tough choices are made between all the things that cause my whole body to smile. Singing landed behind a brand-new love: WRITING!

Since I am on the topic of "Generosity With YOU", I will go ahead and reveal my number-one passion during that workshop: Watching my children thrive and shine in their passions.

Too many times in my tumultuous past, that specific passion was used as a weapon to keep me in line. When things got heated between me and the ex, he would deny our kids access to their activity or cancel plans to go out somewhere, to make me pay for whatever he felt were my sins. It broke my heart to see their upset little faces, sometimes already suited up in hand-me-down sports gear, knowing it was their chance to be normal and have fun with other kids—a colossal, highly treasured treat for my isolated, homeschooled children.

Now that there is only one teen left in our house pursuing a passion, she gets my full-court-press attention! She has played competitive soccer for many years—a sport I did not play growing up, so do not understand very well. Before turning 40, I decided to lace up some cleats and finally learn the game.

A few years later, my team was making appearances at the 'over 35' provincial finals, and I thought—maybe I could re-live some of my unrealized sport dreams and make it to a national arena *(my fantasies are epidemically out of control)*. However, after splitting my eyelid open and getting two, closely timed concussions, the emergency nurses were quite certain I should hang up my grassy shin guards and learn to crochet.

Last season, my daughter joined a team with mostly younger girls, so I was preparing for a drama-filled summer. To my surprise, the girls were very nice to each other, so her challenge became cracking their already tightly formed playing style. She struggled with positioning and felt ineffective when she was on the pitch, even though she was a highly skilled player.

Now, I may not understand soccer rules and positions, but I know what it means to prepare yourself mentally for tough competitions and offered her some advice.

Be vocal!

Lead!

Model your work ethic!

She mucked through a personally frustrating season, but the team ended up going to nationals. They won their first two games of the tournament, then lost in the quarter final, meaning they would be playing for bronze.

When you play outdoor soccer in late October, in a Canadian climate, snow carries a veto card. Both the bronze and gold matches were cancelled without getting rescheduled. An exasperating season ended in a thwarted result, leaving a disheartened little soccer player in a passionless state.

Her situation reminded me of a term I have heard on the soccer pitch, over and over during games: Reset.

This lovely word takes on different meanings, depending on the circumstance.

If a player has made an obvious error in play and teammates want it fixed without blame—reset.

If the team has lost control of the ball or momentum of the play—reset.

If the other team scores—reset.

Anytime a player drifts off or disengages from the play, their teammates and coach voices ring out—reset.

Every player needs this instruction at one time or another. Every player can give it at any time without criticism or judgment. It is a *neutral* reminder to take things back to the start, a place where all manner of potential and developments are possible. All there is to do, is be ready for what is coming next.

GENEROUS WITH YOU

The icon I chose this week is a scrapbook Mum made of her bridal shower and wedding cards. She carefully glued cards, letters, copies of invitations, and RSVPs into what I see as a collection of love. These were her people. Some I know, some I was named after, and some I will never know, but all are part of a story suggesting she honored the generosity of her tribe within this keepsake.

This brings me back to resetting, and why the notion has been playing through my mind and heart this week. I recently disappointed a dear friend, after making plans a month in advance that ensured we would have enough time together to connect and unwind. I cancelled at the last minute.

I was in anguish to give her that news. I truly regretted not being able to keep my commitment and knew it would be hard to relay. It felt like I should run and hide for a while, until her hurt was lessened; Then maybe I could reach out again when it felt more comfortable.

This did not seem like the most generous thing to do. In fact, it felt rather cowardly. I was quite certain in that moment what I could not do: Act like it did not happen. But what would I do instead?

I made a mistake, misread the play, and lost a scoring opportunity. I will accept my error bravely, listening for a gutsy teammate to call out, "Reset!"

Then this week held the classic commotion of arguing with an adult child—never a pleasant thing. For the most part, I attempt to stay out of their business, giving encouragement when I can and looking for chances to transition into that sweet friendship zone. This week, when a clash of opinions became 'the hill to die on', I was the one disappointed in how quickly our trust eroded, breaking communication lines and emotional connection. When a difficult discussion ends without resolution, how does the relationship move forward?

Blaming and hurt rolls off our tongue, we lose momentum, and get ready to grudge, before remembering that some things do not have a resolution. Reset.

Reset is forgiveness, in a way that is not begged for, not taken for granted, and not forgotten as possible.

May we all reset for ourselves and for each other, and reset generously!

Week Forty-Seven

GENEROSITY'S LAST BREATH

My topic of generosity started with a critical look at balance and how the most generous thing I can do for myself is to work on creating it. Because I have so often swung dramatically from one side to the other, my goal was to find a way to moderate how far my pendulum would go before realizing a correction is needed, or—to put it a different way—to stop burning out.

So, for this week, "Generosity with US", I have a chance to reflect on how generosity flows toward my circle of connections. I am picking up the theme of balance, hopefully to further my grasp on this delicate concept.

It has been hard connecting Mum to this topic of generosity. Why, you ask? I know this does not come as a surprise, but she was an imperfect woman. Her faults do not disappear simply because she vacated her earthly life quicker than expected. Dying young does not automatically make someone beyond reproach.

It is heartbreaking to admit, but I would not describe Mum as generous, at least not in the way that is starting to matter most to me.

Yes, she stayed up late sewing Halloween costumes for me and my brother and got up early to bake biscuits Sunday morning.

Yes, she drove us to every sporting event, piano recital, science fair, and social excursion we had half a mind to pursue, dropping us off with dollars in our hands to spend how we chose.

Yes, she brokered my living arrangements for college, mediated with border guards trying to deny me access to the U.S., and sold raffle tickets to everyone who passed through her office so I could be crowned Miss Lumberjack—but I do not remember ever hearing her say, "I love you".

> The trouble is, you think you have TIME.
> ~ Buddha

Twenty-two years of being my mum, and I have no recollection of that phrase coming out of her mouth. I joked about the only signs of actual love between us was when I pounced on her like a puppy, licking her face, and she returned the favor by pinching my bottom. I assume because I always felt like she loved me, the words did not seem to be missing.

For an icon this week, I am using a memory from the day Mum took her last breath. Trying to remember her speaking affectionate words transports me to a quiet bedside, where we watched her body shut down. A stubborn tumor outsmarted brain surgery, aggressive drugs, and multiple prayers, and caused her to slip in and out of consciousness. In the days leading up to this, she intuitively made a point to speak individually to each family member. I have no idea what she wanted to say to her austere parents, her loyal twin sister, her tender brother, her rekindled husband, or her steadfast son, but she kept asking, so people kept coming to her side… while I waited to be next.

I dreaded it. From the onset of her diagnosis I was in fervent denial that she was sick—weak. How could she be? She was the strongest, most capable and intelligent woman I knew. I supported her bald-headed, hospital-gowned, IV-tubed declaration of complete healing, which kept a smile on her face and a laugh in her heart. She would get better!

But *my* talk never happened. Before I had a chance to sit and be guided by her one final time *(perhaps the only time I may have welcomed her advising)*, the swelling on her brain had become too great for her to open her eyes or speak. She would occasionally squeeze my hand, showing she was still somewhere in there. Once the flurry of hospital workers making her comfortable and close friends saying good-bye had gone home, we finally had our moment to sit alone. All she could do by then was raise her finger in the air, slowly waving it back and forth as if she was making a point.

Yes, Mum, I hear you.

Yes, Mum, I know.

Yes, Mum, we are alright.

Okay, Mum, rest now.

If it had not yet occurred to me that this cancer was going to kill her, it flooded me with full force at that moment. I felt she could not go just yet, there being much left unsaid and much more left unlived, but I needed to somehow make this easier for her, so—I put on a brave face, lowered my head, and told God it was okay take her.

I sobbed in anger. I did not know this lady well enough yet. I did not have the chance to call her a friend. I had not shown enough appreciation for the things she said and did to help me become a decent adult. I felt jilted at losing my chance to say how sorry I was for any mean looks I gave her, for my frustrated tone when she wanted to convey something to me, and for being downright unpleasant every morning.

As my tears dried, and Mum's hand rested down along her side again, peace came over me. She was sleeping.

Resting.

She was tired. She fought cancer hard and worked immeasurably hard in her short forty-seven years of life.

Sleep is good.

Dad and brother joined me in her room. We were talking quietly to each other, listening to Mum's raspy breaths through the oxygen tube feeding her dying brain.

Sitting.

Waiting.

Worrying.

Reminiscing.

Laughing.

Without an obvious signal, the room shifted. It seemed to tilt on an angle in strange and gentle, warming waves. I suddenly felt like someone was watching us from above, listening to our conversation and looking at our faces with deep love. When I became aware of what I was sensing, my attention quickly snapped to Mum's chest, which had stopped rising and falling, her breath no longer audible.

Gone

I ran to the nurse's station to tell them she had stopped breathing. They followed calmly and confirmed—her lungs had quit. I called out to my aunt, who responded, "Oh no, not yet. So soon? So soon..." I could not understand why a medical team was not rushing in with carts and machines, like seen on TV—why no one was trying to save her life, make her breathe again. Then a nurse took her hand, looked compassionately at her puffy, pale face and said, "Well, dear. That's a beautiful way to go."

Breath Gone

Life Gone

GENEROSITY WITH US

This is why these fifty-two weeks have been so vital. I have not been trying to recreate my mum's life or become her. I want to take the things she modelled in the short time I had to know her and use them to benefit the ones I have the privilege to love. I do not want to be at the end of my time without my children hearing a permanent soundbite of my voice on repeat: *I love you. I am proud of you.*

I want to keep trying to connect with my family, even when the prickly thorns of personality come out. I want to keep extending olive branches, even though it feels uncomfortable or vulnerable. I will continue trying to be gracious enough to handle my children's youthful barbs, and brave enough to listen to them voicing truth.

I think I have given to my family as much as Mum did, in terms of my time, money, and creativity, in order to help them chase what they love. But I have also enhanced what she modelled by coaching their sports, chaperoning their field trips, and chasing them down for conversations. I did this to engage with them all I could, every chance I could, AND make myself emotionally available for whatever relationship they might seek from me.

My parenting has not always felt balanced. It has been riddled with upheavals and hurdles, stumbles and restarts. There have been critics and adversaries sabotaging it along the way. I have swayed dramatically to achieve any semblance of middle ground, which continues to allude and tease—if it even exists. Maybe equilibrium in parenting cannot truly exist.

Perhaps it is better to release this notion of holding firm to a steady line and instead absorb the shifting waves as they swell and recede, seeing the beauty and fun in an ocean of change. As more family members are added to our brood, and more friends become dear to my heart, my scope gets larger, my sights go further, and I see the end of the tunnel that will beckon us all one day. But before that last breath, I must generously do these few things Mum was not fully able to achieve:

Accept US.

Affirm US.

Adore US… Unashamedly.

You are ALL my truest loves, and will always be, in this life and after.

Week Forty-Eight

GIVE IT AWAY, GIVE IT AWAY, GIVE IT AWAY, GIVE IT AWAY NOW

Generosity. For THEM.

Where to begin?

I recently visited my oldest aunt, who has succumbed to the limitations of an aging brain, resulting in her no longer recognizing my face. The last time I saw her, several months ago, she called me by Mum's name, which pleased me beyond words.

It was initially upsetting to see her declining health. I sympathetically looked at her weakened body and sunken cheek bones, her brow furrowed as she uncomfortably shifted her legs while continuing to sleep the afternoon away. As I sat there in the quiet of her room, gazing upon her and recalling the bits of life where our paths had intersected, I felt compelled to be happy for her.

Last week, I described the sacred moment of Mum passing onto whatever follows one's last breath on earth. This week is not going to be another story about watching loved ones pass on, even though it is likely the last time I will see my aunt earth-side.

This week is very much about recognizing a good life. I feel fortunate to have had a large extended family growing up, who gathered many times throughout the year. I would have weekend sleepovers with my cousins, and we all went camping together in the summer. There were no shortages of positive interactions with my oldest aunt and the rest of my big family, but here are my top three dearest memories of this sweetheart:

She and my uncle adopted their three children. In my eyes, it takes a special kind of person to adopt. I looked at them with awe, even as a child.

Because I did not have a mother to help me with childcare, Aunty generously came to babysit my first child, while I worked two jobs and ex went on 'vacation' from his unemployment.

I received a gift from her on a random occasion. She thought of me when seeing a white T-shirt nightgown sporting a swirling, rainbow-colored, musical staff. The fancy black font read:

Without Music
Life would be a Mistake
~ Friedrich Neitzsche

Indeed.

She and I both shared a love for singing, as did most of her other siblings, especially my father. Singing was ingrained in my young heart, as I both listened and performed intently when given the opportunity at church, school, or family functions. Music was always welcome. Well, maybe not in grade two, in Mrs. M's class. She specifically asked my parents to discourage me from constantly volunteering solos at 'show and tell' time. Aunty would never have stopped any of my songs!

Much history and wisdom were gleaned from the times I had her close, talking about things Mum and I never had the chance to, and listening to her explain why she chose my uncle over any other suitor. It was the life she wanted. She chose it.

Aunty told me it was not always easy being a minister's wife. They moved often, living frugally. They had tricky family moments like all normal families do, but with the added pressure of a parish audience judging every decision. Still—she smiled, and loved, and told funny stories in dramatic voices, giving me every reason to believe I was probably her favorite niece.

It was these thoughts that started to shift my focus from the shell of the woman I saw laying in that bed, to thoughts of the life she lived and the people she loved.

My cousin messaged me after the visit to share how her heart was breaking to see her helpless mother, which I completely understood. However, I also could not help but count the number of years she'd had with her mom, the amount alone a blessing, and then admit how many wishes I have whispered in vain to have been a witness to Mum growing old, using up her entire life, until she had no more to live.

But just living your life up does not seem to fit what was happening to Aunty. It looked to me like she had *loved* her life out.

She had given it all—loved through it all.

GENEROSITY WITH THEM

My eyes were opening to a different perspective, seeing more than her outside appearance. I saw her heart and felt her spirit. She had soared among the greatest, when it came to taking care of the world. So, it seemed logical that I could not be the only person she touched by the huge heart still beating under her now belabored chest. I am certain many others were blessed by her wit, humility, and her gracious ability to put people at ease. One of the coolest things about my aunt was that she was married three times, after my uncle and her second husband died earlier than expected. She never gave up on love!

For the couple minutes she woke while I visited, she could not verbalize her needs, nor did she seem to comprehend my words. But amid the scrambled messages her brain was attempting to decode, she clearly recognized one thing: LOVE

When I said, *"I love you—we all love you very much."* she smiled. A momentary release of stress came from her creased brow, then she closed her eyes to rest some more.

I came home that night and immediately told my girls to not feel sorry for me when I am no longer able to function, and to not let it break their hearts. The clever retort I got was, "We will just pull the plug, Mama." I am used to their overwhelming sensitivity, just as they are used to me talking about how they ought to cope when I die. It is all very therapeutic for us... I think.

I am also thinking that living generously, in a global sense, has something to do with loving yourself completely out. Because I have had many weeks focused on balancing the demands and desires of life, I am not suggesting that being generous with a larger community means we must sacrifice our sanity or health to say yes to everything and care for everyone. I think generosity stems from more than a quantity of public-minded good deeds. It is worth revisiting that great Maya Angelou quote—as I believe she was describing this concept: "I've learned that people will forget what you SAID, people will forget what you DID, but people will never forget how you made them FEEL."

I get so wrapped up in overthinking the most sensitive thing to say or figuring out the perfect thing to do. Perhaps this is a waste of energy, chasing phantoms that lack impact. Maybe all I need to offer people is a present moment, accompanying them even for a brief period, without specific words or deeds lining up—simply giving them time and love. Currently, I would like to be a better aunt, a better neighbor, a better co-worker, a better steward of resources available within my privileged birthright of North American descendance.

My icon for this week is one of Mum's most prized scarves: A silk, watercolor inspired, bird-motif scarf. She wore many scarves and was quite skilled at creatively tying them for various outfits. She attended a scarf-training session, where she learned many techniques and happily shared those with others. *I guess trying to look like her was met with generosity, but don't try to COOK like her!* This scarf reminds me of our brief and precious lives. We flit, we float, we fly.

I pray Aunty soon flies. I ended my visit by singing some old tunes for her. As the songs came pouring out of my heart, I felt she was ready to flex her well-matured wings, woven from years of loving with every piece of her heart.

That will be how I remember her. She is what love looks like after a lifetime of generously giving it away. In this light, she could not have been more beautiful.

This is the kind of legacy I would like to leave in the world. The kind where family, friends, and strangers alike can recount a moment of magic, where it was nothing I SAID, nothing I DID, and yet it FELT like everything.

I plan to use up every last ounce of love in me, and if the cost means lying quietly asleep to wait for the day of my last exhale, it is the life I want.

I choose it.

AJ

When are you stingy with yourself? When are you stingy with others?

What characteristics are most needed by people in our world?

What is stopping US from being more like that?

CHAPTER THIRTEEN

CREATIVITY

You can't use up creativity.
The more you use, the more you have.
~ Maya Angelou

Week Forty-Nine

A WORK IN PROGRESS

This is the beginning of my last topic!

Finally, here it is: CREATIVITY!

I have saved, what I anticipate being, the best for last. Why? Because creativity is so amazing! Everyone has it in one form or another. Some make it very public, while others keep it under wraps and express it privately. Creativity is so intriguing. Here is a fun little riddle for it:

What is started, but never finished?

Used, but never old?

Ignited with sparks, but invisible?

Kids exude it, while adults avoid it?

Rattle that one off at your next office party. Creativity is going to be a powerhouse in my fifty-two-week estimation, and at the risk of giving too much away, it has the potential to play a key role in assuring physical vitality and emotional longevity.

But before we get into all of that, let's start things off with—you guessed it—a story.

Most of you will not know this about me, but I am deathly afraid of getting my hair cut. Clearly not my Mum's daughter when it comes to hair upkeep, since she adhered to a meticulous schedule of salon appointments to maintain her gorgeous hair. Even after my phase of wanting to imitate her hair flair had passed, our likeness remained noticeable, as proven in this photo for my icon of the week.

Now—back to my fear. Obviously, haircuts are somewhat necessary, particularly if a certain business or fashion appearance is required to secure employment, but also to keep your hair growing healthy—or so says Google. Multiple hair truths are only a tap or a click away, which is where I found this gem: Tonsurephobia!

Tonsure is Greek for 'to cut'. People suffering from tonsurephobia have an aversion to sharp, pointy objects being too close to their ears and skull, the onset typically occurring in childhood during a first haircut experience with a pair of scary shears… or shortly after watching the movie, Edward Scissorhands.

I can see how this fear could unfold for sweet, little eyes, especially when a plastic cloak is placed over the client, in the event they get nicked and spring a leak!

As far as I know, I had positive experiences in my childhood with haircuts, and I am not afraid of scissors, or any other hairstyling instrument. I bravely sported a variety of styles growing up—short, long, curly, straight, and everything else in between.

So why does it bother me now? The article I read about tonsurephobia, said that one of the ways to get over it as an adult, besides therapy, is to simply go do it.

HAH! *Bite the bullet, Princess, and deal with it!*

This is the advice!?

Alrighty then—sounds like a challenge I will accept.

I decide to take the matter into own hands *(not literally, like Week Twenty-One where I shaved my head bald)*, but I resolved to do this haircut thing. Soon.

Very, very, soon-ish.

After several weeks of procrastination, an undeniable opportunity approached.

I was running late for a wedding reception. I thought, *Sure would be nice to have someone else do-up my hair—fast and pretty—and I could get a cut while I was at it.* This sounded reasonable, but with no plan and no appointment, my options were limited.

I often complain about the price I pay for a haircut I detest *(which is unfortunately all of them)*, so I thought some more.

Why not just go to a walk-in salon? That way, when I end up wearing a hat and ponytail for three months after, it will have only cost me $16. 99 + tax.

Yes! *That is a good idea.* Fear is taking the back seat today!

To build my resolve, I stated aloud how I trusted the universe to guide me to a safe stylist, who would magnificently craft a masterpiece upon my head. I drove to the strip mall two minutes from home with a giant grin upon my face and roaring with confidence.

She had a melodious name and her hair was long and shiny. Her warm smile met me as I entered the salon. She was obviously the answer to my universal decree, so I happily sat down. I envisioned the matte cape wrapping around me as a protective shield from anything bad happening in that chair, and without hesitation, I asked her to cut layers into my long, straight mane.

She took good care with the lengths, which was a perfect first impression, so I slowly slipped into a coma-like state, while she continued to whittle her scissors along my split strands.

La-dah-dee-dah-dah… I was in the zone. Cool and vibin' with the universe. I began to daydream about completing the look. My outfit, make-up, shoes—and a fabulous hairdo.

Like this one I found on Google:

This is fab hair...   *Or this REALLY fab hair!*

My first hint of a there being a slight problem with achieving the glamourous hair vision pictured above, was the severe lack of hair products or tools at her station.

The second was the fact that walk-in salons do not include a wash, meaning my hair would contain yesterday's natural oils and such, and unless a product was used to fluff it right up—well—see first hint above.

A third clue was noticing that after she managed to hunt down a curling iron, the cord would not reach fully, so she turned my chair away from the mirror. *Blind faith now, baby*. Nothing else to do but wait for the universe to have my back.

The fourth and final tip-off was a burning, chemical smell from whatever bottled substance was being applied before she curled each section of hair. I managed an investigative glance at this bottle, which she noticed me do, and volunteered that it was a heat protector. Whew! *Such a relief, because something smelled very hot!*

When I was spun back around, and the 'hairspray' bottle was set down with its label toward me… ALL the evidence added up too late in my terror-filled brain.

Apparently, I described my hair vision to look like a slimy, partially grey version of Shirley Temple.

I did not know whether to scream or cry. She asked to spray it some more so it would hold—I politely declined.

I paid *(extra, in fact)* for the styling. I tipped. Then thanked her *(because I am Canadian)* and ran.

On the drive home, I assured myself that I could tease this out. Loosen it a bit to make it work, slap on some make-up and all would be well. The fact that it felt crunchy when I reluctantly placed my hand up to survey the damage, was just a technicality.

Daughter, who was playing sweet notes at home on the piano, stared in horror when I walked through the door. But before she could utter a potentially snarky teenager comment, another declaration made its way through my lips: *The universe must hate me!*

There.

I said it.

I was thinking it, and certainly feeling it, so I tossed it out there to be properly heard.

Daughter empathized but confirmed—there was no teasing out for this 'hairdo'. She suggested a high pressurized washer wand or running through a carwash, but lucky for me *(now running even later for the reception)*, a regular showerhead did the trick.

As I hurried out the door, I began to regret my last proclamation. It did sound very negative and not a message I would want seeping into my daughter's recall. Time for a perspective shift.

CREATIVITY WITH ME

If I believe it is possible to continually move toward a better version of myself, sometimes without knowing it, then I must trust the same thing is happening for others.

Newsflash:

"The universe is taking care of everyone else, too."

Maybe the hairstylist needed a chance to practice on a safe client.

Maybe the chat we had about parenting complex kids encouraged both of us, as we shared what love looks like in bumpy relationships.

Maybe creating a new standard for my outward appearance is in order, one that avoids drawing upon the power of the universe to make *(or break)* moments.

After all, I create my reality. I create how the image staring back from the mirror is defined. I create who I am willing to let myself continue to be, and who I am willing to blame when I do not get what I want. *My apologies, universe.*

If I thought creativity was going to be about how fancy I can paint a riverscape *(which I can't)*, or how artistically I might arrange the patio furniture *(also unattainable)*, then I have missed a whole other side to what creativity has to offer ME.

This creativity is a life-art—an artistry of moments—a creation for the soul.

A hairdo does not define ME. It starts growing and changing into something different immediately after it is complete. Whether I think my hair is favorable or not, it transforms each time it is deemed complete, no matter how much hairspray is applied.

Transformation—progressing toward the person I choose to be, is requiring so much love—and patience— and lots and lots of creativity. It feels so powerful to believe I will never stop growing.

This is not how I end.

I get to keep creating ME.

Choose a Final ICON for Creativity:

LAST UPDATE:

January–April 2017

Winter has been mild this year. Celebrating Christmas with only two out of five kids was tough. I love to spoil them with presents and food and feel disappointed when not able.

Hubby and I are back on track, taking time to getaway and remember who we were before grandparenting became the best and hardest thing we ever did. We each forget to remember that the other is a pretty good person, and if we just talk about stuff, it usually feels better. Simple. Beautiful. I am a lucky gal.

Hubby is also supporting me through a delicate and personal incident that happened before we met. Through the process of my writing, I have mustered the courage to speak up about this violation and have begun the steps necessary to bring a resolution to this hurtful event. Because it is currently under investigation, I cannot discuss it in public. I gently, but firmly told myself it would be safe to relive and report this terrifying and humiliating experience if it meant protecting others. I know now, even as I wait for more information to be shared, this was the right thing for me to do. I am facing my fear and pain, and replacing it with honor and wisdom—for myself, my voice, and my story. It is not about punishing someone who has done me wrong. That, I leave in the hands of a higher power. This is for me. I need to know that I can tell my truth and be okay. Darkness says keep quiet, but I live in the light—and light shines.

Mad Marvin has mysteriously disappeared off the face of the planet, again. Rumor mill has him pegged hiding out somewhere in Southeast Asia...

There is other news through the grapevine. Another grandchild is on the way, but not from older son, who is in a committed relationship abroad, or the younger sister who is courting a soccer scholarship with a private university. No.

It isn't our younger son who has been living with a girlfriend after the wheels came off the reconciliation bus with his biological mother, yet he still will not come home.

It is my little runaway. A while ago, when he was 15 and in jail, he had told me I was going to be a grandma. He was so proud to think of himself as a father. He gushed out promises of how he would take care of that baby better than he had been raised. Meanwhile, I did the math and assured him that, if there was to be a baby, it was not possible for it to be his.

Four years later, he is now getting his shot. I have been denied meeting his girlfriend, not surprisingly, but sister stays connected under the condition that she keep their conversations private. When does this division end?

In these moments, the most difficult thing for me to do is forgive myself for the pain I allowed them to experience because I stayed with their father. They were born innocent and sweet, with a sincere desire to do the right thing, but quickly learned there was no safety for them in a house of war. Yes, I still work through guilt and shame, recalling my worst parenting moments as though they were yesterday.

One story I promised to get back to in Week Fourteen, but have not brought myself to write about, was earlier in the relationship when the violence was just beginning. I had done something worthy of wrath; A scratch on the white fridge door was immediately noticed and instead of fessing up to the crime, I gave the oldest toddler up as a potential scapegoat. I expected my ex to go easy on our little son due to his age, and thereby negating any consequence for this misdemeanor.

This was not the case. To my surprise, he spanked my boy who did not understand why, while I wailed for his mercy, yet did not fess up to receive my own punishment. That never happened again. I crawled out of that lowest mothering moment to take as much blame and responsibility for things going wrong as possible. I took strikes for them, did penance for them, as hearing them cry would remind me of the one time I had caused it.

I earnestly seek chances to replace tough memories with brighter encounters, which have been too few for my liking. I have one photo of my grown kids together, taken last summer on that glorious reunion day. My heart hopes for another day like it before I leave this earth.

Love hear my prayer!

Week Fifty

DO YOU GET CREATIVE?

FIFTY WEEKS! *Are ya kiddin' me?*

I will hold off on celebrating this current milestone for the bigger one coming up… even though I am certainly proud to have made it this far! And YOU should be too—so let's stop and give ourselves a warm hug—I mean it! Close your eyes. Squeeze and breathe. This chapter can wait.

Alright, picking up on where we left creativity last, the icon I chose to suit this fifty-week milestone is a crochet pattern Mum used to create little dresses for all the baby girls in our church.

She would wrap this dainty item in a box with fancy paper and frilly bows, the outside appearance just as important as what was inside, then smile as she handed over the goods, her head tilted down slightly, not wanting the person receiving her gift to think she was proud of her accomplished work.

Since she gave all the dresses away, I do not have a sample to show. But I do have two hands, some yarn that looks like it might work, and a brain that can read a pattern. So, I have dared myself to create one of these dresses for my baby grand-daughter before she turns 1. That is four months from now. Lots of time, right?

Hah! Turns out, real crocheting is almost as terrifying for me as going to the hairdresser.

The pattern is intimidating, using words like 'essential', and 'perfect result'. Perhaps the address included on the back of the pattern for overwhelmed crafters will give the right advice, should I need it.

I could not find a print date on the pattern but judging from this little gal's white sock/shoe combo, I am guessing the origin to be sometime in the late 60s to early 70s. Certainly, Emu Wools Ltd of London, England is still located at 15 Woodstock Street—NOPE. Google says Emu dissolved in 1997, so there is no help on the way from them!

My question is this: Will the practice of making this item truly be about creativity or just trying to stay sane? Hopefully four months is long enough to get my clunky fingers moving. In the meantime, to deconstruct what "Creativity with YOU" is all about, I have a little story to get things rollin'...

257

Right before Mum found out she was sick, she attended my first college play, where I was cast as a dual character: A barmy Court Guard in Act I, and a drunken Old Man in Act II. My theatrical roles historically consisted of playing males, not only because more characters are written for men, but because I have a deeper and raspier voice than most ladies—*and ever-so-slightly masculine, squared off shoulders.*

I have never played the role of a young, pretty ingénue, who gets swept away by her prince to a blissful ever after. I was a bit envious of the girls that were cast for their 'princess-like' qualities, but so what? It was still inexplicably rewarding to put on a costume, transform into an alternate person, and lose myself for a while.

Mum said hello to me in the ladies dressing room before the performance. I am not sure it was an intentional hello, or if she was just looking for a washroom, but she heard me sneeze from around a wall of lockers, cleared her throat, and announced she could "recognize that sneeze anywhere." Her voice and face were a comfort to my jittery, opening-night nerves, but I did my best to act like I was completely calm and confident. I tossed her a goofy grin through my stage makeup, anticipating some form of encouragement from my steady ma.

Perhaps because she did not know any customary greetings for actors about to take stage, or because she was not happy to be there, I did not hear "break a leg" or receive a bouquet of flowers from her that night. She looked uncomfortable, like she was preparing for an unpleasant evening, and quietly exited while I finished getting ready.

Mum did not get my creativity, which felt very much like rejection.

Yes, a change of heart during her illness did help me resolve the mostly negative view she emanated for the passions I pursued *(recap if you need in Week Twenty-Five)*, but I still lived more of my life *(like, 99 percent more)* with the thought that she did not understand me, and worse, did not approve.

Now Dad on the other hand—HE got me. We shared probably hundreds of performances, ranging from small family gatherings to large formal audiences. Road trips to and from the various venues, were perfect chances to laugh about directors, rehearse lines, warm up our vocal cords with goofy exercises, and relish the time spent enjoying what made us happy.

Although I loved getting this kind of affirmation from my father, a part of me always watched jealously for Mum's eyes to see me and shine with delight.

Now—I am thinking it, so will just say it and it is going to sound bad—but had she not taken ill, I might not have heard her praise. If she was not facing death, I may never have heard her appreciating my talents. And even though I have lived many hard years without her physical presence, I think it would have been much worse to live my entire life believing my creativity had disappointed her.

Guuulp. Brace yourself. Welcome to the creativity roller coaster ride.

CREATIVITY WITH YOU

So—I am *staring* at the crochet pattern.

The directions are intimidating.

The measurements are in Imperial.

The abbreviations are complex, with confusing repetitions.

My imagination conjures up wild visions of crocheting projects taking over the world. *Google also has an imagination…*

This is over my head!

I seem to recall Mum crocheting things while watching TV, holding a conversation, or playing cards *(maybe even while she weeded the potato plants)*, the crochet hook a natural extension of her fingers, yarn slipping gracefully through her nimble and obedient hands.

My hands? HAH! They are engrossed with distractions: Over-looping threads, rogue pattern gaps that rebel against the chain, chain, chain. My fingers swing hopeful at the intended target and miss— sometimes with considerable force—coming up fast and short, and close to gouging out my eyes with the hook.

Laaaawd, have mercy! This creativity could be my demise.

It does not compute.

It is scary.

I want to back away slowly, before anyone reads this post, and take myself off the 'hook' and never think of this pattern again.

I am not having a good time and am NOT 'getting it'.

And then the penny drops. *Ooooohh...*

Of course, I don't *get it*. This is not *my* creativity. It is hers.

I am guessing Mum felt the same way about witnessing my nonsensical performances as I feel about crocheting this intricate pattern. Our creativity takes on different forms of expression.

How could Mum's creativity have been concealed in my mind for so long? I have already shown examples of it in some of my weekly icons. Her hobbies—gardening, crafts, cooking—and even her professional dealings were drenched in artistic flare and imagination. She could see beyond a sapling in a pot, and feel the shade of its full, mature branches. Her meals were intentionally colorful, with complimentary textures and diverse flavors that came from a huge stock of herbs and spices.

She invested in her art. Honed her craft with trial and error. Shared the fruits of her efforts with those around her *(recipes being the exception)*.

Wow.

If Mum can surprise me after twenty-six years of being gone, I would do well to believe YOU will surprise me with YOUR creativity.

May I have the strength of sight to see it.

Week Fifty-One

MANURE AND MIRACLES

Week Fifty-One—the continuation of my very LAST topic, creativity. It was supposed to be lighthearted and fun—reminiscent of sweet and not-so-sweet moments from life lessons learned during difficult days.

During this time, I have reflected, pro-ooooo-cessed, articulated, and changed *(really, really changed)*, healing bits of my core that seemed unreachable until I was determined to get at them, get through them, and give LOVE permission to gently smooth those painful scars away.

Has this scar-work been effective? Do I now exhibit the kind of freedom and attention that have become the crux of my sojourn? Or am I simply clanging away at my gong, busy with my 'busy', singing like a free bird, but still stuck inside a cage of fear, worry, guilt, anger, and other such sorted manure.

Yup, we are about to get into the mess. When stuck in a cage, manure can pile up rather quickly. If you have not already guessed, the US of my focus this week is going to be a bit stinky.

Alright… a lot stinky.

Surprise, AJ! Life can still turn to 'hooey' after fifty-one weeks of articulate work. I am wondering if my spirit is actually free.

Why? Why would I allow any type of confinement to still exist within me after breaking out into glorious freedom? I should want nothing more than to burn any structure or remnant of that ratchet, gnarly, internal prison… yet a cage structure remains.

- Maybe cages are a permanent construct for finite lives, holding immature souls together until they gain enough wisdom to stand confidently in who they are meant to become.
- Perhaps cages are teachers of how to overcome an obstacle, how to defeat darkness while learning about grace, about unconquerable love, and infallible hope.
- Perhaps a cage structure will always remain, but the door is under the captives' control.

If that last point were true, what would stop me from noticing my power to access the cage-door?

Emotions?

Tunnel Vision?

Lack of Imagination?

Whatever limited perspective kept me from seeing an exit, I refused to budge toward insight for years.

My liberty came with a price tag. I think tough choices are never free, but if the cost of staying confined means losing your life—is there really a choice?

I gratefully rejoice in the hard-fought freedom warranted to me and my children, yet I have watched parts of me walk back into that prison, effortlessly. It is a familiar place, predictable, and holds fond memories of my kids growing up, but (*oh wow*) the odor is stifling!

Arguably, the best icon I can use from Mum's dwindling basket of treasures that started this whole experience, is her favorite perfume. Now, I was never a fan of this scent, finding it very powerful, which is probably why she liked it. The thought of applying the perfume to my skin makes me a bit nauseated (*sorry, Mum*), so I will take a small whiff each morning, hoping it helps neutralize the cage-odor offending my senses currently.

CREATIVITY WITH US

The stinky pile I am sitting on now started in my first marriage. But there is more than a pile. This mountain of nonsense could be divided and categorized into an entire library.

In no particular order, here are the Top Three Factors that ultimately led me to find and then escape through that available cage door:

1. I believed I would die; By his hand, or by my own decision to stop breathing.

I am still alive, and doing pretty well, so I guess facing a life or death outcome was an effective behaviour modifier.

2. The kids witnessed a traumatic event unfold between me and their father, so I could no longer convince myself the violence was happening in secret.

The kids are now witnessing a relationship built on laughter, respect, tricky conversations, playfulness, differences of opinion, acceptance, and 'true love conquers all'—even in long seasons of storms. Perfect imperfections. And it is so, so good. Hubby gets most of the credit here, but taking a second chance on love with him, is my favorite decision in the last ten years.

So far, no manure piling up here. Factor #2 just takes some intention and awareness to maintain a happy, calm home environment. Which leaves Factor #3 ...

3. Wanting to model real love to my kids, maybe saving them from being ill-treated, or from abusing anyone else.

This is where the colossal caa-caa breeds pain so deep into my heart that I think I know how it would feel to be defibrillated while conscious. Seeing my children suffer as they try to reconcile a skewed sense of right, transform a twisted view on love, and redefine their Divine, is almost impossible to bear as the mom who did not understand the harm sooner.

It was the hardest corner to turn, and finally admit: This family, this situation, these kids having two (*unhealthy*) parents care for them, was more destructive to their development than having one parent struggling for a different life.

Lesson learned.

Each of my kids are stretching independent wings, wrestling their giants—sometimes within socially acceptable expressions consistent with new adulthood, like:

- Challenging authority
- Perceiving their safety as guaranteed
- Putting as much distance from home as possible

And sometimes they stretch *outside* of society and its norms with:

- Drug Use
- Premarital Pregnancy
- Homelessness
- Incarceration

Because these behaviors deviate from what society is comfortable talking about, the people connected to them are often judged to be failing. Living with these labels attached to the lives of my children, I have a VERY different viewpoint. While I would not say these choices are easy or healthy avenues, it is *their* road to travel. As their mom, and a person with some 'travelling' experience, I know certain roads hurt. Some scar.

Some routes are direct. Some take a lifetime.

Sometimes people get lost, going around and round, repeating the hurts over and over until finally grasping their bearings and recalculating a different route.

I promised to write a bit about the depression that gripped me for many months in the aftermath of first son who ran away. This was not a case of being near the manure pile, it was being buried deep under a bleak and raunchy emotional desolation. Light was not present here. My desire for living evaporated a little more every day.

Our wedding briefly outshone the darkness, but it returned thicker and heavier than before, and hubby was starting to worry. I stopped working. I stopped bathing. I shut off my phone and media, not caring who got disconnected. I sat like a rock on the porch each day, stoic and silent—maybe waiting to see his face—and each day more depressed when that did not happen. Hubby prompted me to seek medical care.

I went. I wanted to get better. I did not know how. If the answer did not include my boy back safe in his bed, the darkness should surely continue. It was not a quick journey back. There were lots of steps forward, then falling back further. If I had to describe depression in one easy word, it would be: HOPELESS. Sheer hopelessness for anything and everyone.

My hope is restored now, but it looks very different. This was my giant to wrestle, just as I know my children have their own.

"No fire?
No phoenix rising."

But these struggles are not deal breakers for me. I know Love is bigger than these challenges. The love for my children grew deeper when I forced myself to ask, *"What would I not be able to bear as their mother?"* Up to this point, the answer to that has been *"nothing"*. I would bear it all.

I have.

I do.

And have found a way to breathe in it, and *(as much as it hurts)* to laugh in it.

When I feel complete despair, I have even found a way… to hope in it.

So where is this AJ now? I cannot see her through the old, rusty bars she ran back into after learning her child has now adopted the enemy of our freedom— domestic violence.

When one child asks in earnest for feedback on whether they act like their father, afraid to become like him, it means they *are* already not like him! This reflection alone allows them the chance to become who they want to be—and become better. My reassuring arms can wrap around tight to confirm that *"this monster is not inside you, my dear."*

When another child abandons their previous fight against oppression, and instead becomes the oppressor—this is the smell of rotting cruelty, the odor of corrupted memories, the foulness of rejection, the stench of undisciplined power and manipulation, all piled up right where I left them, in a dark cage steaming with anguish and misery.

This child has now done what I feared would be among the hardest possibilities, personifying the violent and inhuman attributes of the devil I divorced. As the mother—the one who nursed, held, worried over, labored to guide, desperately sought out for countless days and sleepless nights while continuing to believe the best was possible—how do I love through this?

> Some of the greatest battles will be fought
> within the silent chambers of your own soul.
> ~ Ezra Taft Benson

My arms and words have long since been rejected. I cannot fight the beast holding my child.

I slip silently back. The darkness has waited.

Ignorantly walking toward a reeking cage, stinging tears disguise my senses.

I step through the door. Shame and guilt team up to cast tricks so convincing that I no longer see light… or have air. No breath—just death here.

The sobbing river from my eyes moves the pain. *Thank God for that.* With each tear, a prayer for strength, wisdom, patience, and protection from fiends that would swallow up my hard-fought joy, the sweat-soaked peace, and the fierce confidence found within love.

Always—it comes right back to love.

Big, big love.

Remembering—love will heal. Reminded—love will forgive. Thankful—love will make everything better.

Trusting, I wait here—for OUR miracle.

Week Fifty-Two!

CELEBRATE ALL TIMES

I would *like* to say this week feels EPIC, being the *last* week of my *last* topic, but epic seems almost anticlimactic. Especially since I do not want to STOP writing! I alluded to a potential prologue after my fifty-two weeks were complete, so have comforted myself that the writing will not stop entirely, meaning I have no reason to prolong this inevitable moment any further.

I hope this is proof *(if only to myself)* that with some patience, kindness, and generosity, this gal *(prone to leaving projects incomplete)* can and WILL finish anything she sets her mind to doing.

So, fellow fifty-two'ers… this is happening now! Here is *(BUP, BUP, BA-DAH)*: "Creativity with THEM".

I am fascinated how people in the world exude creativity. I think it exists in many areas of our lives, whether we are aware of it or not. I asked an old college mate, who has a dazzling abundance of creativity, to describe what being creative felt like:

Captain Thunderpants: "It feels like digesting, and then birthing a new, wonderful, weird brain baby."

Oooooh-kay! Google the Captain later to see more nuggets from his twirling tornado of genius. I need to get to work on my 'weird brain baby'!

Starting a topic quest by searching Google is not my default approach, but this time it proved quite helpful. Below is a list of characteristics that resonated for me when I thought about how creativity has shown up in my life.

CREATIVE PEOPLE ARE…

1. easily bored
2. risk takers
3. color outside the lines
4. think with their hearts
5. make lots of mistakes
6. hate the rules
7. work independently
8. change their mind a lot
9. have a reputation for eccentricity
10. dream big

Any of these fit for you? I think we should feel good about uncovering these traits, especially if it means something creative is about to happen.

I read this list a few more times and realized these attributes were not always viewed as positive. So, I changed the *title* of the list to:

QUALITIES DESCRIBING YOUR NEIGHBORS AND COLLEAGUES

This felt unsettling. Any previous encouragement I had, disappeared. I suddenly saw people as potential failures, if too many of these characteristics showed up during brief interactions.

So, I changed the title again to:

TOP TEN PROBLEMS WITH KIDS

This felt even worse, knowing I have been guilty of inadvertently robbing many children of their creative tendencies by seeing them as problems.

Yup... there is some work to do here, which means that it is story time.

A friend in grade one admonished me for coloring outside the lines AND using the flesh colored crayon on the skin portions of the barbies we were embellishing in her new coloring book. She let me know that I was not welcome to share her book until I promised to mend my coloring habits, and reform to her standards.

That stung! Here I was, completely absorbed in placing bright hues to stark, black-lined figures and watching them come to life with each stroke bursting through my fingers. My goal? To use every space available, filling up each blank, and saturating all possible voids with color. Glorious color. *Ahhh, deliciously simple!*

Then—from one 6-year-old to another—coloring 'outside the lines' is uniformly deemed intolerable.

Unacceptable.

Reform or relinquish your crayons!

Since I truly loved my friend *(and still do)*, I wanted to make her happy, as well as keep coloring in her book, so I promised to correct my wayward habits.

Peer to peer, parent to child, colleague to colleague, it seems we are in the business of annihilating creativity that does not fit our standards.

Don't believe me? Let me translate the original list to what I think happens to creative people showing their true colors:

1. Easily bored = ADHD. *There's a pill for that.*
2. Risk taker = Being careless and short sighted. *You end up broke or in the hospital.*
3. Coloring outside the lines = Messy and undisciplined. *Maybe joining the military could fix this.*

Shall I go on?

4. Think with their heart = Illogical. *That's a problem.*
5. Make lots of mistakes = Brain dead. *Another problem.*
6. Hate the rules = Defiant, disrespectful, or rude. *Really big problem…*

We live in a society that acknowledges isolated strengths of creative people. If we can achieve rock-star status and draw crowds of fans to admire us for certain moments of time, then it is acceptable. I personally sought that status for years, hoping to stumble across the elusive break necessary to bring my creativity to an ultimate level. Not to be.

In its place, I have the experience of travelling down streets I may never have gone if I were not chasing a dream. Multiple rejections instilled courage when hopeful roads led to dead ends. I have learned to navigate sharp corners, gained faith to point myself in any direction, and still *(somehow)* always found my way home.

It seems in this world of 'mold fitters', it is only acceptable to talk about breaking molds, and stepping out of the box, if it is a trendy topic, or a good financial living can be made from it. There seems to be very little room for recognizing creativity just for what it is: A different process, a shift in perspective, an alternate focus on details that 'the mold' misses.

What if every time someone expressed a difference of opinion, thought, or belief, we celebrated it like bravery and marveled at the direction leading to that destination? It might eliminate some of the pity, shame, or judgement that usually accompanies diverse expressions.

What if our sports heroes, musicians, artists, and top achievers in any discipline were given intrinsically motivated rewards, instead of financial gains? Would they all stop trying to be awesome? I doubt it. I would not trade the years I spent honing my craft, even though very little financial benefits were gained.

During my current career, I have managed to utilize many of my creative skills, even though it makes me stand out as a bit odd. I am not the cookie-cutter version one might expect for a cop. Creativity offers me something fresh each day. It offers freedom. It fuels my love for life and urges my heart to care for others, which overrides my compulsion to maintain a mold.

When I was in training, one instructor said: "Wipe that grin off your face because it will get you in trouble out there." Thirteen years later, I am glad I did not quit expressing who I am. I can safely say that my smile 'saved my bacon' many times, helping conflicts ease or anxieties to decrease.

No rock-star wage. No cameras feeding my ego. No stage to perform my good works. Just a girl doing her job.

That is all of us.

I love seeing one of our office custodians walking to work in his oxfords, trench coat and carrying an attaché case; Doing his thing, like a Pro.

The friendliest service I got this week was from a middle-aged woman serving coffee at a diner, her rotted front teeth looking like she had seen rough days, but her smiling face and eyes told another story. I would say she is rocking it.

Parents who offers unconditional encouragement and support for their child's success, blind to comparison and void of pressure. Those folks inspire me.

A mum who quietly steps outside the lines of her surroundings to claim her own style, boldly wearing hats like this:

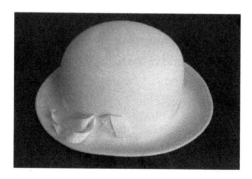

She wore it well.

These are the kind of people who shine in my eyes. I hope they keep radiating and are never dulled by what others believe they are supposed to look like, are supposed to do, or are supposed to think.

I want to value the creativity people share within our world, even when hurtful experiences or harsh exposures to difficult things in life almost extinguish them. I admire the ones who can take the faintest glowing ember left after a devastating blow and fan their fire big enough to take that next step toward home.

And with that, may creativity always lead us home.

AJ

If you hear a voice within you say, "You cannot paint", then by all means paint, and that voice will be silenced.
~ Vincent Van Gogh

What is that *voice* saying you cannot do?

Conditions for creativity are to be puzzled;
to concentrate; to accept conflict and tension;
to be born every day; to feel a sense of self.
~Erich Fromm

How does conflict and tension show up on the road to your dreams?

Knowing creative conflict is normal,
how does this change your view on what is success?

Wrapping Up the Weeks

I do not sit down at my desk to put into verse something that is already clear
in my mind. If it were clear in my mind, I should have no incentive or need to
write about it. We do not write in order to be understood;
we write in order to understand.
~ C. S. Lewis

PART ONE

Well, well, well... There is much to wrap up! The growth and healing that has
transpired during this adventure will be hard to capture in 1300 words or less.
I simply must have two parts to cover it all. It will be my pleasure to attempt
dissecting all the goodness learned in these dynamic and brilliant fifty-two weeks.

Let's start with a recap. My mission was:

First—*HONOR my mum, whom I lost too soon*

And what a mission! It was WAAAYYY more than I imagined it would be—reflecting, processing, articulating, then applying it all to my everything (*a tall order at
which I failed many times*). Yet, each day starts anew, one step in front of the last,
and here it is—a better day, a richer view, a deeper intention of regarding people
and life as precious. So precious.

I must share one LAST memories of my mum. All the pictures and objects—
turned into icons for helping me focus every week—were fun reminders of why

I chose this pilgrimage. This last item is possibly the BEST artifact I kept from her, and a fitting end to this incredible exploration.

I have a personal note from Mum, handwritten a few weeks before she died. You may remember my lament in Week Forty-Seven over not having that final conversation with Mum before she slipped into a full coma.

If anything should have been said on her deathbed, I believe she wrote it here. Her written words—which were ironically discovered through focusing on my own written words—helped me to honor Mum and find my better self along the way.

She wrote:

> "Good morning! I love you. You are my special rose; More sweeter than its fragrance, more beautiful than its appearance."

She goes on to thank me for going into a thrift store with her, even though she knows it makes my head itch to walk into that kind of place. As her writing tapers off onto the right side of the page, I cannot make out what else she was trying to say, although I have no doubt it was something to do with shopping. Perfectly true to her nature, right to the end.

Second—*HEAL hurts from my past and soften life's scars*

It was so easy to bury my pain with numbing behaviors, touting an invincible façade to project wellness into my life. Drinking, promiscuity, and pursuits of reckless freedom did nothing to offer healing for my emotional injuries, my spiritual trauma, or my physical recovery.

Adrenalin made it feel like I was soaring; Flying over barriers I dared never before to fly. I felt powerful, with nothing to fear. Time did not hold me. I held time—swooping higher and higher away from all the hurts that confined me for so long. A year went by before I could no longer flap my emancipated wings. Exhausted, I stopped to look around, and did not recognize where *(or who)* I was.

I—was still lost.

This—was still a cage.

My life—was still as infected with an illness I had worked so hard to escape.

Thankfully, one night, through a fog of alcohol and the pressure to prove I was healing just fine, I looked at a strange man I had gone home with, took a deep, sobering breath and said, *"I am tired."*

And I meant it. I took what was left of my beat-up heart, headed out that stranger's door, and set my path toward finding the parts of me that had been shoved so far down inside, they threatened never to surface again. This is when I heard it.

The voice of Love.

It was entreating me through the many other voices of people who had held me for a moment, as well as those who had held me since birth. It whispered to me, recalling memories of all the times it had showed up, reminding me of a truth I had long forgotten.

Love is here.

Peace is waiting.

Your hurt is temporary.

ALL will be restored.

Really? Restored? I have lost so much during this life: My mum, relationships with my kids, my faith, my identity—and all this is going to be restored?

The voice rang out a simple, quiet… "Yes."

1944   *1966*

These pictures are proof that life is leaning toward restoration. They are loving reminders of bonds that are created by all the regular times, the everyday slugfests of grinding out a good living for ourselves and our families, which is never wasted time. Stuff may be lost for a moment—unnoticed or unappreciated—sometimes downright rejected, but Love allows space for it all to return. Not so that it may be exactly the way it was, though. The point of restoration is that it comes back to you *better*.

So. Much. Better.

And finally—*LIVE how I want to be remembered when I am gone*

Patient, Positive, Kind, Grateful, Gracious, Humorous, Strong, Clever, Generous, Encouraging, Sensitive, Curious, and Creative...

All these got my undivided attention. After analyzing these thirteen characteristics that have grown in my life, I am ready to explore a fourteenth topic!

Restoration

To paraphrase the words of the biblical prophet Joel: "Love RESTORES to you, the years the swarming locust have eaten." I have held this message close to my heart in the nine years since Love spoke it, and continue to cling tightly to this encouragement, as one swarm of locusts dissipates and another gnarly throng grows closer.

I know I am not alone in experiencing 'locust' droughts or hurts that can seem like personal attacks. I have invited some of my locust attackers in, allowing them to multiply as they consume my vitality and hospitality to ensure their own survival. It is in them to eat, use up, and devour all they see. Sometimes, they kill each other to get enough.

My heart weeps in the wake of public tragedies week after week. Our world has always had natural chaos—hurricanes, fires, floods—where no one is to blame, so the trauma just IS. Calamity caused by human error or carelessness is harder to understand, although I think acceptance is possible for those seeking closure. It is almost impossible to understand people who can control their behavior and yet choose to hurt or destroy those who are innocent and vulnerable. What kinds of strategies can we employ against this kind of human destruction?

I do not have the answer. However, from my experiences of days that feel like continual plagues—where depression rises from abounding pain—where hope is blocked by a constant buzzing of tormenters—these are the moments that require my daily resolve to define for myself who I will be, how I will engage within the world given to me, and what legacy I will create for anyone following my footsteps. This requires complex reflection and PATIENCE, but ultimately LOVE—for ME and others—to overcome darkness and be restored.

As I said, this theme started nine years ago, so it is well overdue to be picked up again. My heart is bursting with all the restorative, life-giving elements born from these revolutionary fifty-two weeks. I feel extremely fortunate to have been generously gifted with keepsakes other people had saved from Mum. Thank you for the stories, the photos, and the mementos shared with me. It is a rich treasure to be surrounded by such sweet souls.

I am so humbled and honored to share this next amazing list with everyone.

Things Restored in my Fifty-Two Weeks:
(in no specific order, because they are all very epic)

- Relationship with my oldest son
- Tablecloths Mum made
- Old family photos
- My sanity
- A healthy weight
- Crafts Mum made
- Photos of Mum
- A decorative bag Mum gifted to a dear friend
- Connection with the friend Mum named me after
- Untold stories from people about Mum's impact on their lives
- Reunited with another son *(one more to go—Love willing)*
- Surpassed Mum's biggest regret by becoming a grandma
- Outlived Mum
- Fully recovered from a brain injury
- Unwavering peace, unending joy and immeasurable love

Peace uprooted the nagging fear of an unchallenged lie that said healing was not possible. AND Peace exposed the biggest lie of all: That I... YOU... WE... THEY—are not worth the effort.

We are. You are. I am. It is worth every effort.

Joy has faithfully persisted in lightening my heavy load and brightened my wanderings enough to stay grounded in hope. Joy told me to trust the process and not be ashamed of the lessons along the way.

Love kept showing up to surround my deepest pains and stayed with me through hell-bent nights. For years, I fought to overcome demons real and imagined. Time did not produce any healing. LOVE did.

So, what will I *do* now with this restoration?

Keep reading...

PART TWO

With tears streaming down my face, bittersweet is the sound of my fingernails clicking against familiar letters on a well-used keyboard frame. *Finding HER Stuff...* you have been good for me.

Half of me wants to ignore a conclusion of this journey, denying that an end has come to this miraculous inspection of self, terminating the incredible honor it has been to connect my life to Mum's—flaws and all. The other half of me is ready to break out some intense celebration, for accomplishing this reflective and regenerative feat, and define how all of this gets to be a life changer.

Wipe those tears, girl. It's time to light a fire.

At this point, writing has officially become one of the greatest passions I have—not surpassing my passionate love for Jesus, for hubby, or for my kids.

This fifty-two-week query has pulled out two major themes which appeared as central pillars in my writing.

First theme under the microscope—Restoration.

I addressed this in Part One, but I want to keep seeking how to respond to things that get torn apart in our lives, define the kind of patience and hope it takes to see an uncertain future fall into place, and confirm the courage it takes to allow joy to exist throughout each storm.

The second pillar that has emerged, is tackling the stigma and mystery shrouding victims of domestic abuse. Combing through this quagmire consumed a lot of my reflection during the early weeks. Slowly, my focus changed from dwelling on the traumatic hurts of yesterday, to the goodness showing up TODAY.

That was a miracle in itself—but there is more!

I was deeply afraid, when beginning this soul campaign, of whether I could manage the darkness waiting inside old, painful memories. Having battled the demons of depression and knowing they are fierce adversaries, I worried I could not keep engaging positively with the ones who count on me for attention.

The answer became clear: I could.

I did. The dark moments came. I wrestled and argued, blamed and excused. I released it ALL, only to grab hold of it again. Releasing again, then grabbing hold and repeating the process—all while Light quietly waited for an invitation to speak. Her gentle warmth never blinded or surged in a desperate effort to reveal my flaws. Her soft glow persisted each time I exhaled another sentence onto the keyboard.

Darkness does not win when I write. Instead, a power I did not know before, arrives.

This. Is. Passion.

Passion like this has only come in one other form that has held top reign since I was 10 years old. I did not anticipate anything uprooting my love for singing, but here it is. I am drawn to writing. Fed by it. Lose sleep for it. Find balance in it. And purpose—so much purpose that I can hardly wait to announce what is coming next:

My Second Book!

WOW, right?!

The writing has already begun, and the plot is set. It will be a 'story' that tells my story, but from an interesting angle and through an unexpected voice. This winter will likely find me curled up at the computer with my comfy socks on, my journals and diaries out, and ready to tackle this content with integrity and respect.

How can I ever express enough thanks for how a tiny spark of persuasion has morphed into this roaring flame of passion, taking me down twisty roads, dead ends, and beautiful beginnings, like no other exercise of my heart has been able to achieve.

Fearlessly, without any plans or procedures, I asked Love to show me what I should do next—with my stories and with my life—and the answer came back more certain than if it had been handwritten in the sky by angels' wings:

SHARE. You are ready.

> Share my hurts. Out loud. For those who need healing, and for the ones who strive to heal others. For those who need freedom, and the ones providing sanctuary. For those who cry out in loneliness, and the ones who offer comfort.

CELEBRATE. It is time.

> Celebrate life with more music. Sing, dance, record silly music videos that make people smile. Maybe even branch off into the YouTube world. How do people feel about some slick '*Finding 52*' swag? AJ bobble heads and hummingbird fidget spinners. 'HER Stuff' tees and hoodies. Okay, maybe the bobble heads would be taking it too far, but the music videos? Coming soon to a social media site near you!

Pipe dream? Unrealistic? Pie in the Sky?

Probably.

"Dare to DREAM."

Daydreams are my specialty. It does not matter if they come true. Dream, I must. From the depth of my core these schemes churn, but also overflow if attempted to be contained. It is self-preservation to run with these passions, even if I fail. Failure is a far lesser risk to my health than not running at all.

I have no idea what kinds of opportunities may be appropriate for my voice, but I am willing to find out.

On-FIRE willing.

AJ

What has been restored to you?

Is there a theme YOU want to explore next?

(I would be HONORED to hear about your chosen adventure!)

Connect with AJ:

Email: AJ@Finding52.ca
Facebook: Finding 52
Instagram: ajfinding52

Thank you for taking part in these dynamic, diverse, scary, and sacred fifty-two-weeks. All of us deserve huge kudos for this year—or however long it actually took—of stretching our hearts and testing our emotional strength. WE are on the other side of some tough stuff, more 'whole' and more 'well' than we ever knew was possible.

> **"With every deep and steady heartbeat,**
> **Believe confidently—you were made for this.**
> **Please, Love—don't quit.**
> **Keep finding HER stuff."**

CPSIA information can be obtained
at www.ICGtesting.com
Printed in the USA
LVHW050717020721
691686LV00015B/2174